W9-ARW-709

SUPREME COURT
WATCH 2004

Highlights of the 2001–2003 Terms
Preview of the 2004 Term

DAVID M. O'BRIEN
UNIVERSITY OF VIRGINIA

W · W · **NORTON & COMPANY** · NEW YORK · LONDON

W. W. Norton & Company has been independent since its founding in 1923, when William Warder Norton and Mary D. Herter Norton first published lectures delivered at the People's Institute, the adult education division of New York City's Cooper Union. The Nortons soon expanded their program beyond the Institute, publishing books by celebrated academics from America and abroad. By mid-century, the two major pillars of Norton's publishing program—trade books and college texts—were firmly established. In the 1950s, the Norton family transferred control of the company to its employees, and today—with a staff of four hundred and a comparable number of trade, college, and professional titles published each year—W. W. Norton & Company stands as the largest and oldest publishing house owned wholly by its employees.

Composition by Cathy Lombardi.
Manufacturing by Victor Graphics, Inc.
Production manager: Benjamin Reynolds.

ISBN 0-393-92678-8 (pbk.)

W. W. Norton & Company, Inc., 500 Fifth Avenue, New York, NY 10110
www.wwnorton.com
W. W. Norton & Company Ltd., Castle House, 75/76 Wells Street,
London W1T 3QT

1 2 3 4 5 6 7 8 9 0

CONTENTS

CHAPTER 8 ■ *The Fifth Amendment Guarantee against Self-Accusation*   177

CHAPTER 9 ■ *The Rights to Counsel and Other Procedural Guarantees*   187

PREFACE

Supreme Court Watch 2004 examines the changes and decisions made during the Supreme Court's 2001, 2002, and 2003 terms. In addition to highlighting the major constitutional rulings in excerpts from leading cases, I discuss in section-by-section introductions other important decisions and analyze recent developments in various areas of constitutional law. I also preview here the important cases that the Court has granted review and will decide in its 2004 term. To offer even more information in an efficient format, special boxes titled "The Development of Law" and "Inside the Court" are also included.

The favorable reception of previous editions of the *Watch* has been gratifying, and I hope that this 2004 edition will further contribute to students' understanding of constitutional law, politics, and history, as well as to their appreciation for how the politics of constitutional interpretation turns on differing interpretations of constitutional politics and the role of the Supreme Court. I am most grateful to Aaron Javsicas for doing a terrific and expeditious job of producing this edition.

D.M.O.
June 28, 2004

SUPREME COURT WATCH 2004
VOLUME ONE

2

Law and Politics in the Supreme Court: Jurisdiction and Decision-Making Process

A | *Jurisdiction and*
Justiciable Controversies

In its 2003–2004 term, the Court dismissed *Johnson v. California,* 124 S.Ct. 1833 (2004), underscoring that petitioners raising a federal claim when appealing a state court ruling must first exhaust all state appeals as the Court will not exercise jurisdiction until a "final judgment" has been rendered by the highest court in the state. The petitioner failed to include (as required under the Court's rules) in an appendix to the petition for *certiorari* all opinions and final decisions in the case. Here, the state appellate court published only part of its decision (and, like other state and federal appellate courts in the last thirty years, withheld publication of part of its judgment, due to the mounting number of decisions handed down annually). Johnson included in the appendix only the published opinion and not the unpublished portion (which, like other unpublished opinions, was nonetheless available on Lexis). When the Court discovered from the unpublished opinion that the state appellate court's decision was not in all respects final, it dismissed the case. The Court thereby signaled petitioners to append any published and unpublished opinions of state high courts in order to establish that the decision appealed is indeed "final." See also *Vieth v. Jubelirer* (2004) (excerpted here in Vol. 1, Ch. 8) on the justiciability of challenges to political gerrymandering.

Finally, the Court avoided the heated controversy over whether requiring schoolchildren to recite the Pledge of Allegiance violates the First Amendment by denying standing to raise the issue in *Elk Grove Unified School District v. Newdow* (2004) (excerpted below). Writing for the Court, Justice Stevens held that Michael A. Newdow, who challenged the policy on behalf of his daughter, even though he was not her legal custodian, lacked "prudential standing" to bring the suit. In other words, when legal claims made on behalf of another person are based on domestic relations law, a field largely left to states, "the prudent course is for the federal court to stay its hand rather than reach out to resolve a weighty question of federal constitutional law." But in separate concurring opinions, Chief Justice Rehnquist and Justices O'Connor and Thomas dismissed the majority's theory as "novel" and "like the proverbial excursion ticket—good for this day only." They would have granted standing and rejected Newdow's claims, though for different reasons.

Elk Grove Unified School District v. Newdow
124 S.CT. 2301 (2004)

In 2000, Michael A. Newdow, an atheist, challenged the constitutionality of Elk Grove Unified School District's requirement that teachers lead their classes in reciting the Pledge of Allegiance. Because the Pledge contains the words "under God," he contended that the practice amounts to religious indoctrination and violates the First Amendment. At the time, his daughter was in kindergarten and Newdow was in a custody battle with her mother, Sandra Banning. Banning and Newdow were awarded shared "physical custody," but Banning had "exclusive legal custody." A federal district court dismissed Newdow's complaint, but the Court of Appeals for the Ninth Circuit reversed, holding Newdow had standing as a parent to sue and that the school district's policy violated the (Dis)establishment clause. Banning then filed a motion to have the case dismissed on the ground that she was the sole legal custodian and that she did not feel that it was in her daughter's interest to be a party to the suit. The Ninth Circuit, nonetheless, reaffirmed Newdow's standing to challenge allegedly unconstitutional governmental practices and that under California law he retained the right to expose his child to his religious views, even though they contradicted her mother's Christian views. The school district appealed that decision to the Supreme Court, which granted review. Subsequently, Newdow filed a motion requesting Justice Scalia to recuse himself due to his off-the-bench comments criticizing the Ninth Circuit's ruling that the school district's policy violated the First Amendment.

The Ninth Circuit's decision was unanimously reversed, with Justice Scalia not participating. Justice Stevens delivered the opinion for the Court, holding that Newdow lacked "prudential standing" to raise the challenge on behalf of his daughter and declined to reach the merits of the case. In three separate concurring opinions, Chief Justice Rehnquist and Justices O'Connor and Thomas indicate that Newdow had standing and they would, though each for different reasons, uphold the school district's policy over First Amendment objections.

☐ *Justice STEVENS delivered the opinion of the Court.*

As part of the nationwide interest in commemorating the 400th anniversary of Christopher Columbus' discovery of America, a widely circulated national magazine for youth proposed in 1892 that pupils recite the following affirmation: "I pledge allegiance to my Flag and the Republic for which it stands: one Nation indivisible, with Liberty and Justice for all." In the 1920's, the National Flag Conferences replaced the phrase "my Flag" with "the flag of the United States of America."

In 1942, in the midst of World War II, Congress adopted, and the President signed, a Joint Resolution codifying a detailed set of "rules and customs pertaining to the display and use of the flag of the United States of America." This resolution, which marked the first appearance of the Pledge of Allegiance in positive law, confirmed the importance of the flag as a symbol of our Nation's indivisibility and commitment to the concept of liberty.

Congress revisited the Pledge of Allegiance 12 years later when it amended the text to add the words "under God." The resulting text is the Pledge as we know it today: "I pledge allegiance to the Flag of the United States of America, and to the Republic for which it stands, one Nation under God, indivisible, with liberty and justice for all." . . .

We granted the School District's petition for a writ of *certiorari* to consider two questions: (1) whether Newdow has standing as a noncustodial parent to challenge the School District's policy, and (2) if so, whether the policy offends the First Amendment. . . .

The command to guard jealously and exercise rarely our power to make constitutional pronouncements requires strictest adherence when matters of great national significance are at stake. Even in cases concededly within our jurisdiction under Article III, we abide by "a series of rules under which [we have] avoided passing upon a large part of all the constitutional questions pressed upon [us] for decision." *Ashwander v. TVA*, 297 U.S. 288 (1936) (BRANDEIS, J., concurring).

Consistent with these principles, our standing jurisprudence contains two strands: Article III standing, which enforces the Constitution's case or controversy requirement; and prudential standing, which embodies "judicially self-imposed limits on the exercise of federal jurisdiction," *Allen [v. Wright,* 468 U.S. 737 (1984)]. . . . Although we have not exhaustively defined the prudential dimensions of the standing doctrine, we have explained that prudential standing encompasses "the general prohibition on a litigant's raising another person's legal rights, the rule barring adjudication of generalized grievances more appropriately addressed in the representative branches, and the requirement that a plaintiff's complaint fall within the zone of interests protected by the law invoked." *Allen.*

One of the principal areas in which this Court has customarily declined to intervene is the realm of domestic relations. Long ago we observed that "[t]he whole subject of the domestic relations of husband and wife, parent and child, belongs to the laws of the States and not to the laws of the United States." *In re Burrus*, 136 U.S. 586 (1890). [W]hile rare instances arise in which it is necessary to answer a substantial federal question that transcends or exists apart from the family law issue, in general it is appropriate for the federal courts to leave delicate issues of domestic relations to the state courts. . . .

Newdow's standing derives entirely from his relationship with his daughter, but . . . the interests of this parent and this child are not parallel and, indeed, are potentially in conflict.

Newdow's parental status is defined by California's domestic relations law. Our custom on questions of state law ordinarily is to defer to the interpretation of the Court of Appeals for the Circuit in which the State is located. In this case, the Court of Appeals, which possesses greater familiarity with California law, concluded that state law vests in Newdow a cognizable right to influence his daughter's religious upbringing. . . . Animated by a conception of "family privacy" that includes "not simply a policy of minimum state intervention but also a presumption of parental autonomy," the state cases create a zone of private authority within which each parent, whether custodial or noncustodial, remains free to impart to the child his or her religious perspective. . . .

In our view, it is improper for the federal courts to entertain a claim by a plaintiff whose standing to sue is founded on family law rights that are in dispute when prosecution of the lawsuit may have an adverse effect on the person who is the source of the plaintiff's claimed standing. When hard questions of domestic relations are sure to affect the outcome, the prudent course is for the federal court to stay its hand rather than reach out to resolve a weighty question of federal constitutional law. There is a vast difference between Newdow's right to communicate with his child—which both California law and the First Amendment recognize—and his claimed right to shield his daughter from influences to which she is exposed in school despite the terms of the custody order. We conclude that, having been deprived under California law of the right to sue as next friend, Newdow lacks prudential standing to bring this suit in federal court.

□   CHIEF JUSTICE REHNQUIST, *with whom Justice O'CONNOR joins, and with whom Justice THOMAS joins as to Part I, concurring in the judgment.*

The Court today erects a novel prudential standing principle in order to avoid reaching the merits of the constitutional claim. I dissent from that ruling. On the merits, I conclude that the Elk Grove Unified School District policy that requires teachers to lead willing students in reciting the Pledge of Allegiance, which includes the words "under God," does not violate the Establishment Clause of the First Amendment.

[T]he Court does not dispute that respondent Newdow satisfies the requisites of Article III standing. But curiously the Court incorporates criticism of the Court of Appeals' Article III standing decision into its justification for its novel prudential standing principle. The Court concludes that respondent lacks prudential standing, under its new standing principle, to bring his suit in federal court.

We have, in the past, judicially self-imposed clear limits on the exercise of federal jurisdiction. In contrast, here is the Court's new prudential standing principle: "[I]t is improper for the federal courts to entertain a claim by a plaintiff whose standing to sue is founded on family law rights that are in dispute when prosecution of the lawsuit may have an adverse effect on the person who is the source of the plaintiff's claimed standing." . . .

First, the Court relies heavily on *Ankenbrandt v. Richards*, 504 U.S. 689 (1992), in which we discussed both the domestic relations exception and the abstention doctrine. . . . We . . . conclude[ed] that the domestic relations exception only applies when a party seeks to have a district court issue a "divorce, alimony, and child custody decree." We further held that abstention was inappropriate because "the status of the domestic relationship ha[d] been determined as a matter of state law, and in any event ha[d] no bearing on the underlying torts alleged."

The Court['s] conclusion does not follow from *Ankenbrandt's* discussion of the domestic relations exception and abstention; even if it did, it would not be applicable in this case because, on the merits, this case presents a substantial federal question that transcends the family law. . . .

Although the Court may have succeeded in confining this novel principle almost narrowly enough to be, like the proverbial excursion ticket—good for this day only—our doctrine of prudential standing should be governed by general principles, rather than ad hoc improvisations. . . .

The phrase "under God" in the Pledge seems, as a historical matter, to sum up the attitude of the Nation's leaders, and to manifest itself in many of our public observances. Examples of patriotic invocations of God and official acknowledgments of religion's role in our Nation's history abound.

At George Washington's first inauguration on April 30, 1789, . . . "Washington put his right hand on the *Bible*, opened to Psalm 121:1:'I raise my eyes toward the hills. Whence shall my help come.' The Chancellor proceeded with the oath:'Do you solemnly swear that you will faithfully execute the office of President of the United States and will to the best of your ability preserve, protect and defend the Constitution of the United States?' The President responded, 'I solemnly swear,' and repeated the oath, adding, 'So help me God.' He then bent forward and kissed the Bible before him."

Later the same year, after encouragement from Congress, Washington issued his first Thanksgiving proclamation, which began: "Whereas it is the duty of all Nations to acknowledge the providence of Almighty God, to obey His will, to be grateful for his benefits, and humbly to implore his protection and favor—and whereas both Houses of Congress have by their joint Committee requested me 'to recommend to the People of the United States a day of public thanksgiving and prayer to be observed by acknowledging with grateful hearts the many signal favors of Almighty God especially by affording them an opportunity peaceably to establish a form of government for their safety and happiness.'"

Almost all succeeding Presidents have issued similar Thanksgiving proclamations. Later Presidents, at critical times in the Nation's history, have likewise invoked the name of God. . . .

The motto "In God We Trust" first appeared on the country's coins during the Civil War. [I]n 1956, Congress declared that the motto of the United States would be "In God We Trust."

Our Court Marshal's opening proclamation concludes with the words "God save the United States and this honorable Court." . . .

I do not believe that the phrase "under God" in the Pledge converts its recital into a "religious exercise" of the sort described in *Lee* [*v. Weisman*, 505 U.S. 577 (1992)]. Instead, it is a declaration of belief in allegiance and loyalty to the United States flag and the Republic that it represents. The phrase "under God" is in no sense a prayer, nor an endorsement of any religion. . . . Reciting the Pledge, or listening to others recite it, is a patriotic exercise, not a religious one; participants promise fidelity to our flag and our Nation, not to any particular God, faith, or church. . . .

When courts extend constitutional prohibitions beyond their previously recognized limit, they may restrict democratic choices made by public bodies. . . . The Constitution only requires that schoolchildren be entitled to abstain from the ceremony if they choose to do so. To give the parent of such a child a sort of "heckler's veto" over a patriotic ceremony willingly participated in by other students, simply because the Pledge of Allegiance contains the descriptive phrase "under God," is an unwarranted extension of the Establishment Clause, an extension which would have the unfortunate effect of prohibiting a commendable patriotic observance.

☐ *Justice O'CONNOR, concurring in the judgment.*

I join the concurrence of THE CHIEF JUSTICE in full. Like him, I would follow our policy of deferring to the Federal Courts of Appeals in matters that involve the interpretation of state law, and thereby conclude that the respondent does have standing to bring his constitutional claim before a federal court. Like THE CHIEF JUSTICE, I believe that petitioner school district's policy of having its teachers lead students in voluntary recitations of the Pledge of Allegiance does not offend the Establishment Clause. But while the history presented by THE CHIEF JUSTICE illuminates the constitutional problems this case presents, I write separately to explain the principles that guide my own analysis of the constitutionality of that policy. . . .

When a court confronts a challenge to government-sponsored speech or displays, I continue to believe that the endorsement test "captures the essential command of the Establishment Clause, namely, that government must not make a person's religious beliefs relevant to his or her standing in the political community by conveying a message 'that religion or a particular religious belief is favored or preferred.'" *County of Allegheny v. American Civil Liberties Union, Greater Pittsburgh Chapter*, 492 U.S. 573 (1989) (opinion of O'CONNOR, J.).

Endorsement, I have explained, "sends a message to nonadherents that they are outsiders, not full members of the political community, and an accompanying message to adherents that they are insiders, favored members of the political community." In order to decide whether endorsement has occurred, a reviewing court must keep in mind two crucial and related principles.

First, because the endorsement test seeks "to identify those situations in which government makes adherence to a religion relevant . . . to a person's standing in the political community," it assumes the viewpoint of a reasonable observer. Given the dizzying religious heterogeneity of our Nation, adopting a subjective approach would reduce the test to an absurdity. Nearly any government action could be overturned as a violation of the Establishment Clause if a "heckler's veto" sufficed to show that its message was one of endorsement.

The Court has permitted government, in some instances, to refer to or commemorate religion in public life. . . . One such purpose is to commemorate the role of religion in our history. . . . For centuries, we have marked important occasions or pronouncements with references to God and invocations of divine assistance. Such references can serve to solemnize an occasion instead of to invoke divine provenance. . . .

This case requires us to determine whether the appearance of the phrase "under God" in the Pledge of Allegiance constitutes an instance of such ceremonial deism. Although it is a close question, I conclude that it does, based on my evaluation of the following four factors.

HISTORY AND UBIQUITY

The constitutional value of ceremonial deism turns on a shared understanding of its legitimate nonreligious purposes. That sort of understanding can exist only when a given practice has been in place for a significant portion of the Nation's history, and when it is observed by enough persons that it can fairly be called ubiquitous. By contrast, novel or uncommon references to religion can more easily be perceived as government endorsements because the reasonable observer cannot be presumed to be fully familiar with their origins. As a result, in examining whether a given practice constitutes an instance of ceremonial deism, its "history and ubiquity" will be of great importance. . . .

ABSENCE OF WORSHIP OR PRAYER

"[O]ne of the greatest dangers to the freedom of the individual to worship in his own way [lies] in the Government's placing its official stamp of approval upon one particular kind of prayer or one particular form of religious services." *Engel v. Vitale*, 370 U.S. 421 (1962). Because of this principle, only in the most extraordinary circumstances could actual worship or prayer be defended as ceremonial deism. . . .

ABSENCE OF REFERENCE TO PARTICULAR RELIGION

"The clearest command of the Establishment Clause is that one religious denomination cannot be officially preferred over another." *Larson v. Valente*, 456 U.S. 228 (1982). . . . As a result, no religious acknowledgment could claim to be an instance of ceremonial deism if it explicitly favored one particular religious belief system over another.

The Pledge complies with this requirement. It does not refer to a nation "under Jesus" or "under Vishnu," but instead acknowledges religion in a general way: a simple reference to a generic "God." . . . The phrase "under God," conceived and added at a time when our national religious diversity was neither as robust nor as well recognized as it is now, represents a tolerable attempt to acknowledge religion and to invoke its solemnizing power without favoring any individual religious sect or belief system.

MINIMAL RELIGIOUS CONTENT

A final factor that makes the Pledge an instance of ceremonial deism, in my view, is its highly circumscribed reference to God. [T]he brevity of a reference to religion or to God in a ceremonial exercise can be important for several reasons. First, it tends to confirm that the reference is being used to acknowledge religion or to solemnize an event rather than to endorse religion in any way. Second, it makes it easier for those participants who wish to "opt out" of language they find offensive to do so without having to reject the ceremony entirely. And third, it tends to limit the ability of government to express a preference for one religious sect over another. . . .

Michael Newdow's challenge to petitioner school district's policy is a well-intentioned one, but his distaste for the reference to "one Nation under God," however sincere, cannot be the yardstick of our Establishment Clause inquiry. Certain ceremonial references to God and religion in our Nation are the inevitable consequence of the religious history that gave birth to our founding principles of liberty. It would be ironic indeed if this Court were to wield our constitutional commitment to religious freedom so as to sever our ties to the traditions developed to honor it.

□ *Justice THOMAS, concurring in the judgment.*

Because I agree with THE CHIEF JUSTICE that respondent Newdow has standing, I would take this opportunity to begin the process of rethinking the Establishment Clause. I would acknowledge that the Establishment Clause is a federalism provision, which, for this reason, resists incorporation. Moreover, as I will explain, the Pledge policy is not implicated by any sensible incorporation of the Establishment Clause, which would probably cover little more than the Free Exercise Clause.

In *Lee* [*v. Weisman*], the Court held that invocations and benedictions could not, consistent with the Establishment Clause, be given at public secondary school graduations. . . . It brushed aside both the fact that the students were not required to attend the graduation, and the fact that they were not compelled, in any meaningful sense, to participate in the religious component of the graduation ceremony. The Court surmised that the prayer violated the Establishment Clause because a high school student could—in light of the "peer pressure" to attend graduation and "to stand as a group or, at least, maintain respectful silence during the invocation and benediction"— have "a reasonable perception that she is being forced by the State to pray in a manner her conscience will not allow."

Adherence to *Lee* would require us to strike down the Pledge policy, which, in most respects, poses more serious difficulties than the prayer at issue in *Lee*. A prayer at graduation is a one-time event, the graduating students are almost (if not already) adults, and their parents are usually present. By contrast, very young students, removed from the protection of their parents, are exposed to the Pledge each and every day.

Moreover, this case is more troubling than *Lee* with respect to both kinds of "coercion." First, although students may feel "peer pressure" to attend their graduations, the pressure here is far less subtle: Students are actually compelled.

Analysis of the second form of "coercion" identified in *Lee* is somewhat more complicated. It is true that since this Court decided *West Virginia Bd. of Ed. v. Barnette*, 319 U.S. 624 (1943), States cannot compel (in the traditional sense) students to pledge their allegiance. Formally, then, dissenters can refuse to pledge, and this refusal would be clear to onlookers. That is, students have a theoretical means of opting out of the exercise. . . . On *Lee's* reasoning, *Barnette's* protection is illusory, for government officials can allow children to recite the Pledge and let peer pressure take its natural and predictable course. Further, even if we assume that sitting in respectful silence could be mistaken for assent to or participation in a graduation prayer, dissenting students graduating from high school are not "coerced" to pray. At most, they are "coerced" into possibly appearing to assent to the prayer. The "coercion" here, however, results in unwilling children actually pledging their allegiance.

THE CHIEF JUSTICE would distinguish *Lee* by asserting "that the phrase 'under God' in the Pledge [does not] conver[t] its recital into a 'religious exercise' of the sort described in *Lee*." In *Barnette*, the Court addressed a state law that compelled students to salute and pledge allegiance to the flag. The Court described this as "compulsion of students to declare a belief." In its current form, reciting the Pledge entails pledging allegiance to "the Flag of the United States of America, and to the Republic for which it stands, one Nation under God." Under *Barnette*, pledging allegiance is "to declare a belief" that now includes that this is "one Nation under God." It is difficult to see how this does not entail an affirmation that God exists. Whether or not we classify affirming the existence of God as a "formal religious exercise" akin to prayer, it must present the same or similar constitutional problems.

To be sure, such an affirmation is not a prayer, and I admit that this might be a significant distinction. But the Court has squarely held that the government cannot require a person to "declare his belief in God." *Torcaso v. Watkins*, 367 U.S. 488 (1961). . . .

I conclude that, as a matter of our precedent, the Pledge policy is unconstitutional. I believe, however, that *Lee* was wrongly decided. *Lee* depended on a notion of "coercion" that . . . has no basis in law or reason. The kind of coercion implicated by the Religion Clauses is that accomplished "by force of law and threat of penalty." Peer pressure, unpleasant as it may be, is not coercion. But rejection of *Lee*-style "coercion" does not suffice to settle this case. Although children are not coerced to pledge their allegiance, they are legally coerced to attend school. Because what is at issue is a state action, the question becomes whether the Pledge policy implicates a religious liberty right protected by the Fourteenth Amendment.

I accept that the Free Exercise Clause, which clearly protects an individual right, applies against the States through the Fourteenth Amendment. But the Establishment Clause is another matter. The text and history of the Establishment Clause strongly suggest that it is a federalism provision intended to prevent Congress from interfering with state establishments. Thus, unlike the Free Exercise Clause, which does protect an individual right, it makes little sense to incorporate the Establishment Clause. In any case, I do not believe that the Pledge policy infringes any religious liberty right that would arise from incorporation of the Clause. Because the Pledge policy also does not infringe any free-exercise rights, I conclude that it is constitutional.

B | *The Court's Docket and Screening Cases*

The Supreme Court continued its practice of deciding fewer than 1 percent of the cases on its docket. In its 2002–2003 term, the Court heard oral arguments in eighty-four cases from a total docket of 9,406 cases, and in the 2003–2004 term heard arguments in seventy-three cases. As is the Court's practice, it also reversed more of the lower courts' decisions in cases it granted than it affirmed.

The Court's Disposition of Appeals in the 2003 Term

	AFFIRMED	REVERSED OR VACATED
First Circuit		
Second Circuit		3
Third Circuist	1	2
Fourth Circuit	3	1
Fifth Circuit		6
Sixth Circuit	2	6
Seventh Circuit	1	3
Eighth Circuit	1	3
Ninth Circuit	5	19
Tenth Circuit		3
Eleventh Circuit		4
Federal Circuit		1
District of Columbia Circuit		4
Other Federal Courts	1	1
State Courts and Other	2	5
Totals:★	16	61

★Excludes cases decided on original jurisdiction or dismissed for lack of jurisdiction and remanded.

■ INSIDE THE COURT

The Business of the Supreme Court in the 2003–2004 Term

SUBJECT OF COURT OPINIONS*	SUMMARY	PLENARY
Admiralty		
Antitrust		3
Bankruptcy		4
Bill of Rights (other than rights of accused) and Equal Protection	1	4
Commerce Clause		
1. Constitutionality and construction of federal regulation		
2. Constitutionality of state regulation		
Common Law		
Miscellaneous Statutory Construction		21
Due process		
1. Economic interests		
2. Procedure and rights of accused	2	17
3. Substantive due process (noneconomic)		
Impairment of Contract and Just Compensation		
International Law, War, and Peace		4
Jurisdiction, Procedure, and Practice	4	15
Land Legislation		2
Native Americans		1
Patents, Copyright, and Trademarks		
Other Suits against the Government		2
Suits by States		
Taxation (federal and state)		1
Totals	**7**	**73**

*Note: The classification of cases is that of the author and necessarily invites differences of opinion as to the dominant issue in some cases. The table includes opinions in cases whether decided summarily or given plenary consideration, but not cases summarily disposed of by simple orders, opinions dissenting from the denial of review, and those dismissing cases as improvidently granted.

H | *Opinion Days and Communicating Decisions*

■ INSIDE THE COURT

*Opinion Writing during the 2003–2004 Term**

OPINIONS	MAJORITY	CONCURRING	DISSENTING	SEPARATE	TOTALS
Per Curiam	7				7
Rehnquist	9	1	3		13
Stevens	8	8	11	2	29
O'Connor	8	5	2		15
Scalia	8	10	9	2	29
Kennedy	10	7	7	1	25
Souter	9	3	5	1	18
Thomas	9	6	9	3	27
Ginsburg	8	3	4		15
Breyer	7	4	9		20
Totals	83	47	59	9	198

*Note that Court opinions disposing of two or more companion cases are counted only once here. Note also that in *McConnell v. Federal Election Commission*, four justices delivered the opinion of the Court and are counted here separately. In addition, this table includes opinions in cases disposed of either summarily or upon plenary consideration, but does not include cases summarily disposed of by simple orders or concurring or dissenting opinions from the denial of *certiorari*.

■ Inside the Court

Voting Alignments in the Rehnquist Court, 1986–2002 Terms

	REHNQUIST	WHITE	BLACKMUN	STEVENS	O'CONNOR	SCALIA	KENNEDY	SOUTER	THOMAS	BRENNAN	MARSHALL	GINSBURG	BREYER
Rehnquist	—	80.8	55.2	52.1	80.4	78.6	83.1	67.9	79.1	47.6	46.4	63.6	62.6
White	80.8	—	62.2	60.4	72.5	69.8	75.7	73.5	67.7	52.9	52.9		
Blackmun	55.2	62.2	—	72.0	58.4	49.1	57.6	64.8	44.4	77.4	77.0	68.2	
Stevens	52.1	60.4	72.0	—	56.7	46.5	57.6	71.4	44.7	69.9	71.6	77.4	76.3
O'Connor	80.4	72.5	58.4	56.7	—	70.8	78.8	71.6	70.4	49.4	47.9	66.2	71.0
Scalia	78.6	69.8	49.1	46.5	70.8	—	75.7	59.3	87.0	47.5	45.0	54.4	52.1
Kennedy	83.1	75.7	57.6	57.6	78.8	75.7	—	70.4	73.8	53.7	51.2	66.9	65.6
Souter	67.9	73.5	64.8	71.4	71.6	59.3	70.4	—	56.0		54.6	84.5	82.1
Thomas	79.1	67.7	44.4	44.7	70.4	87.0	73.8	56.0	—			52.4	51.1
Brennan	47.6	52.9	77.4	69.9	49.4	47.5	53.7			—	95.0		
Marshall	46.4	52.9	77.0	71.6	47.9	45.0	51.2	54.6		95.0	—		
Ginsburg	63.6		68.2	77.4	66.2	54.4	66.9	84.5	52.4			—	81.5
Breyer	62.6		76.3	71.0	52.1	65.6	82.1	51.1			81.5	81.5	—

Note: The above are average percentages. The percentages for each term are from Table 1 of the *Harvard Law Review*'s annual review of the Supreme Court's term in volumes 101–117 (1986–2003).

3

PRESIDENTIAL POWER, THE RULE OF LAW, AND FOREIGN AFFAIRS

D | *War-Making and Emergency Powers*

■ CONSTITUTIONAL HISTORY

Citizens, Noncitizens, "Enemy Combatants," and Civil Rights in Wartime

Shortly after the attacks on the World Trade Center and the Pentagon on September 11, 2001, President George W. Bush declared war against al Qaeda forces in Afghanistan and international terrorism. He issued an order authorizing the indefinite detention of captured terrorists and their trial by military tribunals, without appeal. Bush's order invited controversy because the detainees were not treated as prisoners of war according to international law. Under the Third Geneva Convention of 1949, prisoners of war are entitled to an independent and impartial trial, the assistance of counsel, and the right of appeal. Less than two months later, Bush signed into law the 342-page USA PATRIOT Act. Its provisions expand surveillance by law enforcement agencies, provide for greater cooperation among federal agencies, and create new crimes. Civil libertarians and other critics contend that the government overreacted, especially in detaining immigrants and holding U.S. citizens as "enemy combatants."

In historical perspective, threats to national security have tended to be exaggerated and civil liberties curbed. When on the verge of war with France, in 1798 Congress enacted the Alien and Sedition Acts, empowering the president to expel any alien deemed dangerous. The Sedition Act made it unlawful to "write, print, utter or publish . . . any false, scandalous and malicious writing . . . against" the government. It led to twenty-five arrests, fifteen indictments, and ten convictions. Those involved were all Jeffersonian-Republican opponents of the Federalists, who were then in power. The laws expired in 1801 and the Supreme Court took the extraordinary step over 150 years later of declaring them unconstitutional in *New York Times Company v. Sullivan*, 376 U.S. 254 (1964) (excerpted in Vol. 2, Ch. 5).

In 1798, Congress also enacted the Enemy Alien Act, still in effect, authorizing the president during a war to detain and expel citizens of a country with which we are at war. James Madison invoked it during the War of 1812; President Woodrow Wilson did so during World War I to arrest over 6,000 German nationals and hold about 2,300 in internment camps; and during World War II President Franklin D. Roosevelt invoked the law to classify almost one million foreigners as "enemy aliens."

World War I brought other restrictions, particularly for immigrants from East Europe and Russia. The Senate debated a bill that would have turned the country into a military zone and made it a crime to publish anything endangering national security, with trials by military tribunals and convictions punishable by death. But President Wilson persuaded Congress to enact the less extreme Espionage Act of 1917, making it a crime to interfere with war efforts. Still, as amended in 1918, the law criminalized any "disloyal, profane, scurrilous or abusive" language about the government. Approximately 2,000 individuals were prosecuted under the law. By the time appeals reached the Court, World War I was over, but the "Red Scare" remained and most of the convictions were upheld. In *Schenck v. United States*, 249 U.S. 47 (1919) (excerpted in Vol. 2, Ch. 5), Justice Oliver Wendell Holmes proposed his "clear and present danger" test for protecting speech, yet upheld the conviction, observing: "When a nation is at war many things that might be said in time of peace are such a hindrance to its effort that their utterance will not be endured so long as men fight." When another appeal reached the Court, *Abrams v. United States*, 250 U.S. 616 (1919), Justices Holmes and Louis D. Brandeis dissented and explained: "The power undoubtedly is greater in time of war than in time of peace because war opens dangers that do not exist at other times. But as against dangers peculiar to war, as against others, the principle of the right of free speech is always the same." [See also *Gitlow v. People of the State of New York*, 268 U.S. 652 (1925) (excerpted in Vol. 2, Ch. 5).]

During World War II and the Cold War, the Court again did not seriously question wartime hysteria or the prosecution of "subversives." Notably, the Court upheld the convictions of leaders of the Communist Party under the Smith Act of 1940, in *Dennis v. United States*, 341 U.S. 494 (1951) (excerpted in Vol. 2, Ch. 5). That law made it a crime "to organize any society . . . advocat[ing] . . . the overthrow or destruction of any government of the United States." Subsequently, Congress enacted the Internal Security Act of 1950 and the Communist Control Act of 1954, aimed at flushing out communists and others belonging to "subversive organizations."

The Cold War in the 1950s and 1960s also led to congressional "witch hunts." The House Un-American Activities Committee (HUAC), established in 1938 and not abolished until 1974, and the Senate Permanent Investigations Subcommittee, chaired by Wisconsin Senator Joseph R. McCarthy, subpoenaed hundreds of individuals to testify about alleged communist activities. In response to challenges to the investigations, the Court ruled that witnesses may refuse to answer vague and irrelevant questions; see *Watkins v. United States*, 354 U.S. 178 (1957); and *Barenblatt v. United States*, 360 U.S. 109 (1959) (both excerpted in Vol. 1, Ch. 5). But, the Court was initially reluctant to check Congress or the executive branch. However, *United States v. Robel*, 389 U.S. 258 (1967), struck down a section of the Internal Security Act, making it unlawful for a member of a communist-action organization to work in a defense facility, for sweeping "too indiscriminately" and "literally establish[ing] guilt by association."

Besides limiting freedom of speech, press, and association, the government has also detained and incarcerated immigrants and citizens, along with suspending other guarantees of the Bill of Rights. In *Ex parte Milligan*, 71 U.S. 2 (1866) (excerpted in Vol. 1, Ch. 3), the Court overruled President Abraham Lincoln's use of military courts to try civilians accused of disloyalty during the Civil War. Yet during World War II it upheld the internment of over 110,000 Japanese-Americans—70,000 of whom were U.S. citizens—as "enemy aliens" without evidence of their disloyalty, in *Korematsu v. United States*, 323 U.S. 214 (1944) (excerpted in Vol. 1, Ch. 3). On the same day *Korematsu* came down, though, the Court ruled, in *Ex parte Endo*, 323 U.S. 283 (1944), that although the evacuation was permissible, the detention of loyal Japanese-Americans was unconstitutional.

During World War II the Court also approved the use of military tribunals to try eight German saboteurs, including one naturalized U.S. citizen, for sabotaging bridges and utility plants. In *Ex parte Quirin*, 317 U.S. 1 (1942), the Court ruled that the president has the "power . . . to carry into effect . . . all laws defining and punishing offenses against the law of nations, including those which pertain to the conduct of war." Chief Justice Stone added that there was no distinction between U.S. citizens and noncitizens deemed belligerents. As he put it: "citizenship in the United States of an enemy belligerent does not relieve him from the consequences of a belligerency which is unlawful."

At the end of World War II, the Court upheld the use of military commissions to try leaders of the Japanese Imperial Military in *In re Yamashita*, 327 U.S. 1 (1946). The Court also held, in *Johnson v. Eisentrager*, 339 U.S. 763 (1950), that federal courts have no jurisdiction over *habeas corpus* petitions filed by foreign nationals held overseas by U.S. military forces. In *Reid v. Covert*, 354 U.S. 1 (1957), though, the Court ruled that U.S. citizens who are dependents of military personnel stationed abroad may not be subject to courts-martial or denied rights guaranteed in the Bill of Rights. For that reason, John Walker Lindh, the young American captured fighting with the Taliban in Afghanistan, was accorded counsel and prosecuted in federal court.

In the aftermath of the 9/11 terrorist attacks, the boundaries between the rights of citizens and noncitizens were once again blurred. International and constitutional law has long recognized that during wartime the government has special powers over foreign nationals from a country with which it is at war. The Bush administration advanced the position that the war against international terrorism was different because it was against al Qaeda and other terrorists, not a nation. Over 3,000 foreign nationals from the Middle East were detained, and another 6,000 targeted for deportation. The administration rejected international criticism of its indefinite and incommunicado detention of about 650 foreign nationals as "enemy combatants" in Guantanamo Bay, Cuba. The administration initially distinguished between the rights of citizens and foreign nationals, but then blurred the line, drawing sharp criticism from commentators and some lower federal courts for its treatment of U.S. citizens as "enemy combatants."

The line between the rights of citizens and foreign nationals has been breached in the past. The Constitution expressly distinguishes the rights of citizenship in certain respects: only citizens may run for elective federal office and their right to vote may not be denied discriminatorily. Yet all other rights are not so literally limited. The Fourth Amendment guarantee against "unreasonable searches and seizures," for instance, extends to all "people." The Fifth and Fourteenth Amendment guarantees of due process and equal protection extend to all "persons," including resident foreign nationals.

Accordingly, the Court has held that neither the First nor the Fifth Amendment "acknowledges any distinction between citizens and resident aliens," *Kwong Hai Chew v. Colding*, 344 U.S. 590 (1953). The Court reaffirmed that "the Due Process Clause applies to all 'persons' within the United States, including aliens, whether their presence here is lawful, unlawful, temporary, or permanent," in *Zadvydas v. Davis*, 533 U.S. 678 (2001). It also has repeatedly held that equal protection is "universal in [its] application to all persons within the territorial jurisdiction, without regard to differences of . . . nationality," *Yick Wo v. Hopkins*, 118 U.S. 356 (1886); see also *Plyer v. Doe*, 457 U.S. 2002 (1982) (excerpted in Vol. 2, Ch. 12, rejecting the denial of public education to children of illegal aliens).

At the same time, citizens and noncitizens are not similarly situated. Although the Court has held that state laws discriminating against aliens may be presumptively invalid, in *Graham v. Richardson*, 403 U.S. 365 (1971), it has permitted states to bar foreign nationals from public employment as police officers, schoolteachers, and probation officers; see *Foley v. Connelie*, 435 U.S. 291 (1978); *Ambach v. Norwick*, 441 U.S. 68 (1979); and *Cabell v. Chavez-Salido*, 454 U.S. 432 (1982).

The status of citizens and noncitizens diverges most sharply with respect to detention, deportation, and immigration. Citizens may not be expelled from the country, whereas noncitizens may be expelled for even minor infractions. As the Court observed in *Mathews v. Diaz*, 426 U.S. 67 (1976): "In the exercise of its broad power over naturalization and immigration, Congress regularly makes rules that would be unacceptable if applied to citizens." The Court has, thus, permitted the exclusion and expulsion of foreign nationals on the basis of their race and if they have committed certain crimes, in *Chae Chan Ping v. United States*, 130 U.S. 581 (1889); and *Yamataya v. Fisher*, 189 U.S. 861 (1903); as well as allowed their deportation because of political associations, in *Shaughnesy v. United States ex rel Mezei*, 345 U.S. 206 (1953).

In *United States v. Salerno*, 481 U.S. 739 (1987), the Court nonetheless blurred the line between citizens and noncitizens when upholding the pretrial detention for two years, without bail, of a citizen as "regulatory, not penal," and hence not a violation of due process. In dictum, referring to times of "war or insurrection," Chief Justice Rehnquist added that "the government may detain individuals whom the government believes to be dangerous." However, in *Zadvydas v. Davis*, 533 U.S. 678 (2001), the Court ruled that legal immigrant felons are entitled to due process and may not be held indefinitely—longer than six months—under deportation orders when countries refuse to take them back. Subsequently, though, a bare majority in *Demore v. Kim*, 538 U.S. 510 (2003), upheld a federal statute mandating preventive detention during deportation proceedings of foreign nationals accused of certain crimes, based on statistics showing that a high percentage of "criminal aliens" commit more offenses after their release and fail to reappear at deportation hearings.

The detentions and deportations of immigrants of Middle East origin in the aftermath of 9/11 gave rise to a new series of litigation. The Immigration and Naturalization Service's (INS) adoption of secret deportation hearings resulted in conflicting lower federal court rulings. The U.S Court of Appeals for the Sixth Circuit held that the First Amendment guarantees a right of access for the press and the media to the proceedings, while the Third and District of Columbia Circuit courts ruled contrariwise. The Supreme Court denied review of the latter decisions (for further discussion of claims to a right of access see Vol. 2, Ch. 5E).

A panel of the Court of Appeals for the Ninth Circuit also ruled against the administration's policy of indefinite detention, without appeal to federal courts, of foreign nationals deemed "enemy combatants," in *Gherebi v. Bush* (2003). The court found no support in the Congress's Authorization for Use of Military Force of 2001 or precedents, such as *Johnson v. Eisentrager*, for denying detainees access to the judicial process. In the words of the panel, "no lawful policy or precedent supports such a counter-intuitive and un-democratic procedure. . . . In our view, the government's position is incon-sistent with fundamental tenets of American jurisprudence and raises serious questions under international law."

The Court had also to consider appeals of the treatment of "enemy combatants" and to clarify the rights of foreign nationals, as well as U.S. citi-zens in the cases of Yaser Esam Hamdi and Jose Padilla. In its 2003–2004 term, the Court reviewed cases involving foreign nationals captured in Afghanistan and Pakistan, *Rasul v. Bush* (2004) (excerpted in this chapter). Both ques-tioned whether federal courts have jurisdiction over challenges to the legality of holding foreign nationals detained in Guantanamo Bay, Cuba. By a six-to-three vote the Court held that federal courts have jurisdiction over foreign nationals detained in Guantanamo Bay, and that these detainees have the right to seek independent review of their detention.

The Court also granted the appeal of a U.S. citizen declared an "enemy combatant," Yaser Esam Hamdi. Hamdi was born in Baton Rouge, Louisiana, but moved as a child to his parents' homeland in Saudi Arabia, where he was raised. He eventually went to Afghanistan, where he was captured fighting alongside the Taliban. He was initially taken to Guantanamo, but once his U.S. citizenship was discovered he was designated an "enemy combatant" and moved to a brig in Norfolk, Virginia. Hamdi challenged his detention and denial of legal representation as a violation of the Fifth and the Fourteenth Amendments. Before the government could respond, a federal district court judge appointed a public defender and ordered the government to allow Hamdi to consult with an attorney. The Bush administration appealed and the Court of Appeals for the Fourth Circuit reversed. The appellate court, however, rejected the administration's position "that, with no meaningful judicial review, any American citizen alleged to be an enemy combatant could be detained indefinitely without charges or counsel on the government's say-so." Instead, the court sanctioned a deferential judicial review and remanded the case to the district court. On remand, the judge directed the government to respond to Hamdi's petition, and it did so with a two-page, nine-paragraph affidavit from the Special Advisor to the Under Secretary of Defense for Policy Michael Mobbs, detailing only the most rudimentary facts of Hamdi's capture. The judge held that the affidavit fell short of supporting Hamdi's detention and ordered the government to turn over copies of all of his statements to interrogators. When the government objected, the judge certified for the Fourth Circuit's review the following question: "[Is] the Mobbs Declaration, standing alone . . . sufficient as a matter of law to allow a meaningful judicial review of Yaser Esam Hamdi's classification as an enemy combatant?" Back in the Fourth Circuit, Chief Judge J. Harvie Wilkinson relied on *Quirin* in reaffirming that courts should defer to the executive branch in cases involving national security; he concluded that the Mobbs declaration was a sufficient basis to justify Hamdi's incarceration. In December 2003, the Bush administration decided to allow Hamdi to consult with an attorney, though maintaining that it could hold him without further judicial hearings. The Court subsequently granted an appeal and held in *Hamdi v. Rumsfeld* (2004) (excerpted in this chapter) that the president had the power to detain U.S. citizens as enemy combatants, but also that Hamdi had the right to contest his detention before an independent tribunal.

Another U.S. citizen detained as an "enemy combatant," Jose Padilla, was seized under very different circumstances. Padilla was detained after deplaning, unarmed, from a flight in Chicago. He was initially held as a "material witness" for allegedly meeting with al Qaeda operatives and conspiring to detonate a radioactive "dirty bomb." Subsequently, he was moved to a New York jail and then, a Navy brig in Charleston, South Carolina. There, he was held without being charged, having access to a lawyer, or given other guarantees of due process. Lawyers challenged the administration's denial of judicial review, access to a lawyer, and the opportunity to contest the detention. A federal district court asked the Court of Appeals for the Second Circuit to decide whether it had jurisdiction and to decide whether Padilla could be held as an "enemy combatant." A panel of the appellate court held that federal courts have jurisdiction and Padilla's detention was not authorized by the Constitution or Congress. Based on Justice Jackson's opinion in *Youngstown Sheet and Tube Co. v. Sawyer*, 343 U.S. 579 (1952) (excerpted in Vol. 1, Ch. 3), the panel ruled that the president has no inherent power to detain U.S. citizens outside of zones of combat. The panel also held that the president had no power to do so under Congress's Authorization for Use of Military Force Joint Resolution of 2001, or the Nondetention Act of 1971, which prohibits detentions of U.S. citizens without specific congressional authorization. But on appeal, a bare majority in *Rumsfeld v. Padilla*, 124 S.Ct. 2711 (2004), ruled that Padilla's lawyer should have filed the petition in a federal court in South Carolina, where Padilla is held, and not in New York. The four dissenters—Justices Stevens, Souter, Ginsburg, and Breyer—would have upheld the court's jurisdiction and held that Padilla had a right to consult with an attorney and to contest the basis for his detention.

Rasul v. Bush
124 S.CT. 2686 (2004)

On September 11, 2001, al Qaeda terrorists hijacked four airliners and used them as missiles to attack the World Trade Center in New York and the Pentagon in Virginia, killing approximately 3,000 people and destroying hundreds of millions of dollars of property. In response, Congress passed a joint resolution, Authorization for Use of Military Force (AUMF), authorizing the president to use "all necessary and appropriate force against those nations, organizations, or persons he determines planned, authorized, committed, or aided the terrorist attacks . . . or harbored such organizations or persons." Pursuant to that authorization, President George W. Bush sent forces into Afghanistan to fight al Qaeda and the Taliban regime that supported it.

Subsequently, two Australian citizens and twelve Kuwaiti citizens who were captured in Afghanistan and held at the U.S. naval base at Guantanamo Bay, Cuba, filed petitions for writ of *habeas corpus*, seeking access to counsel, release from custody, and review by an independent tribunal or federal court. The naval base is occupied by the U.S. pursuant to a 1903 Lease Agreement executed with Cuba in the aftermath of the Spanish-American War. Under the agreement, "the United States recognizes the continuance of the ultimate sovereignty of the Republic of Cuba over the [leased areas]," while "the Republic of Cuba consents that during the period of the occupation by the United States . . . the United States shall exercise complete jurisdiction and control over and within said areas." The federal district court for the District of Columbia dismissed their petitions on the ground that it lacked jurisdiction, since in *Johnson v. Eisentrager*, 339 U.S. 763 (1950), the Court held that "aliens detained outside the sovereign territory of the United States [may not] invok[e] a petition for a writ of *habeas corpus*." The Court of Appeals for the District of Columbia Circuit affirmed and an appeal was made to the Supreme Court, which granted review.

The appellate court's decision was reversed by a vote of six to three. Justice Stevens delivered the opinion of the Court. Justice Kennedy filed a concurring opinion. Justice Scalia filed a dissenting opinion, which Chief Justice Rehnquist and Justice Thomas joined.

☐ *Justice STEVENS delivered the opinion of the Court.*

Congress has granted federal district courts, "within their respective jurisdictions," the authority to hear applications for *habeas corpus* by any person who claims to be held "in custody in violation of the Constitution or laws or treaties of the United States." [U.S. Code, Section 2241(a).] The statute traces its ancestry to the first grant of federal court jurisdiction: Section 14 of the Judiciary Act of 1789 authorized federal courts to issue the writ of *habeas corpus* to prisoners "in custody, under or by colour of the authority of the United States, or committed for trial before some court of the same." In 1867, Congress extended the protections of the writ to "all cases where any person may be restrained of his or her liberty in violation of the constitution, or of any treaty or law of the United States."

Habeas corpus is, however, "a writ antecedent to statute, . . . throwing its root deep into the genius of our common law." The writ appeared in English law several centuries ago, became "an integral part of our common-law heritage" by the time the Colonies achieved independence, and received explicit recognition in the Constitution, which forbids suspension of "[t]he Privilege of the Writ of *Habeas Corpus* . . . unless when in Cases of Rebellion or Invasion the public Safety may require it," Art. I, Sec. 9, cl. 2. . . .

Consistent with the historic purpose of the writ, this Court has recognized the federal courts' power to review applications for *habeas* relief in a wide variety of cases involving Executive detention, in wartime as well as in times of peace. The Court has, for example, entertained the *habeas* petitions of an American citizen who plotted an attack on military installations during the Civil War, *Ex parte Milligan*, 4 Wall. 2 (1866), and of admitted enemy aliens convicted of war crimes during a declared war and held in the United States, *Ex parte Quirin*, 317 U.S. 1 (1942), and its insular possessions, *In re Yamashita*, 327 U.S. 1 (1946).

The question now before us is whether the *habeas* statute confers a right to judicial review of the legality of Executive detention of aliens in a territory over which the United States exercises plenary and exclusive jurisdiction, but not "ultimate sovereignty."

Respondents' primary submission is that the answer to the jurisdictional question is controlled by our decision in *Eisentrager*. In that case, we held that a Federal District Court lacked authority to issue a writ of *habeas corpus* to 21 German citizens who had been captured by U.S. forces in China, tried and convicted of war crimes by an American military commission headquartered in Nanking, and incarcerated in the Landsberg Prison in occupied Germany. The Court of Appeals in *Eisentrager* had found jurisdiction, reasoning that "any person who is deprived of his liberty by officials of the United States, acting under purported authority of that Government, and who can show that his confinement is in violation of a prohibition of the Constitution, has a right to the writ." In reversing that determination, this Court summarized the six critical facts in the case: "We are here confronted with a decision whose basic premise is that these prisoners are entitled, as a constitutional right, to sue in some court of the United States for a writ of *habeas corpus*. To support that assumption we must hold that a prisoner of our military authorities is constitutionally entitled to the writ, even though he (a) is an enemy alien; (b) has never been or resided in the United States; (c) was captured outside of our territory and there held in military custody as a prisoner of war; (d) was tried and convicted by a Military Commission sitting outside the United States; (e) for offenses against laws of war committed outside the United States; (f) and is at all times imprisoned outside the United States." On this set of facts, the Court concluded, "no right to the writ of *habeas corpus* appears."

Petitioners in these cases differ from the *Eisentrager* detainees in important respects: They are not nationals of countries at war with the United States, and they deny that they have engaged in or plotted acts of aggression against the United States; they have never been afforded access to any tribunal, much less charged with and convicted of wrongdoing; and for more than two years they have been imprisoned in territory over which the United States exercises exclusive jurisdiction and control.

Not only are petitioners differently situated from the *Eisentrager* detainees, but the Court in *Eisentrager* made quite clear that all six of the facts critical to its disposition were relevant only to the question of the prisoners' constitutional entitlement to *habeas corpus*. The Court had far less to say on the question of the petitioners' statutory entitlement to *habeas* review. Its only statement on the subject was a passing reference to the absence of statutory authorization: "Nothing in the text of the Constitution extends such a right, nor does anything in our statutes." . . .

Because subsequent decisions of this Court have filled the statutory gap that had occasioned *Eisentrager*'s resort to "fundamentals," persons detained outside the territorial jurisdiction of any federal district court no longer need rely on the Constitution as the source of their right to federal *habeas* review. In *Braden v. 30th Judicial Circuit Court of Ky.*, 410 U.S. 484 (1973), this Court held that the prisoner's presence within the territorial jurisdiction of the district court is not "an invariable prerequisite" to the exercise of district court jurisdiction under the federal *habeas* statute. Rather, because "the writ of *habeas corpus* does not act upon the prisoner who seeks relief, but upon the person who holds him in what is alleged to be unlawful custody," a district court acts "within [its] respective jurisdiction" within the meaning of Sec. 2241 as long as "the custodian can be reached by service of process." . . .

Because *Braden* overruled the statutory predicate to *Eisentrager*'s holding, *Eisentrager* plainly does not preclude the exercise of Sec. 2241 jurisdiction over petitioners' claims. . . .

Application of the *habeas* statute to persons detained at the base is consistent with the historical reach of the writ of *habeas corpus*. At common law, courts exercised *habeas* jurisdiction over the claims of aliens detained within sovereign territory of the realm, as well as the claims of persons detained in the so-called "exempt jurisdictions," where ordinary writs did not run, and all other dominions under the sovereign's control. As Lord Mansfield wrote in 1759, even if a territory was "no part of the realm," there was "no doubt" as to the court's power to issue writs of *habeas corpus* if the territory was "under the subjection of the Crown." *King v. Cowle*, 2 Burr. 834, 97 Eng. Rep. 587 (K. B.). Later cases confirmed that the reach of the writ depended not on formal notions of territorial sovereignty but rather on the practical question of "the exact extent and nature of the jurisdiction or dominion exercised in fact by the Crown." *Ex parte Mwenya*, [1960] 1 Q. B. 241 (C. A.) (Lord Evershed, M. R.).

In the end, the answer to the question presented is clear. Petitioners contend that they are being held in federal custody in violation of the laws of the United States. No party questions the District Court's jurisdiction over petitioners' custodians. Section 2241, by its terms, requires nothing more. We therefore hold that Sec. 2241 confers on the District Court jurisdiction to hear petitioners' *habeas corpus* challenges to the legality of their detention at the Guantanamo Bay Naval Base. . . .

Whether and what further proceedings may become necessary after respondents make their response to the merits of petitioners' claims are matters that we need not address now. What is presently at stake is only whether the federal courts have jurisdiction to determine the legality of the Executive's potentially indefinite detention of individuals who claim to be wholly innocent of wrongdoing. Answering that question in the affirmative, we reverse the judgment of the Court of Appeals and remand for the District

Court to consider in the first instance the merits of petitioners' claims. It is so ordered.

☐ *Justice KENNEDY, concurring in the judgment.*

The Court is correct, in my view, to conclude that federal courts have jurisdiction to consider challenges to the legality of the detention of foreign nationals held at the Guantanamo Bay Naval Base in Cuba. While I reach the same conclusion, my analysis follows a different course. . . . In my view, the correct course is to follow the framework of *Eisentrager.*

Eisentrager considered the scope of the right to petition for a writ of *habeas corpus* against the backdrop of the constitutional command of the separation of powers. . . . The Court began by noting the "ascending scale of rights" that courts have recognized for individuals depending on their connection to the United States. Citizenship provides a longstanding basis for jurisdiction, the Court noted, and among aliens physical presence within the United States also "gave the Judiciary power to act." This contrasted with the "essential pattern for seasonable Executive constraint of enemy aliens." . . . Because the prisoners in *Eisentrager* were proven enemy aliens found and detained outside the United States, and because the existence of jurisdiction would have had a clear harmful effect on the Nation's military affairs, the matter was appropriately left to the Executive Branch and there was no jurisdiction for the courts to hear the prisoner's claims.

The decision in *Eisentrager* indicates that there is a realm of political authority over military affairs where the judicial power may not enter. The existence of this realm acknowledges the power of the President as Commander in Chief, and the joint role of the President and the Congress, in the conduct of military affairs. A faithful application of *Eisentrager*, then, requires an initial inquiry into the general circumstances of the detention to determine whether the Court has the authority to entertain the petition and to grant relief after considering all of the facts presented. A necessary corollary of *Eisentrager* is that there are circumstances in which the courts maintain the power and the responsibility to protect persons from unlawful detention even where military affairs are implicated.

The facts here are distinguishable from those in *Eisentrager* in two critical ways, leading to the conclusion that a federal court may entertain the petitions. First, Guantanamo Bay is in every practical respect a United States territory, and it is one far removed from any hostilities. . . .

The second critical set of facts is that the detainees at Guantanamo Bay are being held indefinitely, and without benefit of any legal proceeding to determine their status. In *Eisentrager*, the prisoners were tried and convicted by a military commission of violating the laws of war and were sentenced to prison terms. Having already been subject to procedures establishing their status, they could not justify "a limited opening of our courts" to show that they were "of friendly personal disposition" and not enemy aliens. Indefinite detention without trial or other proceeding presents altogether different considerations. . . .

In light of the status of Guantanamo Bay and the indefinite pretrial detention of the detainees, I would hold that federal-court jurisdiction is permitted in these cases. This approach would avoid creating automatic statutory authority to adjudicate the claims of persons located outside the United States, and remains true to the reasoning of *Eisentrager*. For these reasons, I concur in the judgment of the Court.

☐ *Justice SCALIA, with whom THE CHIEF JUSTICE and Justice THOMAS join, dissenting.*

The Court today holds that the *habeas* statute, [Section] 2241 extends to aliens detained by the United States military overseas, outside the sovereign borders of the United States and beyond the territorial jurisdictions of all its courts. This is not only a novel holding; it contradicts a half-century-old precedent on which the military undoubtedly relied, *Johnson v. Eisentrager*, 339 U.S. 763 (1950). The Court's contention that *Eisentrager* was somehow negated by *Braden v. 30th Judicial Circuit Court of Ky.*, 410 U.S. 484 (1973)— a decision that dealt with a different issue and did not so much as mention *Eisentrager*—is implausible in the extreme. This is an irresponsible overturning of settled law in a matter of extreme importance to our forces currently in the field. I would leave it to Congress to change Sec. 2241, and dissent from the Court's unprecedented holding. . . .

Hamdi v. Rumsfeld
124 S.Ct. 2637 (2004)

One week after the al Qaeda terrorist attacks on September 11, 2001, Congress passed a resolution, Authorization for Use of Military Force (AUMF), authorizing the president to "use all necessary and appropriate force against those nations, organizations, or persons he determines planned, authorized, committed, or aided the terrorist attacks" or "harbored such organizations or persons, in order to prevent future acts of international terrorism." Shortly thereafter President George W. Bush ordered forces into Afghanistan.

Yaser Esam Hamdi, an American citizen born in Louisiana in 1980, lived with his family in Saudi Arabia as a child. At some point in 2001, he was seized by members of the Northern Alliance in Afghanistan and turned over to the U.S. military. The government initially detained and interrogated Hamdi in Afghanistan and then transferred him to the U.S. naval base in Guantanamo Bay, Cuba, in January 2002. Subsequently, upon learning that Hamdi is a U.S. citizen, the government transferred him to a naval brig in Norfolk, Virginia, where he remained until transferred to a brig in Charleston, South Carolina.

The government designated Hamdi an "enemy combatant" and claimed that that justified holding him indefinitely, without formal charges. In June 2002, Hamdi's father, Esam Fouad Hamdi, filed a petition for a writ of *habeas corpus* in a federal district court. Hamdi claimed that the government held his son illegally and denied him, a U.S. citizen, the full protection of the Constitution, including access to an impartial tribunal and the assistance of counsel.

The district court appointed a public defender as counsel for Hamdi and ordered his access to Hamdi. The government appealed and the

U.S. Court of Appeals for the Fourth Circuit reversed, holding that the district court failed to extend appropriate deference to the government's security and intelligence interests. It directed the district court to conduct a deferential inquiry into Hamdi's status. On remand, the government filed a motion to dismiss the petition and attached in response a declaration from Michael Mobbs, a Special Advisor to the Under Secretary of Defense for Policy. The Mobbs declaration set forth the sole evidentiary support for Hamdi's detention. It stated that Hamdi "traveled to Afghanistan" in July or August 2001, and he became "affiliated with a Taliban military unit and received weapons training." It asserted that Hamdi "remained with his Taliban unit following the attacks of September 11" and that during the time when Northern Alliance forces were "engaged in battle with the Taliban," "Hamdi's Taliban unit surrendered" to those forces, after which he "surrender[ed] his Kalishnikov assault rifle" to them. The declaration also stated that because al Qaeda and the Taliban "were and are hostile forces engaged in armed conflict with the armed forces of the United States," "individuals associated with" those groups "were and continue to be enemy combatants." Mobbs stated that Hamdi was labeled an enemy combatant "[b]ased upon his interviews and in light of his association with the Taliban." According to the declaration, a series of "U.S. military screening team[s]" determined that Hamdi met "the criteria for enemy combatants."

After the government submitted this declaration, the Fourth Circuit directed the district court to proceed in accordance with its earlier ruling and to "'consider the sufficiency of the Mobbs Declaration as an independent matter before proceeding further.'" The district court found the Mobbs declaration to fall "far short" of supporting Hamdi's detention and criticized the hearsay nature of the affidavit, calling it "little more than the government's 'say-so.'" It ordered the government to turn over copies of all of Hamdi's statements and the notes taken from interviews with him; a list of all interrogators who had questioned Hamdi and their names and addresses; statements by members of the Northern Alliance regarding Hamdi's surrender and capture; a list of the dates and locations of his capture and subsequent detentions; and the names and titles of government officials who made the determinations that Hamdi was an enemy combatant. The district court stated that all of these materials were necessary for "meaningful judicial review" of Hamdi's detention and to satisfy the due process clause of the Constitution.

The government appealed the production order and the district court certified the question of whether the Mobbs Declaration, "'standing alone, is sufficient as a matter of law to allow meaningful judicial review of [Hamdi's] classification as an enemy combatant.'" The Fourth Circuit reversed, stressing that because it was "undisputed that Hamdi was captured in a zone of active combat in a foreign theater of conflict," no factual inquiry or evidentiary hearing allowing Hamdi to be heard or to rebut the government's assertions was necessary or proper. The court concluded that the Mobbs Declaration, "if accurate," provided a sufficient basis upon which to conclude that the president had constitutionally detained Hamdi pursuant to the president's war powers. Hamdi's attorney appealed that decision to the Supreme Court, which granted review.

The appellate court's decision was vacated and remanded. Justice O'Connor delivered the opinion for the Court, which Chief Justice Rehnquist and Justices Kennedy and Breyer joined. By a five-to-four vote the Court held that the president was authorized to declare U.S. citizens enemy combatants and to detain them, with Justices Stevens, Scalia, Souter, and Ginsburg dissenting. By a six-to-three vote the Court held that Hamdi nonetheless had a constitutional right to consult an attorney and to contest the basis for his detention before an independent tribunal. Justice Souter filed an opinion in part concurring and dissenting, which Justice Ginsburg joined. Justice Thomas filed a dissenting opinion. Justice Scalia, joined by Justice Stevens, also filed a dissenting opinion.

□ *Justice O'CONNOR announced the judgment of the Court and delivered an opinion, in which THE CHIEF JUSTICE, Justice KENNEDY, and Justice BREYER join.*

We hold that although Congress authorized the detention of combatants in the narrow circumstances alleged here, due process demands that a citizen held in the United States as an enemy combatant be given a meaningful opportunity to contest the factual basis for that detention before a neutral decisionmaker. . . .

The threshold question before us is whether the Executive has the authority to detain citizens who qualify as "enemy combatants." There is some debate as to the proper scope of this term, and the Government has never provided any court with the full criteria that it uses in classifying individuals as such. It has made clear, however, that, for purposes of this case, the "enemy combatant" that it is seeking to detain is an individual who, it alleges, was " 'part of or supporting forces hostile to the United States or coalition partners' " in Afghanistan and who " 'engaged in an armed conflict against the United States' " there. We therefore answer only the narrow question before us: whether the detention of citizens falling within that definition is authorized.

The Government maintains that no explicit congressional authorization is required, because the Executive possesses plenary authority to detain pursuant to Article II of the Constitution. We do not reach the question whether Article II provides such authority, however, because we agree with the Government's alternative position, that Congress has in fact authorized Hamdi's detention, through the AUMF.

Our analysis on that point, set forth below, substantially overlaps with our analysis of Hamdi's principal argument for the illegality of his detention. He posits that his detention is forbidden by 18 U.S.C. Sec. 4001(a). Section 4001(a) states that "[n]o citizen shall be imprisoned or otherwise detained by the United States except pursuant to an Act of Congress." Congress passed Sec. 4001(a) in 1971 as part of a bill to repeal the Emergency Detention Act of 1950, which provided procedures for executive detention, during times of emergency, of individuals deemed likely to engage in espionage or sabotage. Congress was particularly concerned about the possibility that the Act could be used to reprise the Japanese internment camps of World War II. The Government again presses two alternative positions. First, it argues that Sec. 4001(a), in light of its legislative history and its location in Title 18, applies only to "the control of civilian prisons and related detentions," not to military detentions. Second, it maintains that Sec. 4001(a) is satisfied, because Hamdi is being detained "pursuant to an Act of Congress"—the AUMF. Again, because we conclude that the Government's second assertion is correct, we do not address the first. In other words, we conclude that the AUMF is explicit congressional authorization for the detention of individuals in the narrow category we describe (assuming, without deciding, that such authorization is required), and that the AUMF satisfied Sec. 4001(a)'s requirement that a detention be "pursuant to an Act of Congress" (assuming, without deciding, that Sec. 4001(a) applies to military detentions).

The AUMF authorizes the President to use "all necessary and appropriate force" against "nations, organizations, or persons" associated with the September 11, 2001, terrorist attacks. There can be no doubt that individuals who fought against the United States in Afghanistan as part of the Taliban, an organization known to have supported the al Qaeda terrorist network responsible for those attacks, are individuals Congress sought to target in passing the AUMF. We conclude that detention of individuals falling into the limited category we are considering, for the duration of the particular conflict in which they were captured, is so fundamental and accepted an incident to war as to be an exercise of the "necessary and appropriate force" Congress has authorized the President to use.

The capture and detention of lawful combatants and the capture, detention, and trial of unlawful combatants, by "universal agreement and practice," are "important incident[s] of war." *Ex parte Quirin*, 317 U.S. [1 (1942)]. The purpose of detention is to prevent captured individuals from returning to the field of battle and taking up arms once again.

There is no bar to this Nation's holding one of its own citizens as an enemy combatant. In *Quirin*, one of the detainees, Haupt, alleged that he was a naturalized United States citizen. We held that "[c]itizens who associate themselves with the military arm of the enemy government, and with its aid, guidance and direction enter this country bent on hostile acts, are enemy belligerents within the meaning of . . . the law of war." While Haupt was tried for violations of the law of war, nothing in *Quirin* suggests that his citizenship would have precluded his mere detention for the duration of the relevant hostilities. Nor can we see any reason for drawing such a line here. A citizen, no less than an alien, can be "part of or supporting forces hostile to the United States or coalition partners" and "engaged in an armed conflict against the United States;" such a citizen, if released, would pose the same threat of returning to the front during the ongoing conflict.

In light of these principles, it is of no moment that the AUMF does not use specific language of detention. Because detention to prevent a combatant's return to the battlefield is a fundamental incident of waging war, in permitting the use of "necessary and appropriate force," Congress has clearly and unmistakably authorized detention in the narrow circumstances considered here.

Hamdi objects, nevertheless, that Congress has not authorized the indefinite detention to which he is now subject. . . .

It is a clearly established principle of the law of war that detention may last no longer than active hostilities. See Article 118 of the Geneva Convention (III) Relative to the Treatment of Prisoners of War, Aug. 12, 1949, [1955] 6 U.S.T. 3316, 3406, T. I. A. S. No. 3364 ("Prisoners of war shall be released and repatriated without delay after the cessation of active hostilities"). . . .

Hamdi contends that the AUMF does not authorize indefinite or perpetual detention. Certainly, we agree that indefinite detention for the purpose of interrogation is not authorized. Further, we understand Congress' grant of authority for the use of "necessary and appropriate force" to include the authority to detain for the duration of the relevant conflict, and our understanding is based on longstanding law-of-war principles. If the practical circumstances of a given conflict are entirely unlike those of the conflicts that informed the development of the law of war, that understanding may unravel. But that is not the situation we face as of this date. Active combat operations against Taliban fighters apparently are ongoing in Afghanistan. The United States may detain, for the duration of these hostilities, individuals legitimately determined to be Taliban combatants who "engaged in an armed conflict against the United States." If the record establishes that United States troops are still involved in active combat in Afghanistan, those detentions are part of the exercise of "necessary and appropriate force," and therefore are authorized by the AUMF.

Ex parte Milligan, 4 Wall. 2 (1866), does not undermine our holding about the Government's authority to seize enemy combatants, as we define that term today. In that case, the Court made repeated reference to the fact that its inquiry into whether the military tribunal had jurisdiction to try and punish Milligan turned in large part on the fact that Milligan was not a prisoner of war, but a resident of Indiana arrested while at home there. That fact was central to its conclusion. Had Milligan been captured while he was assisting Confederate soldiers by carrying a rifle against Union troops on a Confederate battlefield, the holding of the Court might well have been different. The Court's repeated explanations that Milligan was not a prisoner of war suggest that had these different circumstances been present he could have been detained under military authority for the duration of the conflict, whether or not he was a citizen. . . .

Even in cases in which the detention of enemy combatants is legally authorized, there remains the question of what process is constitutionally due to a citizen who disputes his enemy-combatant status. . . . Our resolution of this dispute requires a careful examination both of the writ of *habeas corpus*, which Hamdi now seeks to employ as a mechanism of judicial review, and of the Due Process Clause, which informs the procedural contours of that mechanism in this instance.

All agree that, absent suspension, the writ of *habeas corpus* remains available to every individual detained within the United States. U.S. Const., Art. I, Sec. 9, cl. 2 ("The Privilege of the Writ of Habeas Corpus shall not be suspended, unless when in Cases of Rebellion or Invasion the public Safety may require it"). Only in the rarest of circumstances has Congress seen fit to suspend the writ. At all other times, it has remained a critical check on the Executive, ensuring that it does not detain individuals except in accordance with law. All agree suspension of the writ has not occurred here. Thus, it is undisputed that Hamdi was properly before an Article III court to challenge his detention under 28 U.S.C. Sec. 2241. Further, all agree that Sec. 2241 and its companion provisions provide at least a skeletal outline of the procedures to be afforded a petitioner in federal *habeas* review. Most notably, Sec. 2243 provides that "the person detained may, under oath, deny any of the facts set forth in the return or allege any other material facts," and Sec. 2246 allows the taking of evidence in *habeas* proceedings by deposition, affidavit, or interrogatories.

The simple outline of Sec. 2241 makes clear both that Congress envisioned that *habeas* petitioners would have some opportunity to present and rebut facts and that courts in cases like this retain some ability to vary the ways in which they do so as mandated by due process. The Government recognizes the basic procedural protections required by the *habeas* statute, but asks us to hold that, given both the flexibility of the *habeas* mechanism and the circumstances presented in this case, the presentation of the Mobbs Declaration to the *habeas* court completed the required factual development. . . .

In response, Hamdi emphasizes that this Court consistently has recognized that an individual challenging his detention may not be held at the will of the Executive without recourse to some proceeding before a neutral tribunal to determine whether the Executive's asserted justifications for that detention have basis in fact and warrant in law. See, e.g., *Zadvydas v. Davis*, 533 U.S. 678 (2001); *Addington v. Texas*, 441 U.S. 418 (1979).

Both of these positions highlight legitimate concerns. And both emphasize the tension that often exists between the autonomy that the Government asserts is necessary in order to pursue effectively a particular goal and the process that a citizen contends he is due before he is deprived of a constitutional right. The ordinary mechanism that we use for balancing such serious competing interests, and for determining the procedures that are necessary to ensure that a citizen is not "deprived of life, liberty, or property, without due process of law," is the test that we articulated in *Mathews v. Eldridge*, 424 U.S. 319 (1976). *Mathews* dictates that the process due in any given instance is determined by weighing "the private interest that will be affected by the official action" against the Government's asserted interest, "including the function involved" and the burdens the Government would face in providing greater process. The *Mathews* calculus then contemplates a judicious balancing of these concerns, through an analysis of "the risk of an erroneous deprivation" of the private interest if the process were reduced and the "probable value, if any, of additional or substitute safeguards." We take each of these steps in turn.

It is beyond question that substantial interests lie on both sides of the scale in this case. Hamdi's "private interest . . . affected by the official action" is the most elemental of liberty interests—the interest in being free from physical detention by one's own government.

Nor is the weight on this side of the *Mathews* scale offset by the circumstances of war or the accusation of treasonous behavior, for "[i]t is clear that commitment for any purpose constitutes a significant deprivation of liberty that requires due process protection," *Jones v. United States*, 463 U.S. 354 (1983), and at this stage in the *Mathews* calculus, we consider the interest of the erroneously detained individual. Moreover, as critical as the Government's interest may be in detaining those who actually pose an immediate threat to the national security of the United States during ongoing international conflict, history and common sense teach us that an unchecked system of detention carries the potential to become a means for oppression and abuse of others who do not present that sort of threat. We reaffirm today the fundamental nature of a citizen's right to be free from involuntary confinement by his own government without due process of law, and we weigh the opposing governmental interests against the curtailment of liberty that such confinement entails.

On the other side of the scale are the weighty and sensitive governmental interests in ensuring that those who have in fact fought with the enemy during a war do not return to battle against the United States. As discussed above, the law of war and the realities of combat may render such detentions both necessary and appropriate, and our due process analysis need not blink at those realities. Without doubt, our Constitution recognizes that core strategic matters of warmaking belong in the hands of those who are best positioned and most politically accountable for making them. . . .

With due recognition of these competing concerns, we believe that neither the process proposed by the Government nor the process apparently envisioned by the District Court below strikes the proper constitutional balance when a United States citizen is detained in the United States as an enemy combatant. That is, "the risk of erroneous deprivation" of a detainee's liberty interest is unacceptably high under the Government's proposed rule, while some of the "additional or substitute procedural safeguards" suggested by the District Court are unwarranted in light of their limited "probable value" and the burdens they may impose on the military in such cases.

We therefore hold that a citizen-detainee seeking to challenge his classification as an enemy combatant must receive notice of the factual basis for his classification, and a fair opportunity to rebut the Government's factual assertions before a neutral decisionmaker. These essential constitutional promises may not be eroded.

At the same time, the exigencies of the circumstances may demand that, aside from these core elements, enemy combatant proceedings may be tailored to alleviate their uncommon potential to burden the Executive at a time of ongoing military conflict. Hearsay, for example, may need to be accepted as the most reliable available evidence from the Government in such a proceeding. Likewise, the Constitution would not be offended by a presumption in favor of the Government's evidence, so long as that presumption remained a rebuttable one and fair opportunity for rebuttal were provided. Thus, once the Government puts forth credible evidence that the habeas petitioner meets the enemy-combatant criteria, the onus could shift to the petitioner to rebut that evidence with more persuasive evidence that he falls outside the criteria. A burden-shifting scheme of this sort would meet the goal of ensuring that the errant tourist, embedded journalist, or local aid worker has a chance to prove military error while giving due regard to the Executive once it has put forth meaningful support for its conclusion that the detainee is in fact an enemy combatant. In the words of *Mathews*, process of this sort would sufficiently address the "risk of erroneous deprivation" of a detainee's liberty interest while eliminating certain procedures that have questionable additional value in light of the burden on the Government. . . .

In sum, while the full protections that accompany challenges to detentions in other settings may prove unworkable and inappropriate in the enemy-combatant setting, the threats to military operations posed by a basic system of independent review are not so weighty as to trump a citizen's core rights to challenge meaningfully the Government's case and to be heard by an impartial adjudicator.

In so holding, we necessarily reject the Government's assertion that separation of powers principles mandate a heavily circumscribed role for the courts in such circumstances. . . . We have long since made clear that a state of war is not a blank check for the President when it comes to the rights of the Nation's citizens. Whatever power the United States Constitution envisions for the Executive in its exchanges with other nations or with enemy organizations in times of conflict, it most assuredly envisions a role for all three branches when individual liberties are at stake. Likewise, we have made clear that, unless Congress acts to suspend it, the Great Writ of *habeas corpus* allows the Judicial Branch to play a necessary role in maintaining this delicate balance of governance, serving as an important judicial check on the Executive's discretion in the realm of detentions. Thus, while we do not question that our due process assessment must pay keen attention to the particular burdens faced by the Executive in the context of military action, it would turn our system of checks and balances on its head to suggest that a citizen could not make his way to court with a challenge to the factual basis for his detention by his government, simply because the Executive opposes making available such a challenge. Absent suspension of the writ by Congress, a citizen detained as an enemy combatant is entitled to this process.

Because we conclude that due process demands some system for a citizen detainee to refute his classification, the proposed "some evidence" standard is inadequate. Any process in which the Executive's factual assertions go wholly unchallenged or are simply presumed correct without any opportunity for the alleged combatant to demonstrate otherwise falls constitutionally short. As the Government itself has recognized, we have utilized the "some evidence" standard in the past as a standard of review, not as a standard of proof. That is, it primarily has been employed by courts in examining an administrative record developed after an adversarial proceeding—one with process at least of the sort that we today hold is constitutionally mandated in the citizen enemy-combatant setting. This standard therefore is ill suited to the situation in which a habeas petitioner has received no prior proceedings before any tribunal and had no prior opportunity to rebut the Executive's factual assertions before a neutral decisionmaker. . . .

There remains the possibility that the standards we have articulated could be met by an appropriately authorized and properly constituted military tribunal. Indeed, it is notable that military regulations already provide for such process in related instances, dictating that tribunals be made available to determine the status of enemy detainees who assert prisoner-of-war status under the Geneva Convention. In the absence of such process, however, a court that receives a petition for a writ of *habeas corpus* from an alleged enemy combatant must itself ensure that the minimum requirements of due process are achieved. . . .

Hamdi asks us to hold that the Fourth Circuit also erred by denying him immediate access to counsel upon his detention and by disposing of the case without permitting him to meet with an attorney. Since our grant of *certiorari* in this case, Hamdi has been appointed counsel, with whom he has met for consultation purposes on several occasions, and with whom he is now being granted unmonitored meetings. He unquestionably has the right to access to counsel in connection with the proceedings on remand. No further consideration of this issue is necessary at this stage of the case.

The judgment of the United States Court of Appeals for the Fourth Circuit is vacated, and the case is remanded for further proceedings.

☐ *Justice SOUTER, with whom Justice GINSBURG joins, concurring in part, dissenting in part, and concurring in the judgment.*

The plurality rejects [the Bush administration's position on the limitations of] the exercise of *habeas* jurisdiction and so far I agree with its opinion. The plurality does, however, accept the Government's position that if Hamdi's designation as an enemy combatant is correct, his detention (at least as to some period) is authorized by an Act of Congress as required by Sec. 4001(a), that is, by the Authorization for Use of Military Force. Here, I disagree and respectfully dissent. The Government has failed to demonstrate that the Force Resolution authorizes the detention complained of here even on the facts the Government claims. If the Government raises nothing further than the record now shows, the Non-Detention Act entitles Hamdi to be released. . . .

The threshold issue is how broadly or narrowly to read the Non-Detention Act, the tone of which is severe: "No citizen shall be imprisoned or otherwise detained by the United States except pursuant to an Act of Congress." Should the severity of the Act be relieved when the Government's stated factual justification for incommunicado detention is a war on terrorism, so that the Government may be said to act "pursuant" to congressional terms that fall short of explicit authority to imprison individuals? With one possible though important qualification, the answer has to be no. For a number of reasons, the prohibition within Sec. 4001(a) has to be read broadly to accord the statute a long reach and to impose a burden of justification on the Government.

First, the circumstances in which the Act was adopted point the way to this interpretation. The provision superseded a cold-war statute, the Emergency Detention Act of 1950, which had authorized the Attorney General, in time of emergency, to detain anyone reasonably thought likely to engage in espionage or sabotage. That statute was repealed in 1971 out of fear that it could authorize a repetition of the World War II internment of citizens of Japanese ancestry; Congress meant to preclude another episode like the one described in *Korematsu v. United States*, 323 U.S. 214 (1944). . . . The fact that Congress intended to guard against a repetition of the World War II internments when it repealed the 1950 statute and gave us Sec. 4001(a) provides a powerful reason to think that Sec. 4001(a) was meant to require clear congressional authorization before any citizen can be placed in a cell. . . .

Second, when Congress passed Sec. 4001(a) it was acting in light of an interpretive regime that subjected enactments limiting liberty in wartime to the requirement of a clear statement and it presumably intended Sec. 4001(a) to be read accordingly. This need for clarity was unmistakably expressed in *Ex parte Endo*, [323 U.S. 283 (1944)], decided the same day as *Korematsu*. *Endo* began with a petition for *habeas corpus* by an interned citizen claiming to be loyal and law-abiding and thus "unlawfully detained." The petitioner was held entitled to *habeas* relief in an opinion that set out this principle for scrutinizing wartime statutes in derogation of customary liberty: "In interpreting a wartime measure we must assume that [its] purpose was to allow for the greatest possible accommodation between . . . liberties and the exigencies of war. We must assume, when asked to find implied powers in a grant of legislative or executive authority, that the law makers intended to place no greater restraint on the citizen than was clearly and unmistakably indicated by the language they used." Congress's understanding of the need for clear authority before citizens are kept detained is itself therefore clear, and Sec. 4001(a) must be read to have teeth in its demand for congressional authorization.

Finally, even if history had spared us the cautionary example of the internments in World War II, even if there had been no *Korematsu*, and *Endo* had set out no principle of statutory interpretation, there would be a compelling reason to read Sec. 4001(a) to demand manifest authority to detain before detention is authorized. The defining character of American constitutional government is its constant tension between security and liberty, serving both by partial helpings of each. . . . A reasonable balance is more likely to be reached on the judgment of a different branch, just as Madison said in remarking that "the constant aim is to divide and arrange the several offices in such a manner as that each may be a check on the other—that the private interest of every individual may be a sentinel over the public rights." The *Federalist* No. 51. Hence the need for an assessment by Congress before citizens are subject to lockup, and likewise the need for a clearly expressed congressional resolution of the competing claims.

Under this principle of reading Sec. 4001(a) robustly to require a clear statement of authorization to detain, none of the Government's arguments suffices to justify Hamdi's detention. . . .

Because I find Hamdi's detention forbidden by Sec. 4001(a) and unauthorized by the Force Resolution, I would not reach any questions of what process he may be due in litigating disputed issues in a proceeding under the *habeas* statute or prior to the *habeas* enquiry itself. For me, it suffices that the Government has failed to justify holding him in the absence of a further Act of Congress, criminal charges, a showing that the detention conforms to the laws of war, or a demonstration that Sec. 4001(a) is unconstitutional. I would therefore vacate the judgment of the Court of Appeals and remand for proceedings consistent with this view. . . .

□ *Justice THOMAS, dissenting.*

The Executive Branch, acting pursuant to the powers vested in the President by the Constitution and with explicit congressional approval, has determined that Yaser Hamdi is an enemy combatant and should be detained. This detention falls squarely within the Federal Government's war powers, and we lack the expertise and capacity to second-guess that decision. As such, petitioners' *habeas* challenge should fail, and there is no reason to remand the case. The plurality reaches a contrary conclusion by failing adequately to consider basic principles of the constitutional structure as it relates to national security and foreign affairs and by using the balancing scheme of *Mathews v. Eldridge*, 424 U.S. 319 (1976). I do not think that the Federal Government's war powers can be balanced away by this Court. Arguably, Congress could provide for additional procedural protections, but until it does, we have no right to insist upon them. But even if I were to agree with the general approach the plurality takes, I could not accept the particulars. The plurality utterly fails to account for the Government's compelling interests and for our own institutional inability to weigh competing concerns correctly. I respectfully dissent. . . .

The Founders intended that the President have primary responsibility—along with the necessary power—to protect the national security and to conduct the Nation's foreign relations. They did so principally because the structural advantages of a unitary Executive are essential in these domains. "Energy in the executive is a leading character in the definition of good government. It is essential to the protection of the community against foreign attacks." The *Federalist* No. 70 (A. Hamilton). The principle "ingredien[t]" for "energy in the executive" is "unity." This is because "[d]ecision, activity, secrecy, and dispatch will generally characterise the proceedings of one man, in a much more eminent degree, than the proceedings of any greater number."

These structural advantages are most important in the national-security and foreign-affairs contexts. To this end, the Constitution vests in the President "[t]he executive Power," Art. II, Sec. 1, provides that he "shall be

Commander in Chief of the" armed forces, Sec. 2, and places in him the power to recognize foreign governments, Sec. 3.

This Court has long recognized these features and has accordingly held that the President has constitutional authority to protect the national security and that this authority carries with it broad discretion. . . .

For these institutional reasons and because "Congress cannot anticipate and legislate with regard to every possible action the President may find it necessary to take or every possible situation in which he might act," it should come as no surprise that "[s]uch failure of Congress . . . does not, 'especially . . . in the areas of foreign policy and national security,' imply 'congressional disapproval' of action taken by the Executive." *Dames & Moore v. Regan,* 453 U.S. 654 (1981). . . .

Undeniably, Hamdi has been deprived of a serious interest, one actually protected by the Due Process Clause. Against this, however, is the Government's overriding interest in protecting the Nation. If a deprivation of liberty can be justified by the need to protect a town, the protection of the Nation, *a fortiori,* justifies it. . . .

☐ *Justice SCALIA, with whom Justice STEVENS joins, dissenting.*

Where the Government accuses a citizen of waging war against it, our constitutional tradition has been to prosecute him in federal court for treason or some other crime. Where the exigencies of war prevent that, the Constitution's Suspension Clause, Art. I, Sec. 9, cl. 2, allows Congress to relax the usual protections temporarily. Absent suspension, however, the Executive's assertion of military exigency has not been thought sufficient to permit detention without charge. No one contends that the congressional Authorization for Use of Military Force, on which the Government relies to justify its actions here, is an implementation of the Suspension Clause. Accordingly, I would reverse the decision below. . . .

The very core of liberty secured by our Anglo-Saxon system of separated powers has been freedom from indefinite imprisonment at the will of the Executive. Blackstone stated this principle clearly: "Of great importance to the public is the preservation of this personal liberty: for if once it were left in the power of any, the highest, magistrate to imprison arbitrarily whomever he or his officers thought proper . . . there would soon be an end of all other rights and immunities. . . . To bereave a man of life, or by violence to confiscate his estate, without accusation or trial, would be so gross and notorious an act of despotism, as must at once convey the alarm of tyranny throughout the whole kingdom. But confinement of the person, by secretly hurrying him to gaol, where his sufferings are unknown or forgotten; is a less public, a less striking, and therefore a more dangerous engine of arbitrary government. . . ."

The gist of the Due Process Clause, as understood at the founding and since, was to force the Government to follow those common-law procedures traditionally deemed necessary before depriving a person of life, liberty, or property. When a citizen was deprived of liberty because of alleged criminal conduct, those procedures typically required committal by a magistrate followed by indictment and trial.

To be sure, certain types of permissible noncriminal detention—that is, those not dependent upon the contention that the citizen had committed a criminal act—did not require the protections of criminal procedure. However, these fell into a limited number of well-recognized exceptions—civil commitment of the mentally ill, for example, and temporary detention in quarantine of the infectious. See *Opinion on the Writ of Habeas Corpus*, 97 Eng. Rep. 29 (H. L. 1758) (Wilmot, J.). It is unthinkable that the Executive could render otherwise criminal grounds for detention noncriminal merely by disclaiming an intent to prosecute, or by asserting that it was incapacitating dangerous offenders rather than punishing wrongdoing.

These due process rights have historically been vindicated by the writ of *habeas corpus*. In England before the founding, the writ developed into a tool for challenging executive confinement. It was not always effective. For example, in *Darnel's Case*, 3 How. St. Tr. 1 (K. B. 1627), King Charles I detained without charge several individuals for failing to assist England's war against France and Spain. The prisoners sought writs of *habeas corpus*, arguing that without specific charges, "imprisonment shall not continue on for a time, but for ever; and the subjects of this kingdom may be restrained of their liberties perpetually." The Attorney General replied that the Crown's interest in protecting the realm justified imprisonment in "a matter of state . . . not ripe nor timely" for the ordinary process of accusation and trial. The court denied relief, producing widespread outrage, and Parliament responded with the Petition of Right, accepted by the King in 1628, which expressly prohibited imprisonment without formal charges. . . .

The writ of *habeas corpus* was preserved in the Constitution—the only common-law writ to be explicitly mentioned. See Art. I, Sec. 9, cl. 2. Hamilton lauded "the establishment of the writ of habeas corpus" in his *Federalist* defense as a means to protect against "the practice of arbitrary imprisonments . . . in all ages, [one of] the favourite and most formidable instruments of tyranny." The *Federalist* No. 84. Indeed, availability of the writ under the new Constitution (along with the requirement of trial by jury in criminal cases, see Art. III, Sec. 2, cl. 3) was his basis for arguing that additional, explicit procedural protections were unnecessary. . . .

Justice O'CONNOR, writing for a plurality of this Court, asserts that captured enemy combatants (other than those suspected of war crimes) have traditionally been detained until the cessation of hostilities and then released. That is probably an accurate description of wartime practice with respect to enemy aliens. The tradition with respect to American citizens, however, has been quite different. Citizens aiding the enemy have been treated as traitors subject to the criminal process. . . .

The proposition that the Executive lacks indefinite wartime detention authority over citizens is consistent with the Founders' general mistrust of military power permanently at the Executive's disposal. In the Founders' view, the "blessings of liberty" were threatened by "those military establishments which must gradually poison its very fountain." The *Federalist* No. 45 (J. Madison). No fewer than 10 issues of the *Federalist* were devoted in whole or part to allaying fears of oppression from the proposed Constitution's authorization of standing armies in peacetime. Many safeguards in the Constitution reflect these concerns. Congress's authority "[t]o raise and support Armies" was hedged with the proviso that "no Appropriation of Money to that Use shall be for a longer Term than two Years." U.S. Const., Art. 1, Sec. 8, cl. 12. Except for the actual command of military forces, all authorization for their maintenance and all explicit authorization for their use is placed in the control of Congress under Article I, rather than the President under Article II. . . .

It follows from what I have said that Hamdi is entitled to a *habeas* decree requiring his release unless (1) criminal proceedings are promptly brought, or (2) Congress has suspended the writ of *habeas corpus*. A suspension of the writ could, of course, lay down conditions for continued detention, similar to those that today's opinion prescribes under the Due Process Clause. But there is a world of difference between the people's representatives' determining the need for that suspension (and prescribing the conditions for it), and this Court's doing so.

The plurality finds justification for Hamdi's imprisonment in the Authorization for Use of Military Force, [but that] is not remotely a congressional suspension of the writ, and no one claims that it is. Contrary to the plurality's view, I do not think this statute even authorizes detention of a citizen with the clarity necessary to satisfy the interpretive canon that statutes should be construed so as to avoid grave constitutional concerns. But even if it did, I would not permit it to overcome Hamdi's entitlement to *habeas corpus* relief. . . .

It should not be thought, however, that the plurality's evisceration of the Suspension Clause augments, principally, the power of Congress. As usual, the major effect of its constitutional improvisation is to increase the power of the Court. Having found a congressional authorization for detention of citizens where none clearly exists; and having discarded the categorical procedural protection of the Suspension Clause; the plurality then proceeds, under the guise of the Due Process Clause, to prescribe what procedural protections it thinks appropriate. It "weigh[s] the private interest . . . against the Government's asserted interest" and—just as though writing a new Constitution—comes up with an unheard-of system in which the citizen rather than the Government bears the burden of proof, testimony is by hearsay rather than live witnesses, and the presiding officer may well be a "neutral" military officer rather than judge and jury. It claims authority to engage in this sort of "judicious balancing" from *Mathews v. Eldridge*, 424 U.S. 319 (1976), a case involving . . . the withdrawal of disability benefits! Whatever the merits of this technique when newly recognized property rights are at issue (and even there they are questionable), it has no place where the Constitution and the common law already supply an answer. . . .

Several limitations give my views in this matter a relatively narrow compass. They apply only to citizens, accused of being enemy combatants, who are detained within the territorial jurisdiction of a federal court. This is not likely to be a numerous group; currently we know of only two, Hamdi and Jose Padilla. Where the citizen is captured outside and held outside the United States, the constitutional requirements may be different. Cf. *Johnson v. Eisentrager*, 339 U.S. 763 (1950); *Rasul v. Bush* (SCALIA, J., dissenting). Moreover, even within the United States, the accused citizen-enemy combatant may lawfully be detained once prosecution is in progress or in contemplation. See, e.g., *County of Riverside v. McLaughlin*, 500 U.S. 44 (1991) (brief detention pending judicial determination after warrantless arrest); *United States v. Salerno*, 481 U.S. 739 (1987) (pretrial detention under the Bail Reform Act). The Government has been notably successful in securing conviction, and hence long-term custody or execution, of those who have waged war against the state. . . .

Many think it not only inevitable but entirely proper that liberty give way to security in times of national crisis—that, at the extremes of military exigency. Whatever the general merits of the view that war silences law or modulates its voice, that view has no place in the interpretation and application of a Constitution designed precisely to confront war and, in a manner that accords with democratic principles, to accommodate it. Because the Court has proceeded to meet the current emergency in a manner the Constitution does not envision, I respectfully dissent.

■ THE DEVELOPMENT OF LAW

The USA PATRIOT Act of 2001, Wiretaps, and the Foreign Intelligence Surveillance Court*

Enacted in response to the terrorist attacks of September 11, 2001, the USA PATRIOT Act authorizes sweeping changes in law enforcement, notably lowering the standards for searching and seizing individuals suspected of terrorism, for example, as well as expanding investigatory powers. Among these changes, the law authorizes

- Roving wiretaps—wiretaps on any telephone used by a person suspected of terrorism; the use of key-logger devices, which register every stroke made on a computer; and Internet wiretaps.
- Police searches of private property without prior notification of the owners and without a search warrant.
- A lower standard for judicial approval of wiretaps for individuals suspected of terrorist activities.
- The attorney general to designate domestic groups as terrorist organizations and to block the entry into the country of foreigners aligned with them.
- The Central Intelligence Agency to investigate Americans suspected of having connections to terrorism.
- The Department of the Treasury to monitor financial transactions— bank accounts, mutual funds, and brokerage deals—and to obtain medical and other electronic records on individuals.
- The detention and deportation of foreigners suspected of having connections to terrorist organizations.

One of the most controversial provisions of the USA PATRIOT Act removes restrictions on information sharing and foreign intelligence gathering. Section 203 requires the attorney general to disclose to the director of the Central Intelligence Agency (CIA) "foreign intelligence" obtained from a federal criminal investigation, including wiretaps and grand jury hearings. The CIA may also share information with domestic law enforcement agencies.

Critics charge that the broad language of the act's disclosure requirements permits the Department of Justice (DoJ) to give the CIA all information related to a foreigner or to a citizen's contacts with a foreign government or organization, not merely that pertaining to international terrorism. Moreover, the act does not establish any standards or safeguards for restricting the

*The full title of the law is Uniting and Strengthening America by Providing Appropriate Tools Required to Intercept and Obstruct Terrorism (USA PATRIOT) Act of 2001. For the text and other information go to http://personalinfomediary.com/USAPATRIOTACT_Text.htm

disclosure of "foreign intelligence information." Critics therefore contend that the intelligence community may collect information about individuals who have committed no crimes but who are involved in lawful protests of American foreign policies.

Furthermore, the USA PATRIOT Act changed the Foreign Intelligence Surveillance (FIS) Act of 1978, which created a special FIS court, staffed by sitting federal judges on special assignments, to approve wiretaps and to ensure that "the sole purpose" of domestic intelligence gathering was to obtain foreign intelligence information. That law was enacted because of abuses in domestic surveillance of anti-Vietnam war protesters and leaders of the civil rights movement in the 1960s and 1970s. Section 218 of the USA PATRIOT Act, however, changed the law so the DoJ need only show that the collection of foreign intelligence information has "a significant purpose," instead of being "the sole purpose" of an investigation.

Based on those provisions in 2002, Attorney General John Ashcroft issued new guidelines allowing federal prosecutors to consult with law enforcement agents conducting foreign intelligence surveillance. Those guidelines were in turn challenged as a violation of the Fourth Amendment and for permitting the use of special FIS wiretaps for investigating and prosecuting ordinary criminals, and not just spies and terrorists. In May 2002, the U.S. Foreign Intelligence Surveillance Court unanimously rejected the new guidelines and for the first time in the history of the court released a published opinion, *In re: All Matters Submitted to the Foreign Intelligence Surveillance Court*, No. Multiple 02-429 F.Supp. 2d C (U.S. Foreign Intel. Surv. Ct., 17 May 2002). Emphasizing the special and intrusive nature of FIS Act surveillance, the seven judges on the court maintained that the "walls" prohibiting criminal prosecutors from conducting investigations of suspected foreign spies and terrorists should not be torn down and that the DoJ's new guidelines were not "reasonably designed."

However, the DoJ successfully appealed that decision to a special three-judge court of appeals, as authorized by the FIS Act and whose judges are assigned from other federal appellate courts by the chief justice of the Supreme Court. Subsequently, the FIS appellate court upheld the DoJ's new guidelines, in *In re: Sealed Case* (U.S. Foreign Intelligence Surveillance Court of Review No. 02-001 and 02-002), available at http://www.cadc.uscourts.gov/common/newsroom/02001.pdf. In doing so, the appellate court stressed that the USA PATRIOT Act aimed to eliminate "walls" between foreign intelligence and domestic law enforcement agencies, and explained: "Effective counterintelligence, as we have learned, requires the whole-hearted cooperation of all the government's personnel who can be brought to the task. A standard which punishes such cooperation could well be thought dangerous to national security." As a result, federal criminal prosecutors may use information against citizens obtained from wiretaps authorized by the FIS court, based on less than probable cause and on more searching surveillance than permitted under traditional wiretaps.

4

THE PRESIDENT AS
CHIEF EXECUTIVE IN
DOMESTIC AFFAIRS

D | *Accountability and Immunities*

In a potentially wide-ranging ruling supporting the powers of the presidency in domestic affairs, the Court limited *United States v. Nixon* (1974) (excerpted in Vol. 1, Ch. 4) in holding that confidentiality may be preserved without invoking executive privilege in *Cheney v. U.S. District Court for the District of Columbia*, 124 S.Ct. 2576 (2004). Shortly after taking office, President George W. Bush appointed Vice President Dick Cheney to head an advisory group on energy policy, the National Energy Policy Development Group (NEPDG). Subsequently, Judicial Watch and the Sierra Club filed a suit seeking copies of all records showing who attended NEPDG meetings under the Federal Advisory Committee Act, which imposes disclosure requirements except for advisory groups composed completely of officers and employees of the federal government. The Judicial Watch contended that energy corporations were so active in the NEPDG's deliberations as to make them de facto members. The district court agreed and the Bush administration appealed to the Court of Appeals for the District of Columbia, asking it to vacate the decision to permit pretrial discovery of the NEPDG's records. The appellate court dismissed the appeal and the administration's claim that rather than being based in executive privilege, confidentiality was based on the principle of separation of powers and disclosure would harm the presidency. That decision was appealed by the administration.

Writing for the Court, Justice Kennedy distinguished *United States v. Nixon*, which rejected the claim of an absolute unreviewable claim of executive privilege within a criminal proceeding, and the dispute in Cheney over the pretrial discovery in a civil suit for executive branch records. Justice Kennedy explained:

The distinction *Nixon* drew between criminal and civil proceedings is not just a matter of formalism. The need for information for use in civil cases, while far from negligible, does not share the urgency or significance of the criminal subpoena requests in *Nixon*. As *Nixon* recognized, the right to production of relevant evidence in civil proceedings does not have the same "constitutional dimensions."

Nixon [also observed] that a "primary constitutional duty of the Judicial Branch [is] to do justice in criminal prosecutions." . . . Withholding the information in this case, however, does not hamper another branch's ability to perform its "essential functions" in quite the same way. The District Court ordered discovery here, not to remedy known statutory violations, but to ascertain whether FACA's disclosure requirements even apply to the NEPDG in the first place. . . .

[In addition, the] discovery requests are directed to the Vice President and other senior Government officials who served on the NEPDG to give advice and make recommendations to the President. The Executive Branch, at its highest level, is seeking the aid of the courts to protect its constitutional prerogatives. [S]pecial considerations control when the Executive Branch's interests in maintaining the autonomy of its office and safeguarding the confidentiality of its communications are implicated. This Court has held, on more than one occasion, that "[t]he high respect that is owed to the office of the Chief Executive . . . is a matter that should inform the conduct of the entire proceeding, including the timing and scope of discovery," *Clinton* [*v. Jones*, 520 U.S. 681 (1997)], and that the Executive's "constitutional responsibilities and status [are] factors counseling judicial deference and restraint" in the conduct of litigation against it, *Nixon v. Fitzgerald*, 457 U.S. [731 (1982)]. . . .

The observation in *Nixon* that production of confidential information would not disrupt the functioning of the Executive Branch cannot be applied in a mechanistic fashion to civil litigation. In the criminal justice system, there are various constraints, albeit imperfect, to filter out insubstantial legal claims. . . . In contrast, there are no adequate checks in the civil discovery process here. . . .

Given the breadth of the discovery requests in this case [for all records] compared to the narrow subpoena orders [for specific White House tape recordings] in *United States v. Nixon*, our precedent provides no support for the proposition that the Executive Branch "shall bear the burden" of invoking executive privilege with sufficient specificity and of making particularized objections. . . .

Nixon does not leave [courts] the sole option of inviting the Executive Branch to invoke executive privilege while remaining otherwise powerless to modify a party's overly broad discovery requests. Executive privilege is an extraordinary assertion of power "not to be lightly invoked." Once executive privilege is asserted, coequal branches of the Government are set on a collision course. The Judiciary is forced into the difficult task of balancing the need for information in a judicial proceeding and the Executive's Article II prerogatives. This inquiry places courts in the awkward position of evaluating the Executive's claims of confidentiality and autonomy, and pushes to the fore difficult questions of separation of powers and checks and balances. These "occasion[s] for constitutional confrontation between the two branches" should be avoided whenever possible.

The case was remanded for further proceedings. Dissenting Justices Ginsburg and Souter maintained that the lower court could "accommodate separation of powers concerns" by limiting discovery at the government's request. Justices Thomas and Scalia, concurring and dissenting in part, accepted Cheney's argument that the Court should bar all pretrial discovery rather than permit the case to proceed.

5

CONGRESS: MEMBERSHIP, IMMUNITIES, AND INVESTIGATORY POWERS

A | Membership and Immunities

In *Department of Commerce v. U.S. House of Representatives*, 525 U.S. 316 (1999), a bare majority ruled that the use of statistical samplings in the 2000 census would violate the Census Clause's requirement for an actual enumeration. In the 2000 census the Census Bureau nonetheless continued using the statistical technique called "hot-deck imputation," which estimated data on missing households in arriving at the final count. As a result, about 1.2 million people were added—less than one-half of 1 percent—to the final count. On that basis North Carolina received a thirteenth seat in the House of Representatives. Utah sued, claiming it deserved a fourth seat and challenging the constitutionality of the use of "hot-deck imputation." A bare majority in *Utah v. Evans*, 536 U.S. 452 (2002), upheld the use of that statistical measure, which Congress had approved and which had been used in four previous census counts. Justice Breyer wrote for the Court and was joined by Chief Justice Rehnquist and Justices Stevens, Souter, and Ginsburg. Justices O'Connor, Scalia, Kennedy, and Thomas dissented.

7

THE STATES AND AMERICAN FEDERALISM

A | *States' Power over Commerce and Regulation*

In its 2004–2005 term the Court will consider a dormant commerce clause challenge to laws in New York and Michigan that require out-of-state wineries to use in-state wholesalers in order to obtain a license, while in-state wineries may sell directly to consumers. The wineries contend that the laws are discriminatory and in violation of the commerce clause, but the states counter that the regulations are permissible and a constitutional exercise of their power to regulate alcohol under the Twenty-first Amendment. The case is *Granholm v. Heald* (No. 03-1116).

The Court will also consider, in *Ashcroft v. Raich* (No. 03-1454), whether, under the commerce clause, the Controlled Substances Act (CSA) supersedes state laws permitting individuals to grow and use marijuana for medical purposes on the recommendation of their doctors.

■ The Development of Law

Other Rulings on State Regulatory Powers in Alleged Conflict with Federal Legislation

CASE	RULING
Kentucky Association of Health Plans, Inc. v. Miller, 538 U.S. 329 (2003)	Writing for a unanimous Court, Justice Scalia held that the Employment Retirement Income

Security Act (ERISA) does not preempt Kentucky's Any Willing Provider (AWP) laws because they are regulations of the insurance industry. Health Maintenance Organizations (HMOs) had exclusive networks with health-care providers and sought to have the state's AWP laws invalidated on the ground they were preempted by ERISA's regulation of employee benefit plans. But the Court held that Kentucky's laws regulated insurance programs and thus HMOs in the state could not restrict access to particular health-care providers.

| *Beneficial National Bank v. Anderson,* 539 U.S. 1 (2003) | Held that the National Bank Act provides the exclusive basis for usury claims against national |

banks and preempts state usury laws.

| *Hillside Dairy Inc. v. Lyons,* 539 U.S. 59 (2003) | Held that California's milk pricing regulations, which favored in-state farmers, were not exempt |

from Congress's interstate commerce power and the Federal Agriculture and Reform Act of 1996.

| *Aetna Health Inc. v. Davila,* 124 S.Ct. 2488 (2004) | Held that Employee Retirement Income Security Act of 1974 (ERISA) preempts the Texas |

Health Care Liability Act and bars suits against health maintenance organizations (HMOs) for their refusal to provide certain services in state courts, rather than federal courts, where the potential liability of HMOs is more limited.

■ THE DEVELOPMENT OF LAW

Other Rulings on State Regulation of Commerce in the Absence of Federal Legislation

CASE	RULING
Pharmaceutical Research and Manufacturers of America v. Walsh, 538 U.S. 644 (2003)	Held that Maine's Act to Establish Fairer Pricing for Prescription Drugs does not violate the dormant commerce clause.

Due to increasing Medicaid costs for prescription drugs, Congress authorized requiring drug companies to pay rebates to states for their Medicaid purchases. Under Maine's program, the state negotiates rebates with drug companies. If a company does not enter into an agreement, then doctors are required to obtain the state's approval for reimbursement for prescription drugs under Medicaid. Writing for the Court, Justice Stevens held that Maine's law, aimed at promoting discount drugs, did not discriminate against out-of-state drug manufacturers in violation of the commerce clause.

American Insurance Association v. Garamendi, 539 U.S. 396 (2003)	Invalidated California's 1999 Holocaust Victim Insurance Relief Act, which required all

insurance companies in the state that sold individual policies in Europe between 1920 and 1945 to disclose the names of policyholders and beneficiaries in order to assist Holocaust survivors in collecting benefits. Writing for the Court, Justice Souter held that the law infringed on the president's foreign policymaking powers, and in particular the German Foundation Agreement, under which the United States and Germany established a fund and a procedure for compensating insurance companies' victims during the Nazi era. Justice Souter also rejected California's assertion that Congress had authorized in the McCarran-Ferguson Act, rather than preempting under its interstate commerce power, state laws of the sort at issue. Justices Ginsburg, Stevens, Scalia, and Thomas dissented.

B | *The Tenth and Eleventh Amendments and the States*

Breaking with a series of rulings on congressional power and states' sovereign immunity from lawsuits under the Eleventh Amendment [see *Kimel v. Florida Board of Regents*, 528 U.S. 62 (2000), and *Seminole Tribe of Florida v. Florida*, 517 U.S. 44 (1996) (excerpted in Vol. I, Ch. 7)], and Congress's enforcement power under Section 5 of the Fourteenth Amendment [see *City of Boerne v. Flores*, 521 U.S. 507 (1997) (excerpted in Vol. I, Ch. 6), and *United States v. Morrison*, 529 U.S. 598 (2000) (excerpted in Vol. I, Ch. 6)], the Court held that Congress had the power to abrogate states' sovereign immunity in authorizing private lawsuits against states for violations of the Family and Medical Leave Act of 1993 in *Nevada Department of Human Resources v. Hibbs* (excerpted below).

The Court also ruled in *Frew v. Hawkins*, 124 S.Ct. 899 (2004), that states do not enjoy immunity from suits forcing compliance with their obligations under a consent decree approved by a federal court. In addition, a bare majority in *Tennessee v. Lane*, 124 S.Ct. 1978 (2004), held that Congress may abrogate state immunity in authorizing suits to enforce Title 2 of the Americans with Disabilities Act (ADA) of 1990, but limited its holding to suits to force states to provide access for the disabled to courthouses and did not address access to other public facilities. Writing for the Court, Justice Stevens found Congress had established a nationwide problem of discrimination against the disabled and their exercise of a fundamental right to justice. On that basis he distinguished *Board of Trustees of University of Alabama v. Garrett*, 531 U.S. 356 (2001), in which for a bare majority Chief Justice Rehnquist held that Congress lacked the authority under Section 5 of the Fourteenth Amendment to abrogate state immunity from lawsuits filed under Title 1 of the ADA, which forbids discrimination against the disabled in state employment. (For a further discussion see THE DEVELOPMENT OF LAW box in this chapter.)

Nevada Department of Human Resources v. Hibbs
538 U.S. 721, 123 S.CT. 1972 (2003)

The Family and Medical Leave Act of 1993 (FMLA) entitles eligible employees to take up to 12 weeks of unpaid leave annually for attending to illnesses within the immediate family. The FMLA also creates a private right of action to seek damages against an employer for violating provisions of the law. Williams Hibbs worked for the Nevada Department of Human Resources and in 1997 sought leave under the FMLA in order to care for his ailing wife. His request was granted but after he had been on leave for 12 weeks the agency notified him that he must return to work. When Hibbs failed to do so, his employment was terminated. Subsequently, Hibbs sued Nevada in federal district court for violations of the FMLA. The district court held that Hibbs was barred from filing the FMLA claim against the state on the basis of the Eleventh Amendment. However, on appeal the Court of Appeals for the Ninth Circuit reversed that decision and ruled that states' sovereign immunity under the Eleventh Amendment was overridden by Congress's power under Section 5 of the Fourteenth Amendment to enact laws aimed at enforcing the equal protection of the law and to address the persistence of gender discrimination. The state appealed that decision and the Supreme Court granted *certiorari*.

The Supreme Court affirmed by a vote of six to three. Chief Justice Rehnquist delivered the opinion for the Court. Justices Souter and Stevens each filed concurring opinions. Justices Scalia and Kennedy filed dissenting opinions; Justice Thomas joined the latter's dissent.

☐ *CHIEF JUSTICE REHNQUIST delivered the opinion of the Court.*

The Family and Medical Leave Act of 1993 (FMLA or Act) entitles eligible employees to take up to 12 work weeks of unpaid leave annually for any of several reasons, including the onset of a "serious health condition" in an employee's spouse, child, or parent. The Act creates a private right of action to seek both equitable relief and money damages "against any employer (including a public agency) in any Federal or State court of competent jurisdiction," Section 2617(a)(2), should that employer "interfere with, restrain, or deny the exercise of" FMLA rights. We hold that employees of the State of Nevada may recover money damages in the event of the State's failure to comply with the family-care provision of the Act. . . .

For over a century now, we have made clear that the Constitution does not provide for federal jurisdiction over suits against nonconsenting States. *Board of Trustees of Univ. of Ala. v. Garrett*, 531 U.S. 356 (2001); *Kimel v. Florida Bd. of Regents*, 528 U.S. 62 (2000); *College Savings Bank v. Florida Prepaid Postsecondary Ed. Expense Bd.*, 527 U.S. 666 (1999); *Seminole Tribe of Fla. v. Florida*, 517 U.S. 44, 54 (1996); *Hans v. Louisiana*, 134 U.S. 1 (1890).

Congress may, however, abrogate such immunity in federal court if it makes its intention to abrogate unmistakably clear in the language of the statute and acts pursuant to a valid exercise of its power under Section 5 of the Fourteenth Amendment. The clarity of Congress's intent here is not fairly debatable. The Act enables employees to seek damages "against any employer (including a public agency) in any Federal or State court of competent jurisdiction," and Congress has defined "public agency" to include both "the government of a State or political subdivision thereof" and "any agency of . . . a State, or a political subdivision of a State." We held in *Kimel* that, by using identical language in the Age Discrimination in Employment Act of 1967 (ADEA),

Congress satisfied the clear statement rule of *Dellmuth* [*v. Muth,* 491 U.S. 223 (1989)]. This case turns, then, on whether Congress acted within its constitutional authority when it sought to abrogate the States' immunity for purposes of the FMLA's family-leave provision.

In enacting the FMLA, Congress relied on two of the powers vested in it by the Constitution: its Article I commerce power and its power under Section 5 of the Fourteenth Amendment to enforce that Amendment's guarantees. Congress may not abrogate the States' sovereign immunity pursuant to its Article I power over commerce. *Seminole Tribe.* Congress may, however, abrogate States' sovereign immunity through a valid exercise of its Section 5 power, for "the Eleventh Amendment, and the principle of state sovereignty which it embodies, are necessarily limited by the enforcement provisions of Section 5 of the Fourteenth Amendment." *Fitzpatrick v. Bitzer,* 427 U.S. 445 (1976). See also *Garrett; Kimel.*

Two provisions of the Fourteenth Amendment are relevant here: Section 5 grants Congress the power "to enforce" the substantive guarantees of Section 1—among them, equal protection of the laws—by enacting "appropriate legislation." Congress may, in the exercise of its Section 5 power, do more than simply proscribe conduct that we have held unconstitutional. "'Congress' power to enforce' the Amendment includes the authority both to remedy and to deter violation of rights guaranteed thereunder by prohibiting a somewhat broader swath of conduct, including that which is not itself forbidden by the Amendment's text." *Garrett; City of Boerne v. Flores,* 521 U.S. 507 (1997); *Katzenbach v. Morgan,* 384 U.S. 641 (1966). In other words, Congress may enact so-called prophylactic legislation that proscribes facially constitutional conduct, in order to prevent and deter unconstitutional conduct.

City of Boerne also confirmed, however, that it falls to this Court, not Congress, to define the substance of constitutional guarantees. "The ultimate interpretation and determination of the Fourteenth Amendment's substantive meaning remains the province of the Judicial Branch." *Kimel.* Section 5 legislation reaching beyond the scope of Section 1's actual guarantees must be an appropriate remedy for identified constitutional violations, not "an attempt to substantively redefine the States' legal obligations." We distinguish appropriate prophylactic legislation from "substantive redefinition of the Fourteenth Amendment right at issue" by applying the test set forth in *City of Boerne*: Valid Section 5 legislation must exhibit "congruence and proportionality between the injury to be prevented or remedied and the means adopted to that end."

The FMLA aims to protect the right to be free from gender-based discrimination in the workplace. We have held that statutory classifications that distinguish between males and females are subject to heightened scrutiny. See, e.g., *Craig v. Boren,* 429 U.S. 190 (1976). For a gender-based classification to withstand such scrutiny, it must "serv[e] important governmental objectives," and "the discriminatory means employed [must be] substantially related to the achievement of those objectives." *United States v. Virginia,* 518 U.S. 515 (1996). The State's justification for such a classification "must not rely on overbroad generalizations about the different talents, capacities, or preferences of males and females." We now inquire whether Congress had evidence of a pattern of constitutional violations on the part of the States in this area.

The history of the many state laws limiting women's employment opportunities is chronicled in—and, until relatively recently, was sanctioned by—this Court's own opinions. For example, in *Bradwell v. State,* 16 Wall. 130 (1873)

(Illinois), and *Goesaert v. Cleary*, 335 U.S. 464 (1948) (Michigan), the Court upheld state laws prohibiting women from practicing law and tending bar, respectively. State laws frequently subjected women to distinctive restrictions, terms, conditions, and benefits for those jobs they could take. In *Muller v. Oregon*, 208 U.S. 412 (1908), for example, this Court approved a state law limiting the hours that women could work for wages, and observed that 19 States had such laws at the time. Such laws were based on the related beliefs that (1) woman is, and should remain, "the center of home and family life," *Hoyt v. Florida*, 368 U.S. 57 (1961), and (2) "a proper discharge of [a woman's] maternal functions—having in view not merely her own health, but the well-being of the race—justif[ies] legislation to protect her from the greed as well as the passion of man." *Muller*. Until our decision in *Reed v. Reed*, 404 U.S. 71 (1971), "it remained the prevailing doctrine that government, both federal and state, could withhold from women opportunities accorded men so long as any 'basis in reason'"—such as the above beliefs—"could be conceived for the discrimination." *Virginia*.

Congress responded to this history of discrimination by abrogating States' sovereign immunity in Title VII of the Civil Rights Act of 1964, and we sustained this abrogation in *Fitzpatrick*. But state gender discrimination did not cease. "[I]t can hardly be doubted that ... women still face pervasive, although at times more subtle, discrimination ... in the job market." *Frontiero v. Richardson*, 411 U.S. 677 (1973). According to evidence that was before Congress when it enacted the FMLA, States continue to rely on invalid gender stereotypes in the employment context, specifically in the administration of leave benefits. Reliance on such stereotypes cannot justify the States' gender discrimination in this area. *Virginia*. The long and extensive history of sex discrimination prompted us to hold that measures that differentiate on the basis of gender warrant heightened scrutiny; here, as in *Fitzpatrick*, the persistence of such unconstitutional discrimination by the States justifies Congress's passage of prophylactic Section 5 legislation.

As the FMLA's legislative record reflects, a 1990 Bureau of Labor Statistics (BLS) survey stated that 37 percent of surveyed private-sector employees were covered by maternity leave policies, while only 18 percent were covered by paternity leave policies. The corresponding numbers from a similar BLS survey the previous year were 33 percent and 16 percent, respectively. While these data show an increase in the percentage of employees eligible for such leave, they also show a widening of the gender gap during the same period. Thus, stereotype-based beliefs about the allocation of family duties remained firmly rooted, and employers' reliance on them in establishing discriminatory leave policies remained widespread.

Congress also heard testimony that "[p]arental leave for fathers ... is rare. Even ... [w]here child-care leave policies do exist, men, both in the public and private sectors, receive notoriously discriminatory treatment in their requests for such leave." (Washington Council of Lawyers). Many States offered women extended "maternity" leave that far exceeded the typical 4- to 8-week period of physical disability due to pregnancy and childbirth, but very few States granted men a parallel benefit: Fifteen States provided women up to one year of extended maternity leave, while only four provided men with the same. This and other differential leave policies were not attributable to any differential physical needs of men and women, but rather to the pervasive sex-role stereotype that caring for family members is women's work.

Finally, Congress had evidence that, even where state laws and policies were not facially discriminatory, they were applied in discriminatory ways. . . .

In sum, the States' record of unconstitutional participation in, and fostering of, gender-based discrimination in the administration of leave benefits is weighty enough to justify the enactment of prophylactic Section 5 legislation.

We reached the opposite conclusion in *Garrett* and *Kimel*. In those cases, the Section 5 legislation under review responded to a purported tendency of state officials to make age- or disability-based distinctions. Under our equal protection case law, discrimination on the basis of such characteristics is not judged under a heightened review standard, and passes muster if there is "a rational basis for doing so at a class-based level, even if it 'is probably not true' that those reasons are valid in the majority of cases." *Kimel*. Thus, in order to impugn the constitutionality of state discrimination against the disabled or the elderly, Congress must identify, not just the existence of age- or disability-based state decisions, but a widespread pattern of irrational reliance on such criteria. We found no such showing with respect to the ADEA and Title I of the Americans with Disabilities Act of 1990 (ADA). *Kimel*.

Here, however, Congress directed its attention to state gender discrimination, which triggers a heightened level of scrutiny. Because the standard for demonstrating the constitutionality of a gender-based classification is more difficult to meet than our rational-basis test—it must "serv[e] important governmental objectives" and be "substantially related to the achievement of those objectives," *Virginia*—it was easier for Congress to show a pattern of state constitutional violations. Congress was similarly successful in *South Carolina v. Katzenbach*, 383 U.S. 301 (1966), where we upheld the Voting Rights Act of 1965: Because racial classifications are presumptively invalid, most of the States' acts of race discrimination violated the Fourteenth Amendment. . . .

Unlike the statutes at issue in *City of Boerne*, *Kimel*, and *Garrett*, which applied broadly to every aspect of state employers' operations, the FMLA is narrowly targeted at the fault line between work and family—precisely where sex-based overgeneralization has been and remains strongest—and affects only one aspect of the employment relationship. . . .

The judgment of the Court of Appeals is therefore Affirmed.

☐ *Justice KENNEDY, with whom Justice SCALIA and Justice THOMAS join, dissenting.*

The Family and Medical Leave Act of 1993 makes explicit the congressional intent to invoke Section 5 of the Fourteenth Amendment to abrogate state sovereign immunity and allow suits for money damages in federal courts. The specific question is whether Congress may impose on the States this entitlement program of its own design, with mandated minimums for leave time, and then enforce it by permitting private suits for money damages against the States. This in turn must be answered by asking whether subjecting States and their treasuries to monetary liability at the insistence of private litigants is a congruent and proportional response to a demonstrated pattern of unconstitutional conduct by the States. If we apply the teaching of these and related cases, the family leave provision of the Act, Section 2612(a)(1)(C), in my respectful view, is invalid to the extent it allows for private suits against the unconsenting States.

Congress does not have authority to define the substantive content of the Equal Protection Clause; it may only shape the remedies warranted by the violations of that guarantee. *City of Boerne.* This requirement has special force in the context of the Eleventh Amendment, which protects a State's fiscal integrity from federal intrusion by vesting the States with immunity from private actions for damages pursuant to federal laws. The Commerce Clause likely would permit the National Government to enact an entitlement program such as this one; but when Congress couples the entitlement with the authorization to sue the States for monetary damages, it blurs the line of accountability the State has to its own citizens. These basic concerns underlie cases such as *Garrett* and *Kimel,* and should counsel far more caution than the Court shows in holding Section 2612(a)(1)(C) is somehow a congruent and proportional remedy to an identified pattern of discrimination.

The Court is unable to show that States have engaged in a pattern of unlawful conduct which warrants the remedy of opening state treasuries to private suits. The inability to adduce evidence of alleged discrimination, coupled with the inescapable fact that the federal scheme is not a remedy but a benefit program, demonstrate the lack of the requisite link between any problem Congress has identified and the program it mandated.

In examining whether Congress was addressing a demonstrated "pattern of unconstitutional employment discrimination by the States," the Court gives superficial treatment to the requirement that we "identify with some precision the scope of the constitutional right at issue." *Garrett.* The Court suggests the issue is "the right to be free from gender-based discrimination in the workplace," and then it embarks on a survey of our precedents speaking to "[t]he history of the many state laws limiting women's employment opportunities." All would agree that women historically have been subjected to conditions in which their employment opportunities are more limited than those available to men. As the Court acknowledges, however, Congress responded to this problem by abrogating States' sovereign immunity in Title VII of the Civil Rights Act of 1964. The provision now before us has a different aim than Title VII. It seeks to ensure that eligible employees, irrespective of gender, can take a minimum amount of leave time to care for an ill relative.

The relevant question, as the Court seems to acknowledge, is whether, notwithstanding the passage of Title VII and similar state legislation, the States continued to engage in widespread discrimination on the basis of gender in the provision of family leave benefits. If such a pattern were shown, the Eleventh Amendment would not bar Congress from devising a congruent and proportional remedy. The evidence to substantiate this charge must be far more specific, however, than a simple recitation of a general history of employment discrimination against women. When the federal statute seeks to abrogate state sovereign immunity, the Court should be more careful to insist on adherence to the analytic requirements set forth in its own precedents. Persisting overall effects of gender-based discrimination at the workplace must not be ignored; but simply noting the problem is not a substitute for evidence which identifies some real discrimination the family leave rules are designed to prevent. . . .

Even if there were evidence that individual state employers, in the absence of clear statutory guidelines, discriminated in the administration of leave benefits, this circumstance alone would not support a finding of a state-sponsored pattern of discrimination. The evidence could perhaps support the charge of disparate impact, but not a charge that States have engaged in a pattern of intentional discrimination prohibited by the Fourteenth Amendment. *Garrett.* . . .

The paucity of evidence to support the case the Court tries to make demonstrates that Congress was not responding with a congruent and proportional remedy to a perceived course of unconstitutional conduct. Instead, it enacted a substantive entitlement program of its own. If Congress had been concerned about different treatment of men and women with respect to family leave, a congruent remedy would have sought to ensure the benefits of any leave program enacted by a State are available to men and women on an equal basis. Instead, the Act imposes, across the board, a requirement that States grant a minimum of 12 weeks of leave per year. This requirement may represent Congress's considered judgment as to the optimal balance between the family obligations of workers and the interests of employers, and the States may decide to follow these guidelines in designing their own family leave benefits. It does not follow, however, that if the States choose to enact a different benefit scheme, they should be deemed to engage in unconstitutional conduct and forced to open their treasuries to private suits for damages. . . .

What is at issue is only whether the States can be subjected, without consent, to suits brought by private persons seeking to collect moneys from the state treasury. Their immunity cannot be abrogated without documentation of a pattern of unconstitutional acts by the States, and only then by a congruent and proportional remedy. There has been a complete failure by respondents to carry their burden to establish each of these necessary propositions. I would hold that the Act is not a valid abrogation of state sovereign immunity and dissent with respect from the Court's conclusion to the contrary.

■ THE DEVELOPMENT OF LAW

Other Rulings on the Eleventh Amendment

CASE	VOTE	RULING
Lapides v. Board of Regents of The University System of Georgia, 534 U.S. 1052 (2002)	9:0	Writing for a unanimous Court, Justice Breyer held a state's removal of a lawsuit filed against it from a state court to a federal court constitutes a waiver of the

state's Eleventh Amendment immunity.

Verizon Maryland v. Public Service Commission of Maryland, 535 U.S. 467 (2002)	8:0	With Justice O'Connor not participating, the Court held unanimously that states are not immune from suits brought over the im- plementation of the Telecom-

munications Act of 1996. Justice Scalia delivered the opinion of the Court and Justices Kennedy and Souter filed concurring opinions.

Federal Maritime Commission v. South Carolina State Ports Authority, 535 U.S. 743 (2002)	5:4	Writing for the Court, Justice Thomas held that states' sovereign immunity bars the Federal Mari- time Commission (FMC) from adjudicating a private party's com-

plaint against a nonconsenting state in an administrative law proceeding. Justice Thomas reasoned that dual sovereignty is a defining feature of the nation and that an integral component of states' sovereignty is their immunity from private suits. Although the Eleventh Amendment provides that the "judicial Power of the United States" does not "extend to any suit, in law or equity," brought by citizens of one state against another state, that provision does not define states' sovereign immunity but is instead only one exemplification of that immunity. Formalized administrative adjudications were virtually unheard of in the eighteenth and nineteenth centuries, so there is little evidence of the framers' intent. However, because of the presumption that the Constitution was not intended to encourage any proceedings against the state that were "anomalous and unheard of when the Constitution was adopted," *Hans v. Louisiana*, 134 U.S. 1 (1890), the Court should attribute great significance to the fact that the states were not subject to private suits in administrative adjudications at the time of the founding. In deciding whether the *Hans* presumption of immunity applies here, Justice Thomas observed that administrative law judges and trial judges play similar roles and that administrative and judicial proceedings share similar features. More specifically, he noted that the FMC adjudications are a proceeding that "walks, talks, and squawks like a lawsuit." In addition, Justice Thomas concluded that it would be strange if Congress were prohibited from exercising its Article I powers to abrogate state sovereign immunity in Article III judicial proceedings but were permitted to create courtlike administrative tribunals to which state sovereign immunity did not apply. Justices Stevens and Breyer each issued dissenting opinions and were joined by Justices Souter and Ginsburg.

Frew v. Hawkins, 124 S.Ct. 899 (2004)   9:0

Writing for the Court, Justice Kennedy held that states are not immune under the Eleventh Amendment from complying with their obligations under a consent degree enforcing federal law, even for monetary damages for retrospective relief for failure to enforce federal laws. Linda Frew sued Texas for failing to provide medical care for her children under the federal Early and Periodic Screening, Diagnostic, and Treatment (EPSDT) program. State officials did not raise an Eleventh Amendment claim or object to the suit in federal court. But after the court approved a consent degree they claimed that it was unenforceable under the Eleventh Amendment. Justice Kennedy ruled that the Eleventh Amendment does not bar enforcement of a consent degree pertaining to states' providing EPSDT services and, although generally not for damages for retrospective relief for a state's failure to comply with federal law, here the damages were enforceable as part of a federal court order that enforced states' compliance with federal law.

Tennessee v. Lane, 124 S.Ct. 1978 (2004)   5:4

Writing for the Court, Justice Stevens held that Congress has the power under Section 5 of the Fourteenth Amendment to authorize lawsuits against states to force their compliance with Title 2 of the Americans with Disabilities Act (ADA) of 1990 and rejected the claim that such suits are barred by the Eleventh Amendment. But the holding was narrow and limited to suits against states to force them to provide access for the disabled to courthouses. The ruling did not address access to other public "services, programs, or activities" where fundamental rights are not at issue. Justice Stevens justified the exercise of Congress's remedial power on finding that "Congress learned that many individuals, in many states across the country, were being excluded from courthouses and court proceedings by reason of their disabilities." On that basis he distinguished the five-to-four decision in *Board of Trustees of University of Alabama v. Garrett,* 531 U.S. 356 (2001), in which Chief Justice Rehnquist held that Title I of the ADA, barring discrimination against people with disabilities in state employment, did not abrogate states' Eleventh Amendment immunity. Writing for the dissenters—Justices Scalia, Kennedy, and Thomas—in *Lane,* Chief Justice Rehnquist maintained that Congress lacked the authority to abrogate state immunity from suits to enforce the ADA under all of its provisions and dismissed evidence of a congressional finding of discrimination against the disabled as merely "anecdotal" and insufficient to establish systematic discrimination. Justice O'Connor cast the pivotal vote in *Garrett* and *Lane.*

8

REPRESENTATIVE GOVERNMENT, VOTING RIGHTS, AND ELECTORAL POLITICS

A | Representative Government and the Franchise

■ THE DEVELOPMENT OF LAW

Other Rulings Interpreting the Voting Rights Act

CASE	VOTE	RULING
Georgia v. Ashcroft, 539 U.S. 461 (2003)	5:4	The Court held that under Section 5 of the Voting Rights Act, legislative and congressional dis-

tricts may be redrawn in ways that shrink black voting majorities in order to create more Democratic-leaning districts. Georgia's redistricting reduced black majorities in three districts to just over 50 percent, down from 55 to 62 percent, in order to increase the likelihood of electing Democrats. A federal district court held that this violated the Voting Rights Act, but the Supreme Court reversed in holding that in assessing the racial regressive effect all factors may be considered, including a minority group's voting participation in a coalitional district. Writing for the Court, Justice O'Connor observed: "Various studies suggest that the most effective way to maximize minority voting strength may be to create more influence or coalitional districts. Section 5 allows States to risk having fewer minority representatives in order to achieve greater overall representation of a minority group by increasing the number of representatives sympathetic to the interests of minority voters." Justices Stevens, Souter, Ginsburg, and Breyer dissented and accused the majority of gutting the act's prohibition against redistricting that is retrogressive for minority voting rights.

B | *Voting Rights and the Reapportionment Revolution*

In its 2003–2004 term, the Court revisited the controversy over whether political gerrymanders are justiciable. In *Davis v. Bandemer*, 478 U.S. 106 (1986), the Court held that political gerrymandering was a justiciable controversy. But a majority could not agree on a standard for adjudicating such disputes. Almost two decades later the Court revised the issue in *Vieth v. Jubelirer* (2004) (excerpted below). There, a plurality—Chief Justice Rehnquist and Justices O'Connor, Scalia, and Thomas—would have overruled *Davis v. Bandemer* and held that political gerrymandering controversies are nonjusticiable. Justice Kennedy, who cast the pivotal vote, would not go along with that and maintained that an enforceable standard might still emerge. The four dissenters—Justices Stevens, Souter, Ginsburg, and Breyer—countered that the Court could formulate standards for adjudicating political gerrymandering disputes, but they could not agree on a standard.

Vieth v. Jubelirer
124 S.Ct. 1769 (2004)

After the 2000 census, Pennsylvania lost two seats in the House of Representatives, and the Republican-controlled legislature redrew the congressional district lines in ways that disadvantaged Democratic candidates. Three Democrats—Richard Vieth, Norman Jean Vieth, and Susan Furey—challenged the constitutionality of that political gerrymander as a violation of the principle of one person, one vote. The Supreme Court held, in *Davis v. Bandemer*, 478 U.S. 109 (1986), that political gerrymandering controversies are justiciable but provided no standard for adjudicating such disputes. Accordingly, the three-judge district court dismissed Vieth's claim, and an appeal was made to the Supreme Court.

The lower court was affirmed by a vote of five to four. Justice Scalia delivered the opinion for the Court, which was joined by Chief Justice Rehnquist and Justices O'Connor and Thomas. They would have overruled *Davis v. Bandemer* and ruled that political gerrymandering controversies are nonjusticiable. In a concurring opinion, however, Justice Kennedy agreed with the result but declined to overrule *Davis* and held out the possibility of developing a standard for adjudicating the constitutionality of political gerrymanders. Dissenting opinions were filed by Justice Souter, joined by Justice Ginsburg, and by Justices Stevens and Breyer.

□ *Justice SCALIA announced the judgment of the Court and delivered an opinion, in which THE CHIEF JUSTICE, Justice O'CONNOR, and Justice THOMAS join.*

In *Davis v. Bandemer* (1986), this Court held that political gerrymandering claims are justiciable, but could not agree upon a standard to adjudicate them. The present appeal presents the questions whether our decision in *Bandemer* was in error, and, if not, what the standard should be. . . .

Political gerrymanders are not new to the American scene. One scholar traces them back to the Colony of Pennsylvania at the beginning of the 18th century, where several counties conspired to minimize the political power of the city of Philadelphia by refusing to allow it to merge or expand into surrounding jurisdictions, and denying it additional representatives. The political gerrymander remained alive and well (though not yet known by that name) at the time of the framing.

It is significant that the Framers provided a remedy for such practices in the Constitution. Article 1, Sec. 4, while leaving in state legislatures the initial power to draw districts for federal elections, permitted Congress to "make or alter" those districts if it wished. . . .

The power bestowed on Congress to regulate elections, and in particular to restrain the practice of political gerrymandering, has not lain dormant. In the Apportionment Act of 1842, Congress provided that Representatives must be elected from single-member districts "composed of contiguous territory." Congress again imposed these requirements in the Apportionment Act of 1862, and in 1872 further required that districts "contai[n] as nearly as practicable an equal number of inhabitants." In the Apportionment Act of 1901, Congress imposed a compactness requirement. The requirements of contiguity, compactness, and equality of population were repeated in the 1911 apportionment legislation but were not thereafter continued. Today, only the single-member-district requirement remains. Recent history, however, attests to Congress's awareness of the sort of districting practices appellants protest and of its power under Article I, Sec. 4, to control them. Since 1980, no fewer than five bills have been introduced to regulate gerrymandering in congressional districting.

Eighteen years ago, we held that the Equal Protection Clause grants judges the power—and duty—to control political gerrymandering, see *Davis v. Bandemer* (1986). It is to consideration of this precedent that we now turn.

As CHIEF JUSTICE MARSHALL proclaimed two centuries ago, "[i]t is emphatically the province and duty of the judicial department to say what the law is." *Marbury v. Madison*, 1 Cranch 137, 177 (1803). Sometimes, however, the law is that the judicial department has no business entertaining the claim of unlawfulness—because the question is entrusted to one of the political branches or involves no judicially enforceable rights. See, e.g., *Nixon v. United States*, 506 U.S. 224 (1993) (challenge to procedures used in Senate impeachment proceedings). . . .

"The judicial Power" created by Article III, Sec. 1, of the Constitution is not whatever judges choose to do, or even whatever Congress chooses to assign them, see *Lujan v. Defenders of Wildlife*, 504 U.S. 555 (1992). It is the power to act in the manner traditional for English and American courts. One of the most obvious limitations imposed by that requirement is that judicial action must be governed by standard, by rule. Laws promulgated by the Legislative Branch can be inconsistent, illogical, and ad hoc; law pronounced by the courts must be principled, rational, and based upon reasoned distinctions.

Over the dissent of three Justices, the Court held in *Davis v. Bandemer* that, since it was "not persuaded that there are no judicially discernible and manageable standards by which political gerrymander cases are to be decided" such cases were justiciable. The clumsy shifting of the burden of proof for the premise (the Court was "not persuaded" that standards do not exist, rather than "persuaded" that they do) was necessitated by the uncomfortable fact that the six-Justice majority could not discern what the judicially discernable standards might be. . . . The lower courts have lived with that assurance of a standard (or more precisely, lack of assurance that there is no standard), coupled with that inability to specify a standard, for the past 18 years. In that time, they have considered numerous political gerrymandering claims; this Court has never revisited the unanswered question of what standard governs. . . .

Eighteen years of judicial effort with virtually nothing to show for it justify us in revisiting the question whether the standard promised by *Bandemer* exists. As the following discussion reveals, no judicially discernible and manageable standards for adjudicating political gerrymandering claims have emerged. Lacking them, we must conclude that political gerrymandering claims are nonjusticiable and that *Bandemer* was wrongly decided.

We begin our review of possible standards with that proposed by Justice WHITE's plurality opinion in *Bandemer* because, as the narrowest ground for our decision in that case, it has been the standard employed by the lower courts. The plurality concluded that a political gerrymandering claim could succeed only where plaintiffs showed "both intentional discrimination against an identifiable political group and an actual discriminatory effect on that group." As to the intent element, the plurality acknowledged that "[a]s long as redistricting is done by a legislature, it should not be very difficult to prove that the likely political consequences of the reapportionment were intended." However, the effects prong was significantly harder to satisfy. Relief could not be based merely upon the fact that a group of persons banded together for political purposes had failed to achieve representation commensurate with its numbers, or that the apportionment scheme made its winning of elections more difficult. Rather, it would have to be shown that, taking into account a variety of historic factors and projected election results, the group had been "denied its chance to effectively influence the political process" as a whole, which could be achieved even without electing a candidate. It would not be enough to establish, for example, that Democrats had been "placed in a district with a supermajority of other Democratic voters" or that the district "departs from pre-existing political boundaries." Rather, in a challenge to an individual district the inquiry would focus "on the opportunity of members of the group to participate in party deliberations in the slating and nomination of candidates, their opportunity to register and vote, and hence their chance to directly influence the election returns and to secure the attention of the winning candidate." A statewide challenge, by contrast, would involve an analysis of "the voters' direct or indirect influence on the elections of the state legislature as a whole." With what has proved to be a gross understatement, the plurality acknowledged this was "of necessity a difficult inquiry." . . .

Because this standard was misguided when proposed, has not been improved in subsequent application, and is not even defended before us today by the appellants, we decline to affirm it as a constitutional requirement. . . .

Our one-person, one-vote cases, see *Reynolds v. Sims*, 377 U.S. 533 (1964); *Wesberry v. Sanders*, 376 U.S. 1 (1964), have no bearing upon this question, neither in principle nor in practicality. Not in principle, because to say that each individual must have an equal say in the selection of representatives, and hence that a majority of individuals must have a majority say, is not at all to say that each discernable group, whether farmers or urban dwellers or political parties, must have representation equivalent to its numbers. And not in practicality, because the easily administrable standard of population equality adopted by *Wesberry* and *Reynolds* enables judges to decide whether a violation has occurred (and to remedy it) essentially on the basis of three readily determined factors—where the plaintiff lives, how many voters are in his district, and how many voters are in other districts; whereas requiring judges to decide whether a districting system will produce a statewide majority for a majority party casts them forth upon a sea of imponderables, and asks them to make determinations that not even election experts can agree upon. . . .

We turn next to consideration of the standards proposed by today's dissenters. . . .

Justice STEVENS would . . . require courts to consider political gerrymandering challenges at the individual-district level. Much of his dissent is addressed to the incompatibility of severe partisan gerrymanders with democratic principles. We do not disagree with that judgment, any more than we disagree with the judgment that it would be unconstitutional for the Senate to employ, in impeachment proceedings, procedures that are incompatible with its obligation to "try" impeachments. See *Nixon v. United States* (1993). The issue we have discussed is not whether severe partisan gerrymanders violate the Constitution, but whether it is for the courts to say when a violation has occurred, and to design a remedy. On that point, Justice STEVENS's dissent is less helpful, saying, essentially, that if we can do it in the racial gerrymandering context we can do it here. . . .

Justice SOUTER recognizes that there is no existing workable standard for adjudicating such claims. He proposes a "fresh start," a newly constructed standard loosely based in form on our Title VII cases, and complete with a five-step prima facie test sewn together from parts of, among other things, our Voting Rights Act jurisprudence, law review articles, and apportionment cases. Even if these self-styled "clues" to unconstitutionality could be manageably applied, which we doubt, there is no reason to think they would detect the constitutional crime which Justice SOUTER is investigating—an "extremity of unfairness" in partisan competition.

Under Justice SOUTER's proposed standard, in order to challenge a particular district, a plaintiff must show (1) that he is a member of a "cohesive political group"; (2) "that the district of his residence . . . paid little or no heed" to traditional districting principles; (3) that there were "specific correlations between the district's deviations from traditional districting principles and the distribution of the population of his group"; (4) that a hypothetical district exists which includes the plaintiff's residence, remedies the packing or cracking of the plaintiff's group, and deviates less from traditional districting principles; and (5) that "the defendants acted intentionally to manipulate the shape of the district in order to pack or crack his group." When those showings have been made, the burden would shift to the defendants to justify the district "by reference to objectives other than naked partisan advantage."

While this five-part test seems eminently scientific, upon analysis one finds that each of the last four steps requires a quantifying judgment that is unguided and ill suited to the development of judicial standards: How much disregard of traditional districting principles? How many correlations between deviations and distribution? How much remedying of packing or cracking by the hypothetical district? How many legislators must have had the intent to pack and crack—and how efficacious must that intent have been (must it have been, for example, a sine qua non cause of the districting, or a predominant cause)? . . . What is a lower court to do when, as will often be the case, the district adheres to some traditional criteria but not others? Justice SOUTER's only response to this question is to evade it: "It is not necessary now to say exactly how a district court would balance a good showing on one of these indices against a poor showing on another, for that sort of detail is best worked out case by case." But the devil lurks precisely in such detail. The central problem is determining when political gerrymandering has gone too far. It does not solve that problem to break down the original unanswerable question (How much political motivation and effect is too much?) into four more discrete but equally unanswerable questions.

Justice SOUTER's proposal is doomed to failure for a more basic reason: No test—yea, not even a five-part test—can possibly be successful unless one knows what he is testing for. Justice SOUTER . . . vaguely describes the harm he is concerned with as vote dilution, a term which usually implies some actual effect on the weight of a vote. But no element of his test looks to the effect of the gerrymander on the electoral success, the electoral opportunity, or even the political influence, of the plaintiff group. We do not know the precise constitutional deprivation his test is designed to identify and prevent. . . .

We agree with much of Justice BREYER's dissenting opinion, which convincingly demonstrates that "political considerations will likely play an important, and proper, role in the drawing of district boundaries." This places Justice BREYER, like the other dissenters, in the difficult position of drawing the line between good politics and bad politics. Unlike them, he would tackle this problem at the statewide level.

The criterion Justice BREYER proposes is nothing more precise than "the unjustified use of political factors to entrench a minority in power." While he invokes in passing the Equal Protection Clause, it should be clear to any reader that what constitutes unjustified entrenchment depends on his own theory of "effective government." While one must agree with Justice BREYER's incredibly abstract starting point that our Constitution sought to create a "basically democratic" form of government, that is a long and impassable distance away from the conclusion that the judiciary may assess whether a group (somehow defined) has achieved a level of political power (somehow defined) commensurate with that to which they would be entitled absent unjustified political machinations (whatever that means).

Justice BREYER provides no real guidance for the journey. Despite his promise to do so, he never tells us what he is testing for, beyond the unhelpful "unjustified entrenchment." . . .

Justice KENNEDY recognizes that we have "demonstrat[ed] the short-comings of the other standards that have been considered to date." He acknowledges, moreover, that we "lack . . . comprehensive and neutral principles for drawing electoral boundaries," and that there is an "absence of rules to limit and confine judicial intervention." From these premises, one might think that Justice KENNEDY would reach the conclusion that political gerry-mandering claims are nonjusticiable. Instead, however, he concludes that courts should continue to adjudicate such claims because a standard may one day be discovered. . . .

Justice KENNEDY asserts that to declare nonjusticiability would be incautious. Our rush to such a holding after a mere 18 years of fruitless litigation "contrasts starkly" he says, "with the more patient approach" that this Court has taken in the past. We think not. . . .

We conclude that neither Article I, Sec. 2, nor the Equal Protection Clause, nor (what appellants only fleetingly invoke) Article I, Sec. 4, provides a judicially enforceable limit on the political considerations that the States and Congress may take into account when districting.

Considerations of *stare decisis* do not compel us to allow *Bandemer* to stand. . . . Eighteen years of essentially pointless litigation have persuaded us that *Bandemer* is incapable of principled application. We would therefore overrule that case, and decline to adjudicate these political gerrymandering claims. The judgment of the District Court is affirmed.

☐ *Justice KENNEDY, concurring in the judgment.*

I would not foreclose all possibility of judicial relief if some limited and precise rationale were found to correct an established violation of the Constitution in some redistricting cases. . . .

The object of districting is to establish "fair and effective representation for all citizens." *Reynolds v. Sims*, 377 U.S. 533 (1964). At first it might seem that courts could determine, by the exercise of their own judgment, whether political classifications are related to this object or instead burden representational rights. The lack, however, of any agreed upon model of fair and effective representation makes this analysis difficult to pursue. . . .

It is not in our tradition to foreclose the judicial process from the attempt to define standards and remedies where it is alleged that a constitutional right is burdened or denied. Nor is it alien to the Judiciary to draw or approve election district lines. Courts, after all, already do so in many instances. A determination by the Court to deny all hopes of intervention could erode confidence in the courts as much as would a premature decision to intervene.

Our willingness to enter the political thicket of the apportionment process with respect to one-person, one-vote claims makes it particularly difficult to justify a categorical refusal to entertain claims against this other type of gerrymandering. The plurality's conclusion that absent an "easily administrable standard," the appellants' claim must be nonjusticiable contrasts starkly with the more patient approach of *Baker v. Carr* (1962), not to mention the controlling precedent on the question of justiciability of *Davis v. Bandemer*, the case the plurality would overrule. . . .

Even putting *Baker* to the side—and so assuming that the existence of a workable standard for measuring a gerrymander's burden on representational rights distinguishes one-person, one-vote claims from partisan gerrymandering claims for justiciability purposes—I would still reject the plurality's conclusions as to nonjusticiability. Relying on the distinction between a claim having or not having a workable standard of that sort involves a difficult proof: proof of a categorical negative. That is, the different treatment of claims otherwise so alike hinges entirely on proof that no standard could exist. This is a difficult proposition to establish, for proving a negative is a challenge in any context.

That no such standard has emerged in this case should not be taken to prove that none will emerge in the future. Where important rights are involved, the impossibility of full analytical satisfaction is reason to err on the side of caution. Allegations of unconstitutional bias in apportionment are most serious claims, for we have long believed that "the right to vote" is one of "those political processes ordinarily to be relied upon to protect minorities." . . .

If suitable standards with which to measure the burden a gerrymander imposes on representational rights did emerge, hindsight would show that the Court prematurely abandoned the field. That is a risk the Court should not take. . . .

☐ *Justice STEVENS dissenting.*

The central question presented by this case is whether political gerrymandering claims are justiciable. Although our reasons for coming to this conclusion differ, five Members of the Court are convinced that the plurality's answer to that question is erroneous. Moreover, as is apparent from our separate writings today, we share the view that, even if these appellants are not entitled to prevail, it would be contrary to precedent and profoundly unwise to foreclose all judicial review of similar claims that might be advanced in the future. That we presently have somewhat differing views—concerning both the precedential value of some of our recent cases and the standard that should be applied in future cases—should not obscure the fact that the areas of agreement set forth in the separate opinions are of far greater significance.

The concept of equal justice under law requires the State to govern impartially. See *Romer v. Evans*, 517 U.S. 620 (1996). . . . In my view, when partisanship is the legislature's sole motivation—when any pretense of neutrality is forsaken unabashedly and all traditional districting criteria are subverted for partisan advantage—the governing body cannot be said to have acted impartially.

Although we reaffirm the central holding of the Court in *Davis v. Bandemer*, we have not reached agreement on the standard that should govern partisan gerrymanderying claims. I would decide this case on a narrow ground. . . .

State action that discriminates against a political minority for the sole and unadorned purpose of maximizing the power of the majority plainly violates the decisionmaker's duty to remain impartial. Gerrymanders necessarily rest on legislators' predictions that "members of certain identifiable groups . . . will vote in the same way." *Mobile v. Bolden*, 446 U.S. 55 (1980). "In the line-drawing process, racial, religious, ethnic, and economic gerrymanders are all species of political gerrymanders." Thus, the critical issue in both racial and political gerrymandering cases is the same: whether a single non-neutral criterion controlled the districting process to such an extent that the Constitution was offended. This Court has treated that precise question as justiciable in *Gomillion* [*v. Lightfoot*, 364 U.S. 339 (1960)] and in the *Shaw* [*v. Reno*, 509 U.S. 630 (1993)] line of cases, and today's plurality has supplied no persuasive reason for distinguishing the justiciability of partisan gerrymanders. Those cases confirm and reinforce the holding that partisan gerrymandering claims are justiciable. . . .

[W]hile political considerations may properly influence the decisions of our elected officials, when such decisions disadvantage members of a minority group—whether the minority is defined by its members' race, religion, or political affiliation—they must rest on a neutral predicate. Thus, the Equal Protection Clause implements a duty to govern impartially that requires, at the very least, that every decision by the sovereign serve some nonpartisan public purpose.

In evaluating a claim that a governmental decision violates the Equal Protection Clause, we have long required a showing of discriminatory purpose. See *Washington v. Davis*, 426 U.S. 229 (1976). That requirement applies with full force to districting decisions. The line that divides a racial or ethnic minority unevenly between school districts can be entirely legitimate if chosen on the basis of neutral factors—county lines, for example, or a natural boundary such as a river or major thoroughfare. But if the district lines were chosen for the purpose of limiting the number of minority students in the school, or the number of families holding unpopular religious or political views, that invidious purpose surely would invalidate the district. . . .

In sum, in evaluating a challenge to a specific district, I would apply the standard set forth in the *Shaw* cases and ask whether the legislature allowed partisan considerations to dominate and control the lines drawn, forsaking all neutral principles. Under my analysis, if no neutral criterion can be identified to justify the lines drawn, and if the only possible explanation for a district's bizarre shape is a naked desire to increase partisan strength, then no rational basis exists to save the district from an equal protection challenge. Such a narrow test would cover only a few meritorious claims, but it would preclude extreme abuses . . . and it would perhaps shorten the time period in which the pernicious effects of such a gerrymander are felt. This test would mitigate the current trend under which partisan considerations are becoming the be-all and end-all in apportioning representatives. . . .

☐ *Justice SOUTER, with whom Justice GINSBURG joins, dissenting.*

The notion of fairness assumed to be denied . . . has been described as "each political group in a State [having] the same chance to elect representatives of its choice as any other political group," and as a "right to 'fair and effective representation.'" It is undeniable that political sophisticates understand such fairness and how to go about destroying it, although it cannot possibly be described with the hard edge of one person, one vote. The difficulty has been to translate these notions of fairness into workable criteria, as distinct from mere opportunities for reviewing courts to make episodic judgments that things have gone too far, the sources of difficulty being in the facts that some intent to gain political advantage is inescapable whenever political bodies devise a district plan, and some effect results from the intent. Thus, the issue is one of how much is too much, and we can be no more exact in stating a verbal test for too much partisanship than we can be in defining too much race consciousness when some is inevitable and legitimate. Instead of coming up with a verbal formula for too much, then, the Court's job must be to identify clues, as objective as we can make them, indicating that partisan competition has reached an extremity of unfairness. . . .

Since this Court has created the problem no one else has been able to solve, it is up to us to make a fresh start. . . . I would therefore preserve *Davis's* holding that political gerrymandering is a justiciable issue, but otherwise start anew. I would adopt a political gerrymandering test analogous to the summary judgment standard crafted in *McDonnell Douglas Corp. v. Green*, 411 U.S. 792 (1973), calling for a plaintiff to satisfy elements of a prima facie cause of action, at which point the State would have the opportunity not only to rebut the evidence supporting the plaintiff's case, but to offer an affirmative justification for the districting choices, even assuming the proof of the plaintiff's allegations. My own judgment is that we would have better luck at devising a workable prima facie case if we concentrated as much as possible on suspect characteristics of individual districts instead of statewide patterns. It is not that a statewide view of districting is somehow less important; the usual point of gerrymandering, after all, is to control the greatest number of seats overall. But, as will be seen, we would be able to call more readily on some existing law when we defined what is suspect at the district level, and for now I would conceive of a statewide challenge as itself a function of claims that individual districts are illegitimately drawn. Finally, in the same interest of threshold simplicity, I would stick to problems of single-member districts; if we could not devise a workable scheme for dealing with claims about these, we would have to forget the complications posed by multimember districts.

For a claim based on a specific single-member district, I would require the plaintiff to make out a prima facie case with five elements. First, the resident plaintiff would identify a cohesive political group to which he belonged, which would normally be a major party, as in this case and in *Davis*. There is no reason in principle, however, to rule out a claimant from a minor political party (which might, if it showed strength, become the target of vigorous hostility from one or both major parties in a State) or from a different but politically coherent group whose members engaged in bloc voting, as a large labor union might do.

Second, a plaintiff would need to show that the district of his residence, see *United States v. Hays*, 515 U.S. 737 (1995) (requiring residence in a challenged district for standing), paid little or no heed to those traditional districting principles whose disregard can be shown straightforwardly: contiguity, compactness, respect for political subdivisions, and conformity with geographic features like rivers and mountains. Because such considerations are already relevant to justifying small deviations from absolute population equality, and because compactness in particular is relevant to demonstrating possible majority-minority districts under the Voting Rights Act of 1965, there is no doubt that a test relying on these standards would fall within judicial competence. . . .

Third, the plaintiff would need to establish specific correlations between the district's deviations from traditional districting principles and the distribution of the population of his group. For example, one of the districts to which appellants object most strongly in this case is District 6, which they say "looms like a dragon descending on Philadelphia from the west, splitting up towns and communities throughout Montgomery and Berks Counties." To make their claim stick, they would need to point to specific protuberances on the draconian shape that reach out to include Democrats, or fissures in it that squirm away from Republicans. They would need to show that when towns and communities were split, Democrats tended to fall on one side and Republicans on the other.

Fourth, a plaintiff would need to present the court with a hypothetical district including his residence, one in which the proportion of the plaintiff's group was lower (in a packing claim) or higher (in a cracking one) and which at the same time deviated less from traditional districting principles than the actual district. This hypothetical district would allow the plaintiff to claim credibly that the deviations from traditional districting principles were not only correlated with, but also caused by, the packing or cracking of his group. Drawing the hypothetical district would, of course, necessarily involve redrawing at least one contiguous district, and a plaintiff would have to show that this could be done subject to traditional districting principles without packing or cracking his group (or another) worse than in the district being challenged.

Fifth, and finally, the plaintiff would have to show that the defendants acted intentionally to manipulate the shape of the district in order to pack or crack his group. See *Washington v. Davis*, 426 U.S. 229 (1976). In substantiating claims of political gerrymandering under a plan devised by a single major party, proving intent should not be hard, once the third and fourth (correlation and cause) elements are established . . . . A plaintiff who got this far would have shown that his State intentionally acted to dilute his vote, having ignored reasonable alternatives consistent with traditional districting principles. I would then shift the burden to the defendants to justify their decision by reference to objectives other than naked partisan advantage. . . . The State might, for example, posit the need to avoid racial vote dilution. . . . This is not, however, the time or place for a comprehensive list of legitimate objectives a State might present. The point here is simply that the Constitution should not petrify traditional districting objectives as exclusive, and it is enough to say that the State would be required to explain itself, to demonstrate that whatever reasons it gave were more than a mere pretext for an old-fashioned gerrymander.

As for a statewide claim, I would not attempt an ambitious definition without the benefit of experience with individual district claims, and for now I would limit consideration of a statewide claim to one built upon a number of district-specific ones. Each successful district-specific challenge would necessarily entail redrawing at least one contiguous district, and the more the successful claims, the more surrounding districts to be redefined. At a certain point, the ripples would reach the state boundary, and it would no longer make any sense for a district court to consider the problems piecemeal. . . .

□ *Justice BREYER, dissenting.*

I start with a fundamental principle. "We the People," who "ordain[ed] and establish[ed]" the American Constitution, sought to create and to protect a workable form of government that is in its "'principles, structure, and whole mass,'" basically democratic. In a modern Nation of close to 300 million people, the workable democracy that the Constitution foresees must mean more than a guaranteed opportunity to elect legislators representing equally populous electoral districts. . . .

Why do I refer to these elementary constitutional principles? Because I believe they can help courts identify at least one abuse at issue in this case. To understand how that is so, one should begin by asking why single-member electoral districts are the norm, why the Constitution does not insist that the membership of legislatures better reflect different political views held by different groups of voters. History, of course, is part of the answer, but it does not tell the entire story. The answer also lies in the fact that a single-member-district system helps to assure certain democratic objectives better than many "more representative" (i.e., proportional) electoral systems. Of course, single-member districts mean that only parties with candidates who finish "first past the post" will elect legislators. That fact means in turn that a party with a bare majority of votes or even a plurality of votes will often obtain a large legislative majority, perhaps freezing out smaller parties. But single-member districts thereby diminish the need for coalition governments. And that fact makes it easier for voters to identify which party is responsible for government decisionmaking (and which rascals to throw out), while simultaneously providing greater legislative stability.

If single-member districts are the norm, however, then political considerations will likely play an important, and proper, role in the drawing of district boundaries. In part, that is because politicians, unlike nonpartisan observers, normally understand how "the location and shape of districts" determine "the political complexion of the area." It is precisely because politicians are best able to predict the effects of boundary changes that the districts they design usually make some political sense.

More important for present purposes, the role of political considerations reflects a surprising mathematical fact. Given a fairly large state population with a fairly large congressional delegation, districts assigned so as to be perfectly random in respect to politics would translate a small shift in political sentiment, say a shift from 51% Republican to 49% Republican, into a seismic shift in the makeup of the legislative delegation, say from 100% Republican to 100% Democrat. Any such exaggeration of tiny electoral changes—virtually wiping out legislative representation of the minority party—would itself seem highly undemocratic.

Given the resulting need for single-member districts with nonrandom boundaries, it is not surprising that "traditional" districting principles have rarely, if ever, been politically neutral. Rather, because, in recent political memory, Democrats have often been concentrated in cities while Republicans have often been concentrated in suburbs and sometimes rural areas, geographically drawn boundaries have tended to "pac[k]" the former.

This is to say that traditional or historically-based boundaries are not, and should not be, "politics free." Rather, those boundaries represent a series of compromises of principle—among the virtues of, for example, close representation of voter views, ease of identifying "government" and "opposition" parties, and stability in government. They also represent an uneasy truce, sanctioned by tradition, among different parties seeking political advantage.

As I have said, reference back to these underlying considerations helps to explain why the legislature's use of political boundary drawing considerations ordinarily does not violate the Constitution's Equal Protection Clause.

The reason lies not simply in the difficulty of identifying abuse or finding an appropriate judicial remedy. The reason is more fundamental: Ordinarily, there simply is no abuse. The use of purely political boundary-drawing factors, even where harmful to the members of one party, will often nonetheless find justification in other desirable democratic ends, such as maintaining relatively stable legislatures in which a minority party retains significant representation.

At the same time, these considerations can help identify at least one circumstance where use of purely political boundary-drawing factors can amount to a serious, and remediable, abuse, namely the unjustified use of political factors to entrench a minority in power. By entrenchment I mean a situation in which a party that enjoys only minority support among the populace has nonetheless contrived to take, and hold, legislative power. By unjustified entrenchment I mean that the minority's hold on power is purely the result of partisan manipulation and not other factors. These "other" factors that could lead to "justified" (albeit temporary) minority entrenchment include sheer happenstance, the existence of more than two major parties, the unique constitutional requirements of certain representational bodies such as the Senate, or reliance on traditional (geographic, communities of interest, etc.) districting criteria. . . .

Courts need not intervene often to prevent the kind of abuse I have described, because those harmed constitute a political majority, and a majority normally can work its political will. Where a State has improperly gerrymandered legislative or congressional districts to the majority's disadvantage, the majority should be able to elect officials in statewide races—particularly the Governor—who may help to undo the harm that districting has caused the majority's party, in the next round of districting if not sooner. And where a State has improperly gerrymandered congressional districts, Congress retains the power to revise the State's districting determinations.

Moreover, voters in some States, perhaps tiring of the political boundary-drawing rivalry, have found a procedural solution, confiding the task to a commission that is limited in the extent to which it may base districts on partisan concerns. . . .

But we cannot always count on a severely gerrymandered legislature itself to find and implement a remedy. The party that controls the process has no incentive to change it. . . . When it is necessary, a court should prove capable of finding an appropriate remedy. Courts have developed districting remedies in other cases. . . . The bottom line is that courts should be able to identify the presence of one important gerrymandering evil, the unjustified entrenching in power of a political party that the voters have rejected. They should be able to separate the unjustified abuse of partisan boundary-drawing considerations to achieve that end from their more ordinary and justified use. And they should be able to design a remedy for extreme cases. . . .

C | *Campaigns and Elections*

In light of the increasing costs and hotly partisan campaigns for state judgeships, the American Bar Association and other organizations have promoted reforms of state judicial elections. However, by a five-to-four vote in *Republican Party of Minnesota v. White* (2002) (excerpted below), the Court struck down restrictions on judicial candidates' announcing their positions on controversial legal and political issues. Notably, Justice Scalia's opinion for the Court and the dissenters advanced rival views of the role of judges and judicial elections.

Besides upholding most of the provisions of the Bipartisan Campaign Reform Act of 2002 in *McConnell v. Federal Election Commission* (2003) (excerpted below), the Court upheld over First Amendment objections a federal law barring corporations, even nonprofit advocacy corporations like the North Carolina Right to Life, Inc., from directly contributing to candidates for federal office in *Federal Election Commission v. Beaumont*, 539 U.S. 146 (2003). Justice Souter delivered the opinion for the Court, and Justice Thomas, joined by Justice Scalia, dissented.

Republican Party of Minnesota v. White
536 U.S. 765, 122 S.Ct. 2528 (2002)

The Minnesota Supreme Court adopted a canon of judicial conduct prohibiting candidates for judicial office from announcing their views on disputed legal and political issues. While running for the position of associate justice on that court, Gregory Wersal filed a lawsuit seeking a declaration that this "announce clause" violates the First Amendment. A federal district court disagreed and the Court of Appeals for the Eighth Circuit affirmed, whereupon the Republican Party appealed.

The appellate court's decision was reversed by a five-to-four vote and Justice Scalia delivered an opinion for the Court. Justices Stevens and Ginsburg filed dissenting opinions, which Justices Souter and Breyer joined.

☐ *Justice SCALIA delivered the opinion of the Court.*

The question presented in this case is whether the First Amendment permits the Minnesota Supreme Court to prohibit candidates for judicial election in that State from announcing their views on disputed legal and political issues. . . .

Before considering the constitutionality of the announce clause, we must be clear about its meaning. Its text says that a candidate for judicial office shall not "announce his or her views on disputed legal or political issues."

We know that "announc[ing] . . . views" on an issue covers much more than promising to decide an issue a particular way. The prohibition extends to the candidate's mere statement of his current position, even if he does not bind himself to maintain that position after election. All the parties agree this is the case, because the Minnesota Code contains a so-called "pledges or promises" clause, which separately prohibits judicial candidates from making "pledges or promises of conduct in office other than the faithful and impartial performance of the duties of the office"—a prohibition that is not challenged here and on which we express no view.

There are, however, some limitations that the Minnesota Supreme Court has placed upon the scope of the announce clause that are not (to put it politely) immediately apparent from its text. The statements that formed the basis of the complaint against Wersal in 1996 included criticism of past decisions of the Minnesota Supreme Court. One piece of campaign literature stated that "[t]he Minnesota Supreme Court has issued decisions which are marked by their disregard for the Legislature and a lack of common sense." The Judicial Board issued an opinion stating that judicial candidates may criticize past decisions, and the Lawyers Board refused to discipline Wersal for the foregoing statements because, in part, it thought they did not violate the announce clause. The Eighth Circuit relied on the Judicial Board's opinion in upholding the announce clause, and the Minnesota Supreme Court recently embraced the Eighth Circuit's interpretation.

There are yet further limitations upon the apparent plain meaning of the announce clause: In light of the constitutional concerns, the District Court construed the clause to reach only disputed issues that are likely to come before the candidate if he is elected judge. The Eighth Circuit accepted this limiting interpretation by the District Court, and in addition construed the clause to allow general discussions of case law and judicial philosophy. The Supreme Court of Minnesota adopted these interpretations as well when it ordered enforcement of the announce clause in accordance with the Eighth Circuit's opinion.

It seems to us, however, that—like the text of the announce clause itself—these limitations upon the text of the announce clause are not all that they appear to be. First, respondents acknowledged at oral argument that statements critical of past judicial decisions are not permissible if the candidate also states that he is against *stare decisis*. Thus, candidates must choose between stating their views critical of past decisions and stating their views in opposition to *stare decisis*. Or, to look at it more concretely, they may state their view that prior decisions were erroneous only if they do not assert that they, if elected, have any power to eliminate erroneous decisions. Second, limiting the scope of the clause to issues likely to come before a court is not much of a limitation at all. One would hardly expect the "disputed legal or political issues" raised in the course of a state judicial election to include such matters as whether the Federal Government should end the embargo of Cuba. Quite obviously, they will be those legal or political disputes that are the proper (or by past decisions have been made the improper) business of the state courts. And within that relevant category, "[t]here is almost no legal or political issue that is unlikely to come before a judge of an American court, state or federal, of general jurisdiction." Third, construing the clause to allow "general" discussions of case law and judicial philosophy turns out to be of little help in an election campaign. At oral argument, respondents gave, as an example of this exception, that a candidate is free to assert that he is a "'strict constructionist.'" But that, like most other philosophical generalities, has little meaningful content for the electorate unless it is exemplified by application to a particular issue of construction likely to come before a court—for example, whether a particular statute runs afoul of any provision of the Constitution. Respondents conceded that the announce clause would prohibit the candidate from exemplifying his philosophy in this fashion. Without such application to real-life issues, all candidates can claim to be "strict constructionists" with equal (and unhelpful) plausibility.

In any event, it is clear that the announce clause prohibits a judicial candidate from stating his views on any specific nonfanciful legal question within the province of the court for which he is running, except in the context of discussing past decisions—and in the latter context as well, if he expresses the view that he is not bound by *stare decisis.*

Respondents contend that this still leaves plenty of topics for discussion on the campaign trail. These include a candidate's "character," "education," "work habits," and "how [he] would handle administrative duties if elected." Indeed, the Judicial Board has printed a list of preapproved questions which judicial candidates are allowed to answer. These include how the candidate feels about cameras in the courtroom, how he would go about reducing the caseload, how the costs of judicial administration can be reduced, and how he proposes to ensure that minorities and women are treated more fairly by the court system. Whether this list of preapproved subjects, and other topics not prohibited by the announce clause, adequately fulfill the First Amendment's guarantee of freedom of speech is the question to which we now turn. . . .

We think it plain that the announce clause is not narrowly tailored to serve impartiality (or the appearance of impartiality). . . . Indeed, the clause is barely tailored to serve that interest at all, inasmuch as it does not restrict speech for or against particular parties, but rather speech for or against particular issues. To be sure, when a case arises that turns on a legal issue on which the judge (as a candidate) had taken a particular stand, the party taking the opposite stand is likely to lose. But not because of any bias against that party, or favoritism toward the other party. Any party taking that position is just as likely to lose. The judge is applying the law (as he sees it) evenhandedly.

It is perhaps possible to use the term "impartiality" in the judicial context (though this is certainly not a common usage) to mean lack of preconception in favor of or against a particular legal view. This sort of impartiality would be concerned, not with guaranteeing litigants equal application of the law, but rather with guaranteeing them an equal chance to persuade the court on the legal points in their case. Impartiality in this sense may well be an interest served by the announce clause, but it is not a compelling state interest, as strict scrutiny requires. A judge's lack of predisposition regarding the relevant legal issues in a case has never been thought a necessary component of equal justice, and with good reason. For one thing, it is virtually impossible to find a judge who does not have preconceptions about the law. . . .

A third possible meaning of "impartiality" (again not a common one) might be described as openmindedness. This quality in a judge demands, not that he have no preconceptions on legal issues, but that he be willing to consider views that oppose his preconceptions, and remain open to persuasion, when the issues arise in a pending case. This sort of impartiality seeks to guarantee each litigant, not an equal chance to win the legal points in the case, but at least some chance of doing so. It may well be that impartiality in this sense, and the appearance of it, are desirable in the judiciary, but we need not pursue that inquiry, since we do not believe the Minnesota Supreme Court adopted the announce clause for that purpose.

Respondents argue that the announce clause serves the interest in openmindedness, or at least in the appearance of openmindedness, because it relieves a judge from pressure to rule a certain way in order to maintain consistency with statements the judge has previously made. The problem is, however, that statements in election campaigns are such an infinitesimal portion of the public commitments to legal positions that judges (or judges-to-be) undertake, that this object of the prohibition is implausible. Before they arrive on the bench (whether by election or otherwise) judges have often committed themselves on legal issues that they must later rule upon. . . .

The short of the matter is this: In Minnesota, a candidate for judicial office may not say "I think it is constitutional for the legislature to prohibit same-sex marriages." He may say the very same thing, however, up until the very day before he declares himself a candidate, and may say it repeatedly (until litigation is pending) after he is elected. As a means of pursuing the objective of open-mindedness that respondents now articulate, the announce clause is so woefully underinclusive as to render belief in that purpose a challenge to the credulous. . . .

There is an obvious tension between the article of Minnesota's popularly approved Constitution which provides that judges shall be elected, and the Minnesota Supreme Court's announce clause which places most subjects of interest to the voters off limits. The disparity is perhaps unsurprising, since the ABA, which originated the announce clause, has long been an opponent of judicial elections. That opposition may be well taken (it certainly had the support of the Founders of the Federal Government), but the First Amendment does not permit it to achieve its goal by leaving the principle of elections in place while preventing candidates from discussing what the elections are about.

The Minnesota Supreme Court's canon of judicial conduct prohibiting candidates for judicial election from announcing their views on disputed legal and political issues violates the First Amendment. Accordingly, we reverse the grant of summary judgment to respondents and remand the case for proceedings consistent with this opinion. It is so ordered.

☐ *Justice GINSBURG, with whom Justice STEVENS, Justice SOUTER, and Justice BREYER join, dissenting.*

Whether state or federal, elected or appointed, judges perform a function fundamentally different from that of the people's elected representatives. Legislative and executive officials act on behalf of the voters who placed them in office; "judge[s] represen[t] the Law." *Chisom v. Roemer*, 501 U.S. 380 (1991) (SCALIA, J., dissenting). Unlike their counterparts in the political branches, judges are expected to refrain from catering to particular constituencies or committing themselves on controversial issues in advance of adversarial presentation. Their mission is to decide "individual cases and controversies" on individual records, *Plaut v. Spendthrift Farm, Inc.*, 514 U.S. 211 (1995) (STEVENS, J., dissenting), neutrally applying legal principles, and, when necessary, "stand[ing] up to what is generally supreme in a democracy: the popular will," SCALIA, The Rule of Law as a Law of Rules, 56 *U. Chi. L. Rev.* 1175 (1989). . . .

The question this case presents is whether the First Amendment stops Minnesota from furthering its interest in judicial integrity through this precisely targeted speech restriction.

The speech restriction must fail, in the Court's view, because an electoral process is at stake; if Minnesota opts to elect its judges, the Court asserts, the State may not rein in what candidates may say.

I do not agree with this unilocular, "an election is an election," approach. Instead, I would differentiate elections for political offices, in which the First Amendment holds full sway, from elections designed to select those whose office it is to administer justice without respect to persons. Minnesota's choice to elect its judges, I am persuaded, does not preclude the State from installing an election process geared to the judicial office.

Legislative and executive officials serve in representative capacities. . . . Judges, however, are not political actors. They do not sit as representatives of particular persons, communities, or parties; they serve no faction or constituency. "[I]t is the business of judges to be indifferent to popularity." *Chisom.* They must strive to do what is legally right, all the more so when the result is not the one "the home crowd" wants. Even when they develop common law or give concrete meaning to constitutional text, judges act only in the context of individual cases, the outcome of which cannot depend on the will of the public.

Thus, the rationale underlying unconstrained speech in elections for political office—that representative government depends on the public's ability to choose agents who will act at its behest—does not carry over to campaigns for the bench. As to persons aiming to occupy the seat of judgment, the Court's unrelenting reliance on decisions involving contests for legislative and executive posts is manifestly out of place. In view of the magisterial role judges must fill in a system of justice, a role that removes them from the partisan fray, States may limit judicial campaign speech by measures impermissible in elections for political office. . . .

Accordingly, I would affirm the judgment of the Court of Appeals for the Eighth Circuit.

☐ *Justice STEVENS, with whom Justice SOUTER, Justice GINSBURG, and Justice BREYER join, dissenting.*

In her dissenting opinion, Justice GINSBURG has cogently explained why the Court's holding is unsound. I therefore join her opinion without reservation. I add these comments to emphasize the force of her arguments and to explain why I find the Court's reasoning even more troubling than its holding. The limits of the Court's holding are evident: Even if the Minnesota Lawyers Professional Responsibility Board (Board) may not sanction a judicial candidate for announcing his views on issues likely to come before him, it may surely advise the electorate that such announcements demonstrate the speaker's unfitness for judicial office. If the solution to harmful speech must be more speech, so be it. The Court's reasoning, however, will unfortunately endure beyond the next election cycle. By obscuring the fundamental distinction between campaigns for the judiciary and the political branches, and by failing to recognize the difference between statements made in articles or opinions and those made on the campaign trail, the Court defies any sensible notion of the judicial office and the importance of impartiality in that context.

The Court's disposition rests on two seriously flawed premises—an inaccurate appraisal of the importance of judicial independence and impartiality, and an assumption that judicial candidates should have the same freedom " 'to express themselves on matters of current public importance' " as do all other elected officials. Elected judges, no less than appointed judges, occupy an office of trust that is fundamentally different from that occupied by policymaking officials. Although the fact that they must stand for election makes their job more difficult than that of the tenured judge, that fact does not lessen their duty to respect essential attributes of the judicial office that have been embedded in Anglo-American law for centuries. . . .

The disposition of this case on the flawed premise that the criteria for the election to judicial office should mirror the rules applicable to political elections is profoundly misguided. I therefore respectfully dissent.

McConnell v. Federal Election Commission
124 S.CT. 619 (2003)

In 2002, Congress enacted and President George W. Bush signed into law the Bipartisan Campaign Reform Act (BCRA), popularly known as "the McCain-Feingold law" after its sponsors, Arizona Republican senator John McCain and Wisconsin Democratic senator Russ Feingold. The most comprehensive reform of campaign finance in over a quarter of a century, it addressed developments since *Buckley v. Valeo*, 424 U.S. 1 (1976) (excerpted in Vol. 1, Ch. 8), particularly the increased use of "soft money"—unregulated money under the Federal Election Campaign Act (FECA) of 1971—and the proliferation of "issue ads" or "attack ads." Proponents of the law contended that soft money had a corrupting influence on the political process. In the 2000 election, nearly half of the money spent—$498 million or 42 percent—by political parties was soft money, that is, money spent in unlimited amounts for get-out-the-vote drives and attack ads. Moreover, 60 percent of that money came from only 800 individuals and organizations. Opponents countered that the restrictions violated the First Amendment guarantees for free speech and association.

Title I of the BCRA restricts political parties, officeholders, and candidates from spending soft money, and Title II prohibits corporations and unions from using their general funds for "issue ads" and other "electioneering communications" aimed at influencing the outcome of federal elections. Titles III, IV, and V contain additional restrictions requiring broadcasters to sell time to qualified candidates forty-five days prior to a primary and sixty days before the general election; and so-called millionaire provisions that specify staggered contribution limits if an opponent spends a triggering amount of personal funds. Title IV forbids individuals "17 years old or younger" from making campaign contributions, and Title V imposes a requirement on broadcasters to keep records of politically related broadcast requests available to the public.

The constitutionality of the BCRA was immediately challenged by Kentucky Republican senator Mitch McConnell and a wide range of interest groups, including the AFL-CIO, the American Civil Liberties

Union, the National Rifle Association, and the National Right to Life Committee. A three-judge panel heard the challenges to the law and issued a 1,698-page decision upholding most of the BCRA, but striking down restrictions on soft money. Subsequently, twelve appeals by different individuals and groups were made to the Supreme Court and consolidated. The Court granted the case an expedited basis and heard four hours of oral arguments in September 2003.

In December 2003, the Supreme Court handed down almost 300 pages of opinions, affirming and reversing in part the lower court. The justices voted five to four on three opinions, eight to one on one, and unanimously on part of one. For the first time in history four justices issued three opinions for the Court. Justices Stevens and O'Connor issued the opinion for the Court upholding the BCRA's restrictions on soft money and issue ads. Chief Justice Rehnquist issued an opinion for the Court denying the petitioners standing to challenge the "millionaire provisions," and striking down the ban on campaign contributions by individuals younger than eighteen. Justice Breyer issued an opinion for the Court upholding the requirement that broadcasters maintain publicly available records on politically related broadcast requests. Justice Stevens filed a dissent from Chief Justice Rehnquist's opinion holding that the challenge to the "millionaire provisions" was nonjusticiable. Chief Justice Rehnquist also filed a dissenting opinion. Justices Kennedy, Scalia, and Thomas each filed opinions in part dissenting and concurring. The lineup of the justices is presented in the table that follows.

☐ *Justice STEVENS and Justice O'CONNOR delivered the opinion of the Court with respect to BCRA Titles I and II [which Justices SOUTER, GINSBURG, and BREYER joined].*

In this opinion we discuss Titles I and II of BCRA. The opinion of the Court delivered by THE CHIEF JUSTICE discusses Titles III and IV, and the opinion of the Court delivered by Justice BREYER discusses Title V. . . .
    BCRA is the most recent federal enactment designed "to purge national politics of what was conceived to be the pernicious influence of 'big money' campaign contributions." [The] 1907 [Tillman Act] completely banned corporate contributions of "money . . . in connection with" any federal election. In 1925 Congress extended the prohibition of "contributions" "to include 'anything of value,' and made acceptance of a corporate contribution as well as the giving of such a contribution a crime." *Federal Election Comm'n v. National Right to Work Comm.*, 459 U.S. 197 (1982). . . . During and shortly after World War II, Congress reacted to the "enormous financial outlays" made by some unions in connection with national elections. Congress first restricted union contributions in the Hatch Act, and it later prohibited "union contributions in connection with federal elections . . . altogether."
    In early 1972 Congress continued its steady improvement of the national election laws by enacting FECA. . . . As the 1972 presidential elections made clear, however, FECA's passage did not deter unseemly fundraising and

Justices in the Majority

HOLDING	VOTE	REHNQUIST	STEVENS	O'CONNOR	SCALIA	KENNEDY	SOUTER	THOMAS	GINSBURG	BREYER
Upheld ban on soft money	5:4		X	X			X		X	X
Upheld restrictions on issue ads by corporations and unions	5:4		X	X			X		X	X
Struck down ban on contributions by individuals under 18	9:0	X	X	X	X	X	X	X	X	X
Upheld requirement that certain ads authorized by a candidate or committee clearly identify them	8:1	X	X	X	X	X	X		X	X
Upheld record-keeping requirement for broadcasters	5:4		X	X			X		X	X

campaign practices. Evidence of those practices persuaded Congress to enact the Federal Election Campaign Act Amendments of 1974. The 1974 amendments closed the loophole that had allowed candidates to use an unlimited number of political committees for fundraising purposes and thereby to circumvent the limits on individual committees' receipts and disbursements. They also limited individual political contributions to any single candidate to $1,000 per election, with an overall annual limitation of $25,000 by any contributor; imposed ceilings on spending by candidates and political parties for national conventions; required reporting and public disclosure of contributions and expenditures exceeding certain limits; and established the Federal Election Commission (FEC) to administer and enforce the legislation. . . .

This Court . . . concluded that each set of limitations raised serious— though different—concerns under the First Amendment. *Buckley v. Valeo* (1976). We treated the limitations on candidate and individual expenditures as direct restraints on speech, but we observed that the contribution limitations, in contrast, imposed only "a marginal restriction upon the contributor's ability to engage in free communication." [W]e determined that limiting contributions served an interest in protecting "the integrity of our system of representative democracy." In the end, the Act's primary purpose—"to limit the actuality and appearance of corruption resulting from large individual financial contributions"—provided "a constitutionally sufficient justification for the $1,000 contribution limitation."

We prefaced our analysis of the $1,000 limitation on expenditures by observing that it broadly encompassed every expenditure "'relative to a clearly identified candidate.'" . . . We concluded . . . that as so narrowed, the provision would not provide effective protection against the dangers of *quid pro quo* arrangements, because persons and groups could eschew expenditures that expressly advocated the election or defeat of a clearly identified candidate while remaining "free to spend as much as they want to promote the candidate and his views." . . . We therefore held that Congress' interest in preventing real or apparent corruption was inadequate to justify the heavy burdens on the freedoms of expression and association that the expenditure limits imposed. . . .

As a preface to our discussion of the specific provisions of BCRA, we comment briefly on the increased importance of "soft money" [and] the proliferation of "issue ads." . . .

Soft Money

Under FECA, "contributions" must be made with funds that are subject to the Act's disclosure requirements and source and amount limitations. Such funds are known as "federal" or "hard" money. FECA defines the term "contribution," however, to include only the gift or advance of anything of value "made by any person for the purpose of influencing any election for Federal office." Donations made solely for the purpose of influencing state or local elections are therefore unaffected by FECA's requirements and prohibitions. As a result, prior to the enactment of BCRA, federal law permitted corporations and unions, as well as individuals who had already made the maximum permissible contributions to federal candidates, to contribute "nonfederal money"—also known as "soft money"—to political parties for activities intended to influence state or local elections.

Shortly after *Buckley* was decided, questions arose concerning the treatment of contributions intended to influence both federal and state elections.

Although a literal reading of FECA's definition of "contribution" would have required such activities to be funded with hard money, the FEC ruled that political parties could fund mixed-purpose activities—including get-out-the-vote drives and generic party advertising—in part with soft money. In 1995 the FEC concluded that the parties could also use soft money to defray the costs of "legislative advocacy media advertisements," even if the ads mentioned the name of a federal candidate, so long as they did not expressly advocate the candidate's election or defeat.

As the permissible uses of soft money expanded, the amount of soft money raised and spent by the national political parties increased exponentially. Of the two major parties' total spending, soft money accounted for 5% ($21.6 million) in 1984, 11% ($45 million) in 1988, 16% ($80 million) in 1992, 30% ($272 million) in 1996, and 42% ($498 million) in 2000. . . .

ISSUE ADVERTISING

In *Buckley* we construed FECA's disclosure and reporting requirements, as well as its expenditure limitations, "to reach only funds used for communications that expressly advocate the election or defeat of a clearly identifiable candidate." As a result of that strict reading of the statute, the use or omission of "magic words" such as "Elect John Smith" or "Vote Against Jane Doe" marked a bright statutory line separating "express advocacy" from "issue advocacy." Express advocacy was subject to FECA's limitations and could be financed only using hard money. The political parties, in other words, could not use soft money to sponsor ads that used any magic words, and corporations and unions could not fund such ads out of their general treasuries. So-called issue ads, on the other hand, not only could be financed with soft money, but could be aired without disclosing the identity of, or any other information about, their sponsors.

While the distinction between "issue" and express advocacy seemed neat in theory, the two categories of advertisements proved functionally identical in important respects. Both were used to advocate the election or defeat of clearly identified federal candidates, even though the so-called issue ads eschewed the use of magic words. Little difference existed, for example, between an ad that urged viewers to "vote against Jane Doe" and one that condemned Jane Doe's record on a particular issue before exhorting viewers to "call Jane Doe and tell her what you think." . . .

BCRA's central provisions are designed to address Congress' concerns about the increasing use of soft money and issue advertising to influence federal elections. . . . Title I is Congress' effort to plug the soft-money loophole. The cornerstone of Title I is new FECA Sec. 323(a), which prohibits national party committees and their agents from soliciting, receiving, directing, or spending any soft money. In short, Sec. 323(a) takes national parties out of the soft-money business.

The remaining provisions of new FECA Sec. 323 largely reinforce the restrictions in Sec. 323(a). New FECA Sec. 323(b) [for example] prevents the wholesale shift of soft-money influence from national to state party committees by prohibiting state and local party committees from using such funds for activities that affect federal elections. These "Federal election activit[ies]," defined in new FECA Sec. 301(20)(A), are almost identical to the mixed-purpose activities that have long been regulated under the FEC's pre-BCRA allocation regime. . . .

In *Buckley* and subsequent cases, we have subjected restrictions on campaign expenditures to closer scrutiny than limits on campaign contributions. See, e.g., *Federal Election Comm'n v. Beaumont* [539 U.S. 146] (2003); see also *Nixon v. Shrink Missouri Government PAC*, 528 U.S. 377 (2000). In these cases we have recognized that contribution limits, unlike limits on expenditures, "entai[l] only a marginal restriction upon the contributor's ability to engage in free communication." . . .

Because the electoral process is the very "means through which a free society democratically translates political speech into concrete governmental action," *Shrink Missouri*, contribution limits, like other measures aimed at protecting the integrity of the process, tangibly benefit public participation in political debate. For that reason, [the] less rigorous standard of review we have applied to contribution limits (*Buckley*'s "closely drawn" scrutiny) shows proper deference to Congress' ability to weigh competing constitutional interests in an area in which it enjoys particular expertise. . . .

Like the contribution limits we upheld in *Buckley*, Sec. 323's restrictions have only a marginal impact on the ability of contributors, candidates, officeholders, and parties to engage in effective political speech. Complex as its provisions may be, Sec. 323, in the main, does little more than regulate the ability of wealthy individuals, corporations, and unions to contribute large sums of money to influence federal elections, federal candidates, and federal officeholders. . . .

NEW FECA SEC. 323(A)'S RESTRICTIONS ON NATIONAL PARTY COMMITTEES

The core of Title I is new FECA §323(a), which provides that "national committee[s] of a political party . . . may not solicit, receive, or direct to another person a contribution, donation, or transfer of funds or any other thing of value, or spend any funds, that are not subject to the limitations, prohibitions, and reporting requirements of this Act."

The main goal of Sec. 323(a) is modest. In large part, it simply effects a return to the scheme that was approved in *Buckley* and that was subverted by the creation of the FEC's allocation regime, which permitted the political parties to fund federal electioneering efforts with a combination of hard and soft money. Under that allocation regime, national parties were able to use vast amounts of soft money in their efforts to elect federal candidates. Consequently, as long as they directed the money to the political parties, donors could contribute large amounts of soft money for use in activities designed to influence federal elections. New Sec. 323(a) is designed to put a stop to that practice.

1. Governmental Interests Underlying New FECA Sec. 323(a)

The Government defends Sec. 323(a)'s ban on national parties' involvement with soft money as necessary to prevent the actual and apparent corruption of federal candidates and officeholders. Our cases have made clear that the prevention of corruption or its appearance constitutes a sufficiently important interest to justify political contribution limits. We have not limited that interest to the elimination of cash-for-votes exchanges. . . .

The question for present purposes is whether large soft-money contributions to national party committees have a corrupting influence or give rise to the appearance of corruption. Both common sense and the ample record in these cases confirm Congress' belief that they do. . . .

The evidence in the record shows that candidates and donors alike have in fact exploited the soft-money loophole, the former to increase their prospects of election and the latter to create debt on the part of officeholders, with the national parties serving as willing intermediaries. Thus, despite FECA's hard-money limits on direct contributions to candidates, federal officeholders have commonly asked donors to make soft-money donations to national and state committees "solely in order to assist federal campaigns," including the officeholder's own. . . .

Despite this evidence and the close ties that candidates and officeholders have with their parties, Justice KENNEDY would limit Congress' regulatory interest only to the prevention of the actual or apparent *quid pro quo* corruption "inherent in" contributions made directly to, contributions made at the express behest of, and expenditures made in coordination with, a federal officeholder or candidate. . . . This crabbed view of corruption, and particularly of the appearance of corruption, ignores precedent, common sense, and the realities of political fundraising exposed by the record in this litigation. . . .

2. New FECA Sec. 323(a)'s Restriction on Spending and Receiving Soft Money

Plaintiffs and THE CHIEF JUSTICE contend that Sec. 323(a) is impermissibly overbroad because it subjects all funds raised and spent by national parties to FECA's hard-money source and amount limits, including, for example, funds spent on purely state and local elections in which no federal office is at stake. Such activities, THE CHIEF JUSTICE asserts, pose "little or no potential to corrupt . . . federal candidates or officeholders." This observation is beside the point. . . .

Access to federal officeholders is the most valuable favor the national party committees are able to give in exchange for large donations. The fact that officeholders comply by donating their valuable time indicates either that officeholders place substantial value on the soft-money contribution themselves, without regard to their end use, or that national committees are able to exert considerable control over federal officeholders.

3. New FECA Sec. 323(a)'s Restriction on Soliciting or Directing Soft Money

Plaintiffs also contend that Sec. 323(a)'s prohibition on national parties' soliciting or directing soft-money contributions is substantially overbroad. The reach of the solicitation prohibition, however, is limited. It bars only solicitations of soft money by national party committees and by party officers in their official capacities. The committees remain free to solicit hard money on their own behalf, as well as to solicit hard money on behalf of state committees and state and local candidates. They also can contribute hard money to state committees and to candidates. In accordance with FEC regulations, furthermore, officers of national parties are free to solicit soft money in their individual capacities, or, if they are also officials of state parties, in that capacity. . . .

4. New FECA Sec. 323(a)'s Application to Minor Parties

The McConnell and political party plaintiffs contend that Sec. 323(a) is substantially overbroad and must be stricken on its face because it impermissibly infringes the speech and associational rights of minor parties such as the

Libertarian National Committee, which, owing to their slim prospects for electoral success and the fact that they receive few large soft-money contributions from corporate sources, pose no threat of corruption comparable to that posed by the RNC and DNC. In *Buckley*, we rejected a similar argument concerning limits on contributions to minor-party candidates, noting that "any attempt to exclude minor parties and independents en masse from the Act's contribution limitations overlooks the fact that minor-party candidates may win elective office or have a substantial impact on the outcome of an election." We have thus recognized that the relevance of the interest in avoiding actual or apparent corruption is not a function of the number of legislators a given party manages to elect. It applies as much to a minor party that manages to elect only one of its members to federal office as it does to a major party whose members make up a majority of Congress. It is therefore reasonable to require that all parties and all candidates follow the same set of rules designed to protect the integrity of the electoral process. . . .

5. New FECA Sec. 323(a)'s Associational Burdens

Finally, plaintiffs assert that Sec. 323(a) is unconstitutional because it impermissibly interferes with the ability of national committees to associate with state and local committees. By way of example, plaintiffs point to the Republican Victory Plans, whereby the RNC acts in concert with the state and local committees of a given State to plan and implement joint, full-ticket fundraising and electioneering programs. The political parties assert that Sec. 323(a) outlaws any participation in Victory Plans by RNC officers, including merely sitting down at a table and engaging in collective decisionmaking about how soft money will be solicited, received, and spent.

We are not persuaded by this argument because it hinges on an unnaturally broad reading of the terms "spend," "receive," "direct," and "solicit." Nothing on the face of Sec. 323(a) prohibits national party officers, whether acting in their official or individual capacities, from sitting down with state and local party committees or candidates to plan and advise how to raise and spend soft money. As long as the national party officer does not personally spend, receive, direct, or solicit soft money, Sec. 323(a) permits a wide range of joint planning and electioneering activity.

New FECA Sec. 323(b)'s Restrictions on State and Local Party Committees

Section 323(b) is designed to foreclose wholesale evasion of Sec. 323(a)'s anticorruption measures by sharply curbing state committees' ability to use large soft-money contributions to influence federal elections. The core of Sec. 323(b) is a straightforward contribution regulation: It prevents donors from contributing nonfederal funds to state and local party committees to help finance "Federal election activity." The term "Federal election activity" encompasses four distinct categories of electioneering: (1) voter registration activity during the 120 days preceding a regularly scheduled federal election; (2) voter identification, get-out-the-vote (GOTV), and generic campaign activity that is "conducted in connection with an election in which a candidate for Federal office appears on the ballot"; (3) any "public communication" that "refers to a clearly identified candidate for Federal office" and "promotes," "supports," "attacks," or "opposes" a candidate for that office; and (4) the services provided by a state committee employee who dedicates more than

25% of his or her time to "activities in connection with a Federal election." The Act explicitly excludes several categories of activity from this definition: public communications that refer solely to nonfederal candidates; contributions to nonfederal candidates; state and local political conventions; and the cost of grassroots campaign materials like bumper stickers that refer only to state candidates. All activities that fall within the statutory definition must be funded with hard money.

Section 323(b)(2), the so-called Levin Amendment, carves out an exception to this general rule. A refinement on the pre-BCRA regime that permitted parties to pay for certain activities with a mix of federal and nonfederal funds, the Levin Amendment allows state and local party committees to pay for certain types of federal election activity with an allocated ratio of hard money and "Levin funds"—that is, funds raised within an annual limit of $10,000 per person. Except for the $10,000 cap and certain related restrictions to prevent circumvention of that limit, Sec. 323(b)(2) leaves regulation of such contributions to the States.

We begin by noting that, in addressing the problem of soft-money contributions to state committees, Congress both drew a conclusion and made a prediction. Its conclusion, based on the evidence before it, was that the corrupting influence of soft money does not insinuate itself into the political process solely through national party committees. Rather, state committees function as an alternate avenue for precisely the same corrupting forces. . . . Section 323(b) thus promotes an important governmental interest by confronting the corrupting influence that soft-money donations to political parties already have.

Congress also made a prediction. Having been taught the hard lesson of circumvention by the entire history of campaign finance regulation, Congress knew that soft-money donors would react to Sec. 323(a) by scrambling to find another way to purchase influence. It was "neither novel nor implausible" for Congress to conclude that political parties would react to Sec. 323(a) by directing soft-money contributors to the state committees, and that federal candidates would be just as indebted to these contributors as they had been to those who had formerly contributed to the national parties. . . .

We accordingly conclude that Sec. 323(b), on its face, is closely drawn to match the important governmental interests of preventing corruption and the appearance of corruption.

NEW FECA SEC. 323(D)'S RESTRICTIONS ON PARTIES' SOLICITATIONS FOR, AND DONATIONS TO, TAX-EXEMPT ORGANIZATIONS

Section 323(d) prohibits national, state, and local party committees, and their agents or subsidiaries, from "solicit[ing] any funds for, or mak[ing] or direct[ing] any donations" to, any organization established under Sec. 501(c) of the Internal Revenue Code that makes expenditures in connection with an election for federal office, and any political organizations established under Sec. 527 "other than a political committee, a State, district, or local committee of a political party, or the authorized campaign committee of a candidate for State or local office." The District Court struck down the provision on its face. We reverse and uphold Sec. 323(d), narrowly construing the section's ban on donations to apply only to the donation of funds not raised in compliance with FECA. . . .

Title II of BCRA, entitled "Noncandidate Campaign Expenditures," is divided into two subtitles: "Electioneering Communications" and "Independent and Coordinated Expenditures."

BCRA Sec. 201's Definition of "Electioneering Communication"

The first section of Title II, Sec. 201, comprehensively amends FECA Sec. 304, which requires political committees to file detailed periodic financial reports with the FEC. The amendment coins a new term, "electioneering communication," to replace the narrowing construction of FECA's disclosure provisions adopted by this Court in *Buckley*. As discussed further below, that construction limited the coverage of FECA's disclosure requirement to communications expressly advocating the election or defeat of particular candidates. By contrast, the term "electioneering communication" is not so limited, but is defined to encompass any "broadcast, cable, or satellite communication" that "(I) refers to a clearly identified candidate for Federal office; "(II) is made within "(aa) 60 days before a general, special, or runoff election for the office sought by the candidate; or "(bb) 30 days before a primary or preference election, or a convention or caucus of a political party that has authority to nominate a candidate, for the office sought by the candidate; and "(III) in the case of a communication which refers to a candidate other than President or Vice President, is targeted to the relevant electorate." . . .

In addition to setting forth this definition, BCRA's amendments to FECA Sec. 304 specify significant disclosure requirements for persons who fund electioneering communications. BCRA's use of this new term is not, however, limited to the disclosure context: A later section of the Act (BCRA Sec. 203) restricts corporations' and labor unions' funding of electioneering communications. Plaintiffs challenge the constitutionality of the new term as it applies in both the disclosure and the expenditure contexts.

The major premise of plaintiffs' challenge to BCRA's use of the term "electioneering communication" is that Buckley drew a constitutionally mandated line between express advocacy and so-called issue advocacy, and that speakers possess an inviolable First Amendment right to engage in the latter category of speech. . . .

That position misapprehends our prior decisions, for the express advocacy restriction was an endpoint of statutory interpretation, not a first principle of constitutional law. . . . [A] plain reading of *Buckley* makes clear that the express advocacy limitation, in both the expenditure and the disclosure contexts, was the product of statutory interpretation rather than a constitutional command. In narrowly reading the FECA provisions in *Buckley* to avoid problems of vagueness and overbreadth, we nowhere suggested that a statute that was neither vague nor overbroad would be required to toe the same express advocacy line.

In short, the concept of express advocacy and the concomitant class of magic words were born of an effort to avoid constitutional infirmities. . . . Nor are we persuaded, independent of our precedents, that the First Amendment erects a rigid barrier between express advocacy and so-called issue advocacy. That notion cannot be squared with our longstanding recognition that the presence or absence of magic words cannot meaningfully distinguish electioneering speech from a true issue ad. Indeed, the unmistakable lesson from the record in this litigation is that *Buckley's* magic-words requirement is functionally meaningless. Not only can advertisers easily evade the line by eschewing the use of magic words, but they would seldom choose to use such words even if permitted. And although the resulting advertisements do not urge the viewer to vote for or against a candidate in so many words, they are no less clearly intended to influence the election. *Buckley's* express advocacy line, in short, has not aided the legislative effort to combat real or apparent corruption, and Congress enacted BCRA to correct the flaws it found in the existing system. . . .

BCRA SEC. 203's PROHIBITION OF CORPORATE AND LABOR DISBURSEMENTS FOR ELECTIONEERING COMMUNICATIONS

Since our decision in *Buckley*, Congress' power to prohibit corporations and unions from using funds in their treasuries to finance advertisements expressly advocating the election or defeat of candidates in federal elections has been firmly embedded in our law. The ability to form and administer separate segregated funds authorized by FECA Sec. 316 has provided corporations and unions with a constitutionally sufficient opportunity to engage in express advocacy. That has been this Court's unanimous view, and it is not challenged in this litigation.

Section 203 of BCRA amends FECA Sec. 316(b)(2) to extend this rule, which previously applied only to express advocacy, to all "electioneering communications" covered by the definition of that term in amended FECA Sec. 304(f)(3). Thus, under BCRA, corporations and unions may not use their general treasury funds to finance electioneering communications, but they remain free to organize and administer segregated funds, or PACs, for that purpose. Because corporations can still fund electioneering communications with PAC money, it is "simply wrong" to view the provision as a "complete ban" on expression rather than a regulation. . . .

We are under no illusion that BCRA will be the last congressional statement on the matter. Money, like water, will always find an outlet. What problems will arise, and how Congress will respond, are concerns for another day. In the main we uphold BCRA's two principal, complementary features: the control of soft money and the regulation of electioneering communications. Accordingly, we affirm in part and reverse in part the District Court's judgment with respect to Titles I and II.

☐ *CHIEF JUSTICE REHNQUIST delivered the opinion of the Court with respect to BCRA Titles III and IV.*

This opinion addresses issues involving miscellaneous Title III and IV provisions of the Bipartisan Campaign Reform Act of 2002 (BCRA). For the reasons discussed below, we affirm the judgment of the District Court with respect to these provisions.

BCRA Sec. 305 amends the federal Communications Act of 1934, which requires that, 45 days before a primary or 60 days before a general election, broadcast stations must sell a qualified candidate the "lowest unit charge of the station for the same class and amount of time for the same period." . . .

The McConnell plaintiffs challenge Sec. 305. They argue that Senator McConnell's testimony that he plans to run advertisements critical of his opponents in the future and that he had run them in the past is sufficient to establish standing. We think not.

Article III of the Constitution limits the "judicial power" to the resolution of "cases" and "controversies." One element of the "bedrock" case-or-controversy requirement is that plaintiffs must establish that they have standing to sue. On many occasions, we have reiterated the three requirements that constitute the "'irreducible constitutional minimum'" of standing. First, a plaintiff must demonstrate an "injury in fact," which is "concrete," "distinct and palpable," and "actual or imminent." Second, a plaintiff must establish "a causal connection between the injury and the conduct complained of—the injury has to be 'fairly trace[able] to the challenged action of the defendant, and not . . . th[e] result [of] some third party not before the court.'" *Lujan v. Defenders of Wildlife*, 504 U. S. 555 (1992). Third, a plaintiff must show the "'substantial likelihood'" that the requested relief will remedy the alleged injury in fact."

Because Senator McConnell's current term does not expire until 2009, the earliest day he could be affected by Sec. 305 is 45 days before the Republican primary election in 2008. This alleged injury in fact is too remote temporally to satisfy Article III standing. [CHIEF JUSTICE REHNQUIST proceeded to deny standing to other plaintiffs' challenges to contribution limits and to the "millionaire provisions," before addressing the challenge to restrictions on campaign contributions by individuals under the age of 18.] . . .

BCRA Sec. 318 prohibits individuals "17 years old or younger" from making contributions to candidates and contributions or donations to political parties. The McConnell and Echols plaintiffs . . . argue that Sec. 318 violates the First Amendment rights of minors. We agree.

Minors enjoy the protection of the First Amendment. See, e.g., *Tinker v. Des Moines Independent Community School Dist.*, 393 U. S. 503 (1969). Limitations on the amount that an individual may contribute to a candidate or political committee impinge on the protected freedoms of expression and association. When the Government burdens the right to contribute, we apply heightened scrutiny. We ask whether the statute is "closely drawn" to avoid unnecessary abridgment of First Amendment freedoms. The Government asserts that the provision protects against corruption by conduit; that is, donations by parents through their minor children to circumvent contribution limits applicable to the parents. But the Government offers scant evidence of this form of evasion. . . .

For the foregoing reasons, we affirm the District Court's judgment finding the plaintiffs' challenges to BCRA Secs. 305, 307, and the millionaire provisions nonjusticiable, striking down as unconstitutional BCRA Sec. 318, and upholding BCRA Sec. 311.

□ *[Justice BREYER delivered the opinion of the Court with respect to BCRA Title V and upheld the constitutionality of Sec. 504, amending the Communications Act of 1934, and requiring broadcasters to keep records of politically related broadcasting requests available to the public. He found no evidence that the requirements impose onerous administrative burdens, lack any offsetting justification, and consequently violate the First Amendment. In addition, he noted that the Court should defer the FEC's interpretation of the requirements.]*

Justice STEVENS, dissenting with respect to Sec. 305 [and which Justices GINSBURG and BREYER join].

THE CHIEF JUSTICE, writing for the Court, concludes that the McConnell plaintiffs lack standing to challenge Sec. 305 of BCRA because Senator

McConnell cannot be affected by the provision until "45 days before the Republican primary election in 2008." I am not persuaded that Article III's case-or-controversy requirement imposes such a strict temporal limit on our jurisdiction. By asserting that he has run attack ads in the past, that he plans to run such ads in his next campaign, and that Sec. 305 will adversely affect his campaign strategy, McConnell has identified a "concrete," "'distinct,'" and "'actual'" injury. That the injury is distant in time does not make it illusory. . . .

Like BCRA's other disclosure requirements, Sec. 305 evenhandedly regulates speech based on its electioneering content. In sum, I would uphold Sec. 305.

☐ *CHIEF JUSTICE REHNQUIST, dissenting with respect to BCRA Titles I and V [and which Justices SCALIA and KENNEDY join].*

The Court fails to recognize that the national political parties are exemplars of political speech at all levels of government, in addition to effective fundraisers for federal candidates and officeholders. . . . Indeed, some national political parties exist primarily for the purpose of expressing ideas and generating debate.

When political parties engage in pure political speech that has little or no potential to corrupt their federal candidates and officeholders, the government cannot constitutionally burden their speech any more than it could burden the speech of individuals engaging in these same activities. . . .

☐ *Justice THOMAS, concurring with respect to BCRA Titles III and IV, except for BCRA Secs. 311 and 318, concurring in the result with respect to BCRA Sec. 318, concurring in the judgment in part and dissenting in part with respect to BCRA Title II, and dissenting with respect to BCRA Titles I, V, and Sec. 311 [and which Justice SCALIA joins in part].*

With breathtaking scope, the Bipartisan Campaign Reform Act of 2002 (BCRA), directly targets and constricts core political speech, the "primary object of First Amendment protection." *Nixon v. Shrink Missouri Government PAC*, 528 U.S. 377 (2000) (THOMAS, J., dissenting). . . .

The very "purpose of the First Amendment [is] to preserve an uninhibited marketplace of ideas in which truth will ultimately prevail." *Red Lion Broadcasting Co. v. FCC*, 395 U.S. 367 (1969). Yet today the fundamental principle that "the best test of truth is the power of the thought to get itself accepted in the competition of the market," *Abrams v. United States*, 250 U.S. 616 (1919) (HOLMES, J., dissenting), is cast aside in the purported service of preventing "corruption," or the mere "appearance of corruption." *Buckley v. Valeo*. . . .

☐ *Justice KENNEDY, concurring in the judgment in part and dissenting in part with respect to BCRA Titles I and II, [which CHIEF JUSTICE REHNQUIST joined and Justices SCALIA and THOMAS joined in part].*

Until today's consolidated cases, the Court has accepted but two principles to use in determining the validity of campaign finance restrictions. First is the anticorruption rationale. The principal concern, of course, is the agreement for a *quid pro quo* between officeholders (or candidates) and those who would seek to influence them. The Court has said the interest in preventing corruption allows limitations on receipt of the *quid* by a candidate or office-holder, regardless of who gives it or of the intent of the donor or officeholder. Second, the Court has analyzed laws that classify on the basis of the speaker's corporate or union identity under the corporate speech rationale. The Court has said that the willing adoption of the entity form by corporations and unions justifies regulating them differently: Their ability to give candidates *quids* may be subject not only to limits but also to outright bans; their electoral speech may likewise be curtailed....

Buckley made clear, by its express language and its context, that the corruption interest only justifies regulating candidates' and officeholders' receipt of what we can call the "*quids*" in the *quid pro quo* formulation. The Court rested its decision on the principle that campaign finance regulation that restricts speech without requiring proof of particular corrupt action withstands constitutional challenge only if it regulates conduct posing a demonstrable *quid pro quo* danger....

The Court ... in effect interprets the anticorruption rationale to allow regulation not just of "actual or apparent *quid pro quo* arrangements," but of any conduct that wins goodwill from or influences a Member of Congress.... The very aim of *Buckley*'s standard, however, was to define undue influence by reference to the presence of *quid pro quo* involving the officeholder. The Court, in contrast, concludes that access, without more, proves influence is undue. Access, in the Court's view, has the same legal ramifications as actual or apparent corruption of officeholders. This new definition of corruption sweeps away all protections for speech that lie in its path....

Today's decision breaks faith with our tradition of robust and unfettered debate....

☐ *Justice SCALIA, concurring with respect to BCRA Titles III and IV, dissenting with respect to BCRA Titles I and V, and concurring in the judgment in part and dissenting in part with respect to BCRA Title II.*

This is a sad day for the freedom of speech. Who could have imagined that the same Court which, within the past four years, has sternly disapproved of restrictions upon such inconsequential forms of expression as virtual child pornography, *Ashcroft v. Free Speech Coalition*, 535 U.S. 234 (2002), tobacco advertising, *Lorillard Tobacco Co. v. Reilly*, 533 U.S. 525 (2001), dissemination of illegally intercepted communications, *Bartnicki v. Vopper*, 532 U.S. 514 (2001), and sexually explicit cable programming, *United States v. Playboy Entertainment Group, Inc.*, 529 U.S. 803 (2000), would smile with favor upon a law that cuts to the heart of what the First Amendment is meant to protect: the right to criticize the government. For that is what the most offensive provisions of this legislation are all about. We are governed by Congress, and this legislation prohibits the criticism of Members of Congress by those entities most capable of giving such criticism loud voice: national political parties and corporations, both of the commercial and the not-for-profit sort. It forbids pre-election criticism of incumbents by corporations, even not-for-profit corporations, by use of their general funds; and forbids national-party use of "soft" money to fund "issue ads" that incumbents find so offensive....

Beyond that, however, the present legislation targets for prohibition certain categories of campaign speech that are particularly harmful to incumbents. Is it accidental, do you think, that incumbents raise about three times as much "hard money"—the sort of funding generally not restricted by this legislation—as do their challengers? ...

I wish to address three fallacious propositions that might be thought to justify some or all of the provisions of this legislation—only the last of which is explicitly embraced by the principal opinion for the Court, but all of which underlie, I think, its approach to these cases.

MONEY IS NOT SPEECH

It was said by congressional proponents of this legislation that since this legislation regulates nothing but the expenditure of money for speech, as opposed to speech itself, the burden it imposes is not subject to full First Amendment scrutiny; the government may regulate the raising and spending of campaign funds just as it regulates other forms of conduct, such as burning draft cards, see *United States v. O'Brien*, 391 U.S. 367 (1968), or camping out on the National Mall, see *Clark v. Community for Creative Non-Violence*, 468 U.S. 288 (1984).

Our traditional view was correct, and today's cavalier attitude toward regulating the financing of speech (the "exacting scrutiny" test of *Buckley* is not uttered in any majority opinion, and is not observed in the ones from which I dissent) frustrates the fundamental purpose of the First Amendment.

In any economy operated on even the most rudimentary principles of division of labor, effective public communication requires the speaker to make use of the services of others. An author may write a novel, but he will seldom publish and distribute it himself. . . . Division of labor requires a means of mediating exchange, and in a commercial society, that means is supplied by money. The publisher pays the author for the right to sell his book; it pays its staff who print and assemble the book; it demands payments from booksellers who bring the book to market. . . . The right to speak would be largely ineffective if it did not include the right to engage in financial transactions that are the incidents of its exercise.

[W]here the government singles out money used to fund speech as its legislative object, it is acting against speech as such, no less than if it had targeted the paper on which a book was printed or the trucks that deliver it to the bookstore. . . .

We have kept faith with the Founders' tradition by prohibiting the selective taxation of the press. *Minneapolis Star & Tribune Co. v. Minnesota Comm'r of Revenue*, 460 U.S. 575 (1983) (ink and paper tax). And we have done so whether the tax was the product of illicit motive or not. These press-taxation cases belie the claim that regulation of money used to fund speech is not regulation of speech itself. . . .

It should be obvious, then, that a law limiting the amount a person can spend to broadcast his political views is a direct restriction on speech. . . .

POOLING MONEY IS NOT SPEECH

Another proposition which could explain at least some of the results of today's opinion is that the First Amendment right to spend money for speech does not include the right to combine with others in spending money for speech. . . . The freedom to associate with others for the dissemination of ideas—not just by singing or speaking in unison, but by pooling financial resources for expressive purposes—is part of the freedom of speech. . . .

If it were otherwise, Congress would be empowered to enact legislation requiring newspapers to be sole proprietorships, banning their use of partnership or corporate form. That sort of restriction would be an obvious violation of the First Amendment, and it is incomprehensible why the conclusion should change when what is at issue is the pooling of funds for the most important (and most perennially threatened) category of speech: electoral speech. . . .

SPEECH BY CORPORATIONS CAN BE ABRIDGED

The last proposition that might explain at least some of today's casual abridgment of free-speech rights is this: that the particular form of association known as a corporation does not enjoy full First Amendment protection. Of course the text of the First Amendment does not limit its application in this fashion. . . . In *First Nat. Bank of Boston v. Bellotti*, 435 U.S. 765 (1978), we held unconstitutional a state prohibition of corporate speech designed to influence the vote on referendum proposals.

The Court changed course in *Austin v. Michigan Chamber of Commerce*, 494 U.S. 652 (1990), upholding a state prohibition of an independent corporate expenditure in support of a candidate for state office. I dissented in that case, and remain of the view that it was error. In the modern world, giving the government power to exclude corporations from the political debate enables it effectively to muffle the voices that best represent the most significant segments of the economy and the most passionately held social and political views. People who associate—who pool their financial resources—for purposes of economic enterprise overwhelmingly do so in the corporate form; and with increasing frequency, incorporation is chosen by those who associate to defend and promote particular ideas—such as the American Civil Liberties Union and the National Rifle Association, parties to these cases. . . .

9

ECONOMIC RIGHTS AND
AMERICAN CAPITALISM

C | The "Takings Clause" and Just Compensation

In an important ruling on land-use regulations, in *Tahoe-Sierra Preservation Council, Inc. v. Tahoe Regional Planning Agency* (2002) (excerpted below), the Court rejected a Fifth Amendment Takings Clause challenge to temporary moratoria on construction by a vote of six to three.

Tahoe-Sierra Preservation Council, Inc. v. Tahoe Regional Planning Agency
535 U.S. 302, 122 S.CT. 1465 (2002)

Lake Tahoe's exceptional clarity is attributed to the absence of algae as a result of the lack of nitrogen and phosphorus in its water. The lake's pristine state, however, has deteriorated during the last forty years. In the 1960s, when the problems associated with burgeoning development began to receive attention, California and Nevada, five counties, several municipalities, and the U.S. Forest Service shared jurisdiction over the lake. In 1968 the legislatures of both states adopted the Tahoe Regional Planning Compact, which Congress approved in 1969. The compact set goals for the preservation of the lake and created the Tahoe Regional

Planning Agency (TRPA) "to coordinate and regulate development" in the lake's basin and "to conserve its natural resources." In 1980 the compact was redefined and the TRPA was directed to develop regional "standards for air quality, water quality, soil conservation, vegetation preservation and noise." Subsequently, the TRPA ordered two moratoria on construction in the basin in order to maintain the status quo while studying the impact of development on the lake. The first, Ordinance 81-5, was in effect from August 24, 1981, to August 26, 1983, and the second, more restrictive Resolution 83-21 was in effect from August 27, 1983, to April 25, 1984. As a result of those directives, virtually all development on substantial areas of the land within the TRPA's jurisdiction was prohibited for thirty-two months.

The constitutionality of the moratoria was challenged as a violation of the Fifth Amendment's Takings Clause. A federal district court held that, although the property owners retained some value in the land, the moratoria temporarily deprived them of "all economically viable use of their land" and therefore constituted a "categorical" takings in violation of the Fifth Amendment, based on the rulings in *Lucas v. South Carolina Coastal Council*, 505 U.S. 1003 (1992), and *First English Evangelical Lutheran Church of Glendale v. County of Los Angeles*, 482 U.S. 304 (1987). On appeal, the U.S. Court of Appeals for the Ninth Circuit reversed that decision and held that the moratoria had only a temporary impact on the property owners' economic interests and thus were not categorical takings. That decision was appealed and the Supreme Court granted *certiorari*.

The appellate court's decision was affirmed by a vote of six to three. Justice Stevens delivered the opinion of the Court and Chief Justice Rehnquist filed a dissent, which Justices Scalia and Thomas joined; the latter also issued a separate dissent.

□ *Justice STEVENS delivered the opinion of the Court.*

Petitioners contend that the mere enactment of a temporary regulation that, while in effect, denies a property owner all viable economic use of her property gives rise to an unqualified constitutional obligation to compensate her for the value of its use during that period. . . . For petitioners, it is enough that a regulation imposes a temporary deprivation—no matter how brief— of all economically viable use to trigger a per se rule that a taking has occurred. Petitioners assert that our opinions in *First English* and *Lucas* have already endorsed their view, and that it is a logical application of the principle that the Takings Clause was "designed to bar Government from forcing some people alone to bear burdens which, in all fairness and justice, should be borne by the public as a whole." *Armstrong v. United States*, 364 U.S. 40 (1960).

We shall first explain why our cases do not support their proposed categorical rule—indeed, fairly read, they implicitly reject it. Next, we shall explain why the *Armstrong* principle requires rejection of that rule as well as the less extreme position advanced by petitioners at oral argument. In our view the answer to the abstract question whether a temporary moratorium effects a taking is neither "yes, always" nor "no, never"; the answer depends upon the particular circumstances of the case.

The text of the Fifth Amendment itself provides a basis for drawing a distinction between physical takings and regulatory takings. Its plain language requires the payment of compensation whenever the government acquires private property for a public purpose, whether the acquisition is the result of a condemnation proceeding or a physical appropriation. But the Constitution contains no comparable reference to regulations that prohibit a property owner from making certain uses of her private property. Our jurisprudence involving condemnations and physical takings is as old as the Republic and, for the most part, involves the straightforward application of per se rules. Our regulatory takings jurisprudence, in contrast, is of more recent vintage and is characterized by "essentially ad hoc, factual inquiries," *Penn Central* [*Transportation Co. v. New York City*, 438 U.S. 104 (1978)], designed to allow "careful examination and weighing of all the relevant circumstances."

When the government physically takes possession of an interest in property for some public purpose, it has a categorical duty to compensate the former owner, regardless of whether the interest that is taken constitutes an entire parcel or merely a part thereof. Thus, compensation is mandated when a leasehold is taken and the government occupies the property for its own purposes, even though that use is temporary. But a government regulation that merely prohibits landlords from evicting tenants unwilling to pay a higher rent; that bans certain private uses of a portion of an owner's property; or that forbids the private use of certain airspace, does not constitute a categorical taking. "The first category of cases requires courts to apply a clear rule; the second necessarily entails complex factual assessments of the purposes and economic effects of government actions." *Yee v. Escondido*, 503 U.S. 519 (1992).

This longstanding distinction between acquisitions of property for public use, on the one hand, and regulations prohibiting private uses, on the other, makes it inappropriate to treat cases involving physical takings as controlling precedents for the evaluation of a claim that there has been a "regulatory taking," and vice versa. . . .

Perhaps recognizing this fundamental distinction, petitioners wisely do not place all their emphasis on analogies to physical takings cases. Instead, they rely principally on our decision in *Lucas v. South Carolina Coastal Council*—a regulatory takings case that, nevertheless, applied a categorical rule—to argue that the *Penn Central* framework is inapplicable here. A brief review of some of the cases that led to our decision in *Lucas*, however, will help to explain why the holding in that case does not answer the question presented here.

As we noted in *Lucas*, it was Justice HOLMES' opinion in *Pennsylvania Coal Co. v. Mahon*, 260 U.S. 393 (1922), that gave birth to our regulatory takings jurisprudence. In subsequent opinions we have repeatedly and consistently endorsed HOLMES' observation that "if regulation goes too far it will be recognized as a taking." Justice HOLMES did not provide a standard for determining when a regulation goes "too far," but he did reject the view expressed in Justice BRANDEIS' dissent that there could not be a taking because the property remained in the possession of the owner and had not been appropriated or used by the public. After *Mahon*, neither a physical appropriation nor a public use has ever been a necessary component of a "regulatory taking."

In the decades following that decision, we have "generally eschewed" any set formula for determining how far is too far, choosing instead to engage in "'essentially ad hoc, factual inquiries.'" Indeed, we still resist the temptation to adopt per se rules in our cases involving partial regulatory takings, preferring to examine "a number of factors" rather than a simple "mathematically precise" formula. Justice BRENNAN's opinion for the Court in *Penn Central* did, however, make it clear that even though multiple factors are relevant in the analysis of regulatory takings claims, in such cases we must focus on "the parcel as a whole": "'Taking' jurisprudence does not divide a single parcel into discrete segments and attempt to determine whether rights in a particular segment have been entirely abrogated. In deciding whether a particular governmental action has effected a taking, this Court focuses rather both on the character of the action and on the nature and extent of the interference with rights in the parcel as a whole—here, the city tax block designated as the 'landmark site.'" This requirement that "the aggregate must be viewed in its entirety" explains why, for example, a regulation that prohibited commercial transactions in eagle feathers, but did not bar other uses or impose any physical invasion or restraint upon them, was not a taking. It also clarifies why restrictions on the use of only limited portions of the parcel, such as set-back ordinances, or a requirement that coal pillars be left in place to prevent mine subsidence, were not considered regulatory takings. In each of these cases, we affirmed that "where an owner possesses a full 'bundle' of property rights, the destruction of one 'strand' of the bundle is not a taking."

While the foregoing cases considered whether particular regulations had "gone too far" and were therefore invalid, none of them addressed the separate remedial question of how compensation is measured once a regulatory taking is established. In his dissenting opinion in *San Diego Gas & Elec. Co. v. San Diego*, 450 U.S. 621 (1981), Justice BRENNAN identified that question and explained how he would answer it: "The constitutional rule I propose requires that, once a court finds that a police power regulation has effected a 'taking,' the government entity must pay just compensation for the period commencing on the date the regulation first effected the 'taking,' and ending on the date the government entity chooses to rescind or otherwise amend the regulation." Justice BRENNAN's proposed rule was subsequently endorsed by the Court in *First English*. *First English* was certainly a significant decision, and nothing that we say today qualifies its holding. Nonetheless, it is important to recognize that we did not address in that case the quite different and logically prior question whether the temporary regulation at issue had in fact constituted a taking. . . .

Similarly, our decision in *Lucas* is not dispositive of the question presented. Although *Lucas* endorsed and applied a categorical rule, it was not the one that petitioners propose. . . . The categorical rule that we applied in *Lucas* states that compensation is required when a regulation deprives an owner of "all economically beneficial uses" of his land. But our holding was limited to "the extraordinary circumstance when no productive or economically beneficial use of land is permitted." . . .

Certainly, our holding that the permanent "obliteration of the value" of a fee simple estate constitutes a categorical taking does not answer the question whether a regulation prohibiting any economic use of land for a 32-month period has the same legal effect. Petitioners seek to bring this case under the rule announced in *Lucas* by arguing that we can effectively sever a 32-month segment from the remainder of each landowner's fee simple estate, and then ask whether that segment has been taken in its entirety by the moratoria. Of course, defining the property interest taken in terms of the very regulation being challenged is circular. With property so divided, every delay would become a total ban; the moratorium and the normal permit process alike would constitute categorical takings. . . .

Neither *Lucas*, nor *First English*, nor any of our other regulatory takings cases compels us to accept petitioners' categorical submission. In fact, these cases make clear that the categorical rule in *Lucas* was carved out for the "extraordinary case" in which a regulation permanently deprives property of all value; the default rule remains that, in the regulatory taking context, we require a more fact specific inquiry. . . .

[T]he ultimate constitutional question is whether the concepts of "fairness and justice" that underlie the Takings Clause will be better served by one of these categorical rules or by a *Penn Central* inquiry into all of the relevant circumstances in particular cases. From that perspective, the extreme categorical rule that any deprivation of all economic use, no matter how brief, constitutes a compensable taking surely cannot be sustained. Petitioners' broad submission would apply to numerous "normal delays in obtaining build-ing permits, changes in zoning ordinances, variances, and the like," as well as to orders temporarily prohibiting access to crime scenes, businesses that violate health codes, fire-damaged buildings, or other areas that we cannot now foresee. Such a rule would undoubtedly require changes in numerous practices that have long been considered permissible exercises of the police power. A rule that required compensation for every delay in the use of prop-erty would render routine government processes prohibitively expensive or encourage hasty decision-making. Such an important change in the law should be the product of legislative rulemaking rather than adjudication. . . .

The concepts of "fairness and justice" that underlie the Takings Clause, of course, are less than fully determinate. Accordingly, we have eschewed any "set formula" for determining when "justice and fairness" require that eco-nomic injuries caused by public action be compensated by the government, rather than remain disproportionately concentrated on a few persons. The outcome instead depends largely "upon the particular circumstances [in that] case." In rejecting petitioners' per se rule, we do not hold that the temporary nature of a land-use restriction precludes finding that it effects a taking; we simply recognize that it should not be given exclusive significance one way or the other.

A narrower rule that excluded the normal delays associated with process-ing permits, or that covered only delays of more than a year, would certainly have a less severe impact on prevailing practices, but it would still impose serious financial constraints on the planning process. Unlike the "extraordi-nary circumstance" in which the government deprives a property owner of all economic use, moratoria like Ordinance 81–5 and Resolution 83–21 are used widely among land-use planners to preserve the status quo while for-mulating a more permanent development strategy. In fact, the consensus in the planning community appears to be that moratoria, or "interim develop-ment controls" as they are often called, are an essential tool of successful development. . . .

[T]he interest in protecting the decisional process is even stronger when an agency is developing a regional plan than when it is considering a permit for a single parcel. In the proceedings involving the Lake Tahoe Basin, for example, the moratoria enabled TRPA to obtain the benefit of comments and criticisms from interested parties, such as the petitioners, during its delib-erations. Since a categorical rule tied to the length of deliberations would likely create added pressure on decisionmakers to reach a quick resolution of land-use questions, it would only serve to disadvantage those landowners and interest groups who are not as organized or familiar with the planning process. . . .

It may well be true that any moratorium that lasts for more than one year should be viewed with special skepticism. But given the fact that the District Court found that the 32 months required by TRPA to formulate the 1984 Regional Plan was not unreasonable, we could not possibly conclude that every delay of over one year is constitutionally unacceptable. Formulating a general rule of this kind is a suitable task for state legislatures. In our view, the duration of the restriction is one of the important factors that a court must consider in the appraisal of a regulatory takings claim, but with respect to that factor as with respect to other factors, the "temptation to adopt what amount to per se rules in either direction must be resisted." There may be moratoria that last longer than one year which interfere with reasonable investment-backed expectations, but as the District Court's opinion illustrates, petitioners' proposed rule is simply "too blunt an instrument," for identifying those cases. We conclude, therefore, that the interest in "fairness and justice" will be best served by relying on the familiar *Penn Central* approach when deciding cases like this, rather than by attempting to craft a new categorical rule.

☐ *CHIEF JUSTICE REHNQUIST, with whom Justice SCALIA and Justice THOMAS join, dissenting.*

Lucas reaffirmed our "frequently expressed" view that "when the owner of real property has been called upon to sacrifice all economically beneficial uses in the name of the common good, that is, to leave his property economically idle, he has suffered a taking." The Court does not dispute that petitioners were forced to leave their land economically idle during this period. But the Court refuses to apply *Lucas* on the ground that the deprivation was "temporary." Neither the Takings Clause nor our case law supports such a distinction. For one thing, a distinction between "temporary" and "permanent" prohibitions is tenuous. The "temporary" prohibition in this case that the Court finds is not a taking lasted almost six years. The "permanent" prohibition that the Court held to be a taking in *Lucas* lasted less than two years. The "permanent" prohibition in *Lucas* lasted less than two years because the law, as it often does, changed. . . .

[E]ven if a practical distinction between temporary and permanent deprivations were plausible, to treat the two differently in terms of takings law would be at odds with the justification for the *Lucas* rule. The *Lucas* rule is derived from the fact that a "total deprivation of use is, from the landowner's point of view, the equivalent of a physical appropriation." The regulation in *Lucas* was the "practical equivalence" of a long-term physical appropriation, i.e., a condemnation, so the Fifth Amendment required compensation. The "practical equivalence," from the landowner's point of view, of a "temporary" ban on all economic use is a forced leasehold. . . .

When a regulation merely delays a final land-use decision, we have recognized that there are other background principles of state property law that prevent the delay from being deemed a taking. We thus noted in *First English* that our discussion of temporary takings did not apply "in the case of normal delays in obtaining building permits, changes in zoning ordinances, variances, and the like."

But a moratorium prohibiting all economic use for a period of six years is not one of the longstanding, implied limitations of state property law. Moratoria are "interim controls on the use of land that seek to maintain the status quo with respect to land development in an area by either 'freezing' existing land uses or by allowing the issuance of building permits for only certain land uses that would not be inconsistent with a contemplated zoning plan or zoning change." Typical moratoria thus prohibit only certain categories of development, such as fast-food restaurants, or adult businesses, or all commercial development.

Such moratoria do not implicate *Lucas* because they do not deprive landowners of all economically beneficial use of their land. As for moratoria that prohibit all development, these do not have the lineage of permit and zoning requirements and thus it is less certain that property is acquired under the "implied limitation" of a moratorium prohibiting all development. Moreover, unlike a permit system in which it is expected that a project will be approved so long as certain conditions are satisfied, a moratorium that prohibits all uses is by definition contemplating a new land-use plan that would prohibit all uses. . . .

Because the prohibition on development of nearly six years in this case cannot be said to resemble any "implied limitation" of state property law, it is a taking that requires compensation. . . .

□ *Justice THOMAS, with whom Justice SCALIA joins, dissenting.*

A taking is exactly what occurred in this case. . . . I would hold that regulations prohibiting all productive uses of property are subject to *Lucas'* per se rule, regardless of whether the property so burdened retains theoretical useful life and value if, and when, the "temporary" moratorium is lifted. To my mind, such potential future value bears on the amount of compensation due and has nothing to do with the question whether there was a taking in the first place. It is regrettable that the Court has charted a markedly different path today.

SUPREME COURT WATCH 2004

VOLUME TWO

3

ECONOMIC RIGHTS AND
AMERICAN CAPITALISM

C | The "Takings Clause" and
Just Compensation

Tahoe-Sierra Preservation Council, Inc. v. Tahoe Regional Planning Agency (2002)
is excerpted in Volume One, Chapter 9 (reprise).

4

THE NATIONALIZATION OF THE BILL OF RIGHTS

B | *The Rise and Retreat of the "Due Process Revolution"*

In its 2002–2003 term the Court revisited the constitutionality of "Megan's Laws," which all fifty states have enacted and which require convicted sex offenders to register with state and local police, as well as to make available to the public their names, addresses, and photographs. These laws were enacted following the death of Megan Kanka, a New Jersey girl who was raped and murdered in 1994 by a sex offender in her neighborhood whose criminal history was unknown to her parents. Two convicted sex offenders challenged the constitutionality of Connecticut's law that, like those in nineteen other states, requires the public disclosure of personal information and DNA samples as well as the posting of the names, addresses, and photographs of convicted sex offenders on the Internet. A federal district court agreed that the publication and posting on the Web of offenders' personal information without first holding a hearing on their danger to society violated the guarantee of due process. The Court of Appeals for the Second Circuit agreed, but on appeal the Supreme Court reversed and found no due process violation because the registry requirement is based on a criminal conviction, not current dangerousness, in *Connecticut Department of Public Safety v. Doe*, 538 U.S. 1 (2003).

■ THE DEVELOPMENT OF LAW

Rulings on Substantive and Procedural Due Process

CASE	VOTE	RULING
Dusenbery v. United States, 534 U.S. 161 (2002)	5:4	Writing for the Court, Chief Justice Rehnquist upheld the forfeiture of private property of a

prison inmate, who was served notice by certified mail and in the absence of a response to the notice of forfeiture, and held that due process does not require "actual notice," only "an attempt to provide actual notice" of forfeiture. Justices Ginsburg, Stevens, Souter, and Breyer dissented.

Kansas v. Crane, 534 U.S. 407 (2002)	7:2	In *Kansas v. Hendricks,* 521 U.S. 346 (1997) (excerpted in Vol. 2, Ch. 4) the Court upheld the state's

Sexually Violent Predator Act, authorizing the continued civil commitment of convicted sexual offenders who have a "mental abnormality or personality disorder" that renders them dangerous to themselves or others. Subsequently, Kansas sought the continued commitment of Michael Crane, but the state supreme court ruled that due process requires a finding that the defendant "cannot control his dangerous behavior." Writing for the Court, Justice Breyer held that there must be a hearing and finding that a dangerous sexual offender lacks self-control, but also emphasized that under *Hendricks* there is no narrow or technical meaning of "lack of control" and that that must be determined on a case by case basis, depending on the circumstances and psychiatric evaluations. Justices Scalia and Thomas dissented.

Connecticut Department of Public Safety v. Doe, 538 U.S. 1 (2003)	9:0	Writing for a unanimous Court, Chief Justice Rehnquist held that due process is not violated by states' requiring convicted sex

offenders to register personal information, including addresses and photographs, which are then posted on a website, because the registry requirement is based on a prior conviction, not the sex offender's current dangerousness.

State Farm Mutual Automobile Insurance v. Campbell, 538 U.S. 408 (2003)	6:3	Writing for the Court, Justice Kennedy held that punitive damages awards must be reasonable and proportionate to the wrong

committed and that "the wealth of a defendant cannot justify an otherwise unconstitutional punitive damages award." Here, the majority overturned a $145 million jury award against State Farm that was 145 times the amount of the injury as "an irrational and arbitrary deprivation of the property of the defendant." Justices Scalia, Thomas, and Ginsburg dissented.

Demore v. Kim, 538 U.S. 51 (2003)   5:4   Writing for the Court, Chief Justice Rehnquist upheld a 1996 federal law authorizing the detention of immigrants, including permanent residents or "green card holders," who have committed certain crimes and served their sentences while the government decides whether to deport them. The majority rejected the due process claim that they are entitled to a hearing on whether they would jump bail or posed a danger to society. In the chief justice's words: "Congress may make rules as to aliens that would be unacceptable if applied to citizens." Justice Souter, joined by Justices Stevens and Ginsburg, filed an opinion in part concurring and dissenting that endorsed the substantive and procedural due process claim. In a separate opinion, Justice Breyer concurred and dissented in part.

Overton v. Bazzetta, 539 U.S. 126 (2003)   9:0   The Court held that prison regulations limiting inmate visitations do not violate freedom of association or substantive due process and are rationally related to penelogical interests.

Sell v. United States, 539 U.S. 166 (2003)   6:3   Writing for the Court, Justice Breyer held that antipsychotic drugs may be administered to a mentally ill defendant without his or her consent if the forced medication (1) is necessary to an "important governmental interest," (2) significantly furthers that interest, (3) is medically necessary without a less intrusive alternative, and (4) is medically appropriate.

5

FREEDOM OF EXPRESSION AND ASSOCIATION

I n *Watchtower Bible & Tract Society of New York, Inc. v. Village of Stratton* (excerpted below) the Court struck down an ordinance requiring a permit for solicitations on private property. The Jehovah's Witnesses challenged the ordinance as a violation of the First Amendment's protection for freedom of speech and religion, and the Court agreed, with only Chief Justice Rehnquist dissenting.

Watchtower Bible & Tract Society of New York, Inc. v. Village of Stratton
536 U.S. 150, 122 S.Ct. 2080 (2002)

The Village of Stratton, Ohio, enacted ordinances prohibiting "canvassers" and others from "going in and upon" private residential property for the purpose of promoting any cause without obtaining a Solicitation Permit from the mayor's office. Once the canvasser had obtained the permit, he or she was authorized to go on the premises listed on the registration form but had to carry the permit and show it if requested to do so by a police officer or resident. The constitutionality of the ordinance was challenged as a violation of the First Amendment's guarantees of freedom of speech and press and of the free exercise of religion by the Watchtower Bible and Tract Society of New York, which coordinates the preaching activities of Jehovah's Witnesses. A federal district court upheld most of the provisions as valid, content-neutral regulations, and the Court of Appeals for the Sixth Circuit affirmed. The latter decision was appealed to the Supreme Court, which granted review.

The lower court's decision was reversed by an eight-to-one vote, and Justice Stevens delivered the opinion of the Court. Justices Breyer and Scalia filed concurring opinions, and Chief Justice Rehnquist issued a dissenting opinion.

☐ *Justice STEVENS delivers the opinion of the Court.*

For over 50 years, the Court has invalidated restrictions on door-to-door canvassing and pamphleteering. It is more than historical accident that most of these cases involved First Amendment challenges brought by Jehovah's Witnesses, because door-to-door canvassing is mandated by their religion. As we noted in *Murdock v. Pennsylvania*, 319 U.S. 105 (1943), the Jehovah's Witnesses "claim to follow the example of Paul, teaching 'publicly, and from house to house.' Acts 20:20. They take literally the mandate of the Scriptures, 'Go ye into all the world, and preach the gospel to every creature.' Mark 16:15. In doing so they believe that they are obeying a commandment of God." Moreover, because they lack significant financial resources, the ability of the Witnesses to proselytize is seriously diminished by regulations that burden their efforts to canvass door-to-door.

Although our past cases involving Jehovah's Witnesses, most of which were decided shortly before and during World War II, do not directly control the question we confront today, they provide both a historical and analytical backdrop for consideration of petitioners' First Amendment claim that the breadth of the Village's ordinance offends the First Amendment. Those cases involved petty offenses that raised constitutional questions of the most serious magnitude—questions that implicated the free exercise of religion, the freedom of speech, and the freedom of the press. From these decisions, several themes emerge that guide our consideration of the ordinance at issue here.

First, the cases emphasize the value of the speech involved. For example, in *Murdock v. Pennsylvania*, the Court noted that "hand distribution of religious tracts is an age-old form of missionary evangelism—as old as the history of printing presses. It has been a potent force in various religious movements down through the years. . . . This form of religious activity occupies the same high estate under the First Amendment as do worship in the churches and preaching from the pulpits. It has the same claim to protection as the more orthodox and conventional exercises of religion. It also has the same claim as the others to the guarantees of freedom of speech and freedom of the press."

In addition, the cases discuss extensively the historical importance of door-to-door canvassing and pamphleteering as vehicles for the dissemination of ideas. In *Schneider v. State (Town of Irvington)*, 308 U.S. 147 (1939), the petitioner was a Jehovah's Witness who had been convicted of canvassing without a permit based on evidence that she had gone from house to house offering to leave books or booklets. Writing for the Court, Justice ROBERTS stated that "pamphlets have proved most effective instruments in the dissemination of opinion. And perhaps the most effective way of bringing them to the notice of individuals is their distribution at the homes of the people. On this method of communication the ordinance imposes censorship, abuse of which engendered the struggle in England which eventuated in the establishment of the doctrine of the freedom of the press embodied in our Constitution. To require a censorship through license which makes impossible the free and unhampered distribution of pamphlets strikes at the very heart of the constitutional guarantees."

Despite the emphasis on the important role that door-to-door canvassing and pamphleteering has played in our constitutional tradition of free and open discussion, these early cases also recognized the interests a town may have in some form of regulation, particularly when the solicitation of money is involved. In *Cantwell v. Connecticut*, 310 U.S. 296 (1940), the Court held that an ordinance requiring Jehovah's Witnesses to obtain a license before soliciting door to door was invalid because the issuance of the license depended on the exercise of discretion by a city official. . . .

The Village argues that three interests are served by its ordinance: the prevention of fraud, the prevention of crime, and the protection of residents' privacy. We have no difficulty concluding, in light of our precedent, that these are important interests that the Village may seek to safeguard through some form of regulation of solicitation activity. We must also look, however, to the amount of speech covered by the ordinance and whether there is an appropriate balance between the affected speech and the governmental interests that the ordinance purports to serve.

The text of the Village's ordinance prohibits "canvassers" from going on private property for the purpose of explaining or promoting any "cause," unless they receive a permit and the residents visited have not opted for a "no solicitation" sign. Had this provision been construed to apply only to commercial activities and the solicitation of funds, arguably the ordinance would have been tailored to the Village's interest in protecting the privacy of its residents and preventing fraud. Yet, even though the Village has explained that the ordinance was adopted to serve those interests, it has never contended that it should be so narrowly interpreted. To the contrary, the Village's administration of its ordinance unquestionably demonstrates that the provisions apply to a significant number of noncommercial "canvassers" promoting a wide variety of "causes." Indeed, on the "No Solicitation Forms" provided to the residents, the canvassers include "Camp Fire Girls," "Jehovah's Witnesses," "Political Candidates," "Trick or Treaters during Halloween Season," and "Persons Affiliated with Stratton Church." The ordinance unquestionably applies, not only to religious causes, but to political activity as well. It would seem to extend to "residents casually soliciting the votes of neighbors," or ringing doorbells to enlist support for employing a more efficient garbage collector.

The mere fact that the ordinance covers so much speech raises constitutional concerns. It is offensive—not only to the values protected by the First Amendment, but to the very notion of a free society—that in the context of everyday public discourse a citizen must first inform the government of her desire to speak to her neighbors and then obtain a permit to do so. Even if the issuance of permits by the mayor's office is a ministerial task that is performed promptly and at no cost to the applicant, a law requiring a permit to engage in such speech constitutes a dramatic departure from our national heritage and constitutional tradition. . . .

The breadth and unprecedented nature of this regulation does not alone render the ordinance invalid. Also central to our conclusion that the ordinance does not pass First Amendment scrutiny is that it is not tailored to the Village's stated interests. Even if the interest in preventing fraud could adequately support the ordinance insofar as it applies to commercial transactions and the solicitation of funds, that interest provides no support for its application to petitioners, to political campaigns, or to enlisting support for unpopular causes. The Village, however, argues that the ordinance is nonetheless valid because it serves the two additional interests of protecting the privacy of the resident and the prevention of crime.

With respect to the former, it seems clear that Section 107 of the ordinance, which provides for the posting of "No Solicitation" signs and which is not challenged in this case, coupled with the resident's unquestioned right to refuse to engage in conversation with unwelcome visitors, provides ample protection for the unwilling listener. The annoyance caused by an uninvited knock on the front door is the same whether or not the visitor is armed with a permit.

With respect to the latter, it seems unlikely that the absence of a permit would preclude criminals from knocking on doors and engaging in conversations not covered by the ordinance. They might, for example, ask for directions or permission to use the telephone, or pose as surveyors or census takers. Or they might register under a false name with impunity because the ordinance contains no provision for verifying an applicant's identity or organizational credentials. Moreover, the Village did not assert an interest in crime prevention below, and there is an absence of any evidence of a special crime problem related to door-to-door solicitation in the record before us.

The rhetoric used in the World War II–era opinions that repeatedly saved petitioners' coreligionists from petty prosecutions reflected the Court's evaluation of the First Amendment freedoms that are implicated in this case. The value judgment that then motivated a united democratic people fighting to defend those very freedoms from totalitarian attack is unchanged. It motivates our decision today.

☐ *Justice SCALIA, with whom Justice THOMAS joins, concurring in the judgment.*

I concur in the judgment, for many but not all of the reasons set forth in the opinion for the Court. I do not agree, for example, that one of the causes of the invalidity of Stratton's ordinance is that some people have a religious objection to applying for a permit, and others (posited by the Court) "have such firm convictions about their constitutional right to engage in uninhibited debate in the context of door-to-door advocacy, that they would prefer silence to speech licensed by a petty official."

If a licensing requirement is otherwise lawful, it is in my view not invalidated by the fact that some people will choose, for religious reasons, to forgo speech rather than observe it. That would convert an invalid free-exercise claim, see *Employment Div., Dept. of Human Resources of Ore. v. Smith*, 494 U.S. 872 (1990), into a valid free-speech claim—and a more destructive one at that. Whereas the free-exercise claim, if acknowledged, would merely exempt Jehovah's Witnesses from the licensing requirement, the free-speech claim exempts everybody, thanks to Jehovah's Witnesses.

As for the Court's fairy-tale category of "patriotic citizens," who would rather be silenced than licensed in a manner that the Constitution (but for their "patriotic" objection) would permit: If our free-speech jurisprudence is to be determined by the predicted behavior of such crackpots, we are in a sorry state indeed.

☐ *CHIEF JUSTICE REHNQUIST, dissenting.*

Stratton is a village of 278 people located along the Ohio River where the borders of Ohio, West Virginia, and Pennsylvania converge. It is strung out along a multi-lane highway connecting it with the cities of East Liverpool to the north and Steubenville and Weirton, West Virginia, to the south. One may doubt how much legal help a village of this size has available in drafting an ordinance such as the present one, but even if it had availed itself of a battery of constitutional lawyers, they would have been of little use in the town's effort. For the Court today ignores the cases on which those lawyers would have relied, and comes up with newly fashioned doctrine. This doctrine contravenes well-established precedent, renders local governments largely impotent to address the very real safety threat that canvassers pose, and may actually result in less of the door-to-door communication it seeks to protect.

More than half a century ago we recognized that canvassers, "whether selling pots or distributing leaflets, may lessen the peaceful enjoyment of a home," and that "burglars frequently pose as canvassers, either in order that they may have a pretense to discover whether a house is empty and hence ripe for burglary, or for the purpose of spying out the premises in order that they may return later." *Martin v. City of Struthers*, 319 U.S. 141 (1943). These problems continue to be associated with door-to-door canvassing, as are even graver ones.

A recent double murder in Hanover, New Hampshire, a town of approximately 7,500 that would appear tranquil to most Americans but would probably seem like a bustling town of Dartmouth College students to Stratton residents, illustrates these dangers. Two teenagers murdered a married couple of Dartmouth College professors, Half and Susanne Zantop, in the Zantops' home. Investigators have concluded, based on the confession of one of the teenagers, that the teenagers went door-to-door intent on stealing access numbers to bank debit cards and then killing their owners. Their modus operandi was to tell residents that they were conducting an environmental survey for school. They canvassed a few homes where no one answered. At another, the resident did not allow them in to conduct the "survey." They were allowed into the Zantop home. After conducting the phony environmental survey, they stabbed the Zantops to death.

In order to reduce these very grave risks associated with canvassing, the 278 "'little people'" of Stratton, who, unlike petitioners, do not have a team of attorneys at their ready disposal, enacted the ordinance at issue here. The residents did not prohibit door-to-door communication, they simply required that canvassers obtain a permit before going door-to-door. And the village does not have the discretion to reject an applicant who completes the application.

The town had little reason to suspect that the negligible burden of having to obtain a permit runs afoul of the First Amendment. For over 60 years, we have categorically stated that a permit requirement for door-to-door canvassers, which gives no discretion to the issuing authority, is constitutional. The District Court and Court of Appeals, relying on our cases, upheld the ordinance. . . .

The double murder in Hanover described above is but one tragic example of the crime threat posed by door-to-door canvassing. . . .

What is more, the Court soon forgets both the privacy and crime interests. It finds the ordinance too broad because it applies to a "significant number of noncommercial 'canvassers.'" But noncommercial canvassers, for example, those purporting to conduct environmental surveys for school, violate no trespassing signs and engage in burglaries and violent crimes just as easily as commercial canvassers can. . . .

The next question is whether the ordinance serves the important interests of protecting privacy and preventing fraud and crime. With respect to the interest in protecting privacy, the Court concludes that "[t]he annoyance caused by an uninvited knock on the front door is the same whether or not the visitor is armed with a permit." True, but that misses the key point: the permit requirement results in fewer uninvited knocks. Those who have complied with the permit requirement are less likely to visit residences with no trespassing signs, as it is much easier for the authorities to track them down.

The Court also fails to grasp how the permit requirement serves Stratton's interest in preventing crime. We have approved of permit requirements for those engaging in protected First Amendment activity because of a common-sense recognition that their existence both deters and helps detect wrongdoing. . . .

A discretionless permit requirement for canvassers does not violate the First Amendment. Today, the Court elevates its concern with what is, at most, a negligible burden on door-to-door communication above this established proposition. Ironically, however, today's decision may result in less of the door-to-door communication that the Court extols. As the Court recognizes, any homeowner may place a "No Solicitation" sign on his or her property, and it is a crime to violate that sign. In light of today's decision depriving Stratton residents of the degree of accountability and safety that the permit requirement provides, more and more residents may decide to place these signs in their yards and cut off door-to-door communication altogether.

B | Obscenity, Pornography, and Offensive Speech

In its 2001–2002 term the Court continued to grapple with how to decide First Amendment challenges to the exclusionary zoning of adult entertainment businesses. As in prior cases, the issue of justifying such zoning restrictions based on the "secondary effects" of adult-oriented businesses continued to fragment the justices. In *City of Los Angeles v. Alameda Books, Inc.* (2002) (excerpted below), only a plurality joined Justice O'Connor's opinion for the Court, upholding an ordinance prohibiting more than one adult establishment from operating at the same location. Justices Scalia and Kennedy filed concurring opinions. Justice Souter filed a dissent, which Justices Stevens, Ginsburg, and Breyer joined.

In *Ashcroft v. Free Speech Coalition* (2002) (excerpted below) the Court struck down sections of the Child Pornography Prevention Act of 1996 that made it a crime to create, distribute, or possess "virtual child pornography" generated by computer images of young adults or simulated images, rather than of actual children. In doing so, the justices split six-and-a-half to two-and-a-half with Chief Justice Rehnquist and Justice

Scalia dissenting, and Justice O'Connor filing a separate opinion in part concurring and dissenting.

City of Los Angeles v. Alameda Books, Inc.
535 U.S. 425, 122 S.Ct. 1728 (2002)

Los Angeles enacted an ordinance prohibiting "the establishment or maintenance of more than one adult entertainment business in the same building, structure or portion thereof." The owners of two adult establishments, each operating a bookstore and a video arcade in the same building, were found in violation of the ordinance and challenged its constitutionality. A federal district court held that the prohibition was a content-based regulation of speech and failed to survive strict scrutiny. The Court of Appeals for the Ninth Circuit affirmed, though on different grounds. The city appealed that decision and the Supreme Court granted review.

The appellate court was reversed in a five-to-four decision. Justice O'Connor delivered the opinion for the Court. Justices Scalia and Kennedy filed concurring opinions. Justice Souter filed a dissenting opinion, which Justices Stevens, Ginsburg, and Breyer joined.

☐ *Justice O'CONNOR announced the judgment of the Court and delivered an opinion, in which THE CHIEF JUSTICE, Justice SCALIA, and Justice THOMAS join.*

In 1977, the city of Los Angeles conducted a comprehensive study of adult establishments and concluded that concentrations of adult businesses are associated with higher rates of prostitution, robbery, assaults, and thefts in surrounding communities. Accordingly, the city enacted an ordinance prohibiting the establishment, substantial enlargement, or transfer of ownership of an adult arcade, bookstore, cabaret, motel, theater, or massage parlor or a place for sexual encounters within 1,000 feet of another such enterprise or within 500 feet of any religious institution, school, or public park.

There is evidence that the intent of the city council when enacting this prohibition was not only to disperse distinct adult establishments housed in separate buildings, but also to disperse distinct adult businesses operated under common ownership and housed in a single structure. The ordinance the city enacted, however, directed that "[t]he distance between any two adult entertainment businesses shall be measured in a straight line . . . from the closest exterior structural wall of each business." Subsequent to enactment, the city realized that this method of calculating distances created a loophole permitting the concentration of multiple adult enterprises in a single structure.

Concerned that allowing an adult-oriented department store to replace a strip of adult establishments could defeat the goal of the original ordinance, the city council amended Section 12.70(C) by adding a prohibition on "the establishment or maintenance of more than one adult entertainment business in the same building, structure or portion thereof." . . .

In *Renton v. Playtime Theatres, Inc.* [475 U.S. 41 (1986)], this Court considered the validity of a municipal ordinance that prohibited any adult movie theater from locating within 1,000 feet of any residential zone, family dwelling, church, park, or school. Our analysis of the ordinance proceeded in three steps. First, we found that the ordinance did not ban adult theaters altogether, but merely required that they be distanced from certain sensitive locations. The ordinance was properly analyzed, therefore, as a time, place, and manner regulation. We next considered whether the ordinance was content neutral or content based. If the regulation were content based, it would be considered presumptively invalid and subject to strict scrutiny. We held, however, that the Renton ordinance was aimed not at the content of the films shown at adult theaters, but rather at the secondary effects of such theaters on the surrounding community, namely at crime rates, property values, and the quality of the city's neighborhoods. Therefore, the ordinance was deemed content neutral. Finally, given this finding, we stated that the ordinance would be upheld so long as the city of Renton showed that its ordinance was designed to serve a substantial government interest and that reasonable alternative avenues of communication remained available. We concluded that Renton had met this burden, and we upheld its ordinance.

The Court of Appeals applied the same analysis to evaluate the Los Angeles ordinance challenged in this case. First, the Court of Appeals found that the Los Angeles ordinance was not a complete ban on adult entertainment establishments, but rather a sort of adult zoning regulation, which *Renton* considered a time, place, and manner regulation. The Court of Appeals turned to the second step of the *Renton* analysis, but did not draw any conclusions about whether the Los Angeles ordinance was content based. It explained that, even if the Los Angeles ordinance were content neutral, the city had failed to demonstrate, as required by the third step of the *Renton* analysis, that its prohibition on multiple-use adult establishments was designed to serve its substantial interest in reducing crime. The Court of Appeals noted that the primary evidence relied upon by Los Angeles to demonstrate a link between combination adult businesses and harmful secondary effects was the 1977 study conducted by the city's planning department. The Court of Appeals found, however, that the city could not rely on that study because it did not "suppor[t] a reasonable belief that [the] combination [of] businesses . . . produced harmful secondary effects of the type asserted."

The central component of the 1977 study is a report on city crime patterns provided by the Los Angeles Police Department. That report indicated that, during the period from 1965 to 1975, certain crime rates grew much faster in Hollywood, which had the largest concentration of adult establishments in the city, than in the city of Los Angeles as a whole. For example, robberies increased 3 times faster and prostitution 15 times faster in Hollywood than citywide. . . .

The Court of Appeals found that the 1977 study did not reasonably support the inference that a concentration of adult operations within a single adult establishment produced greater levels of criminal activity because the study focused on the effect that a concentration of establishments—not a concentration of operations within a single establishment—had on crime rates. The Court of Appeals pointed out that the study treated combination adult bookstore/arcades as single establishments and did not study the effect of any separate-standing adult bookstore or arcade.

The Court of Appeals misunderstood the implications of the 1977 study. While the study reveals that areas with high concentrations of adult establishments are associated with high crime rates, areas with high concentrations of adult establishments are also areas with high concentrations of adult operations, albeit each in separate establishments. It was therefore consistent with the findings of the 1977 study, and thus reasonable, for Los Angeles to suppose that a concentration of adult establishments is correlated with high crime rates because a concentration of operations in one locale draws, for example, a greater concentration of adult consumers to the neighborhood, and a high density of such consumers either attracts or generates criminal activity. The assumption behind this theory is that having a number of adult operations in one single adult establishment draws the same dense foot traffic as having a number of distinct adult establishments in close proximity, much as minimalls and department stores similarly attract the crowds of consumers. Under this view, it is rational for the city to infer that reducing the concentration of adult operations in a neighborhood, whether within separate establishments or in one large establishment, will reduce crime rates. . . .

The error that the Court of Appeals made is that it required the city to prove that its theory about a concentration of adult operations attracting crowds of customers, much like a minimall or department store does, is a necessary consequence of the 1977 study. For example, the Court of Appeals refused to allow the city to draw the inference that "the expansion of an adult bookstore to include an adult arcade would increase" business activity and "produce the harmful secondary effects identified in the Study." . . . The Court of Appeals simply replaced the city's theory—that having many different operations in close proximity attracts crowds—with its own—that the size of an operation attracts crowds. If the Court of Appeals' theory is correct, then inventory limits make more sense. If the city's theory is correct, then a prohibition on the combination of businesses makes more sense. Both theories are consistent with the data in the 1977 study. The Court of Appeals' analysis, however, implicitly requires the city to prove that its theory is the only one that can plausibly explain the data because only in this manner can the city refute the Court of Appeals' logic. . . .

In *Renton*, we specifically refused to set such a high bar for municipalities that want to address merely the secondary effects of protected speech. We held that a municipality may rely on any evidence that is "reasonably believed to be relevant" for demonstrating a connection between speech and a substantial, independent government interest. . . .

Accordingly, we reverse the Court of Appeals' judgment granting summary judgment to respondents and remand the case for further proceedings. It is so ordered.

☐ *Justice SCALIA, concurring.*

I join the plurality opinion because I think it represents a correct application of our jurisprudence concerning regulation of the "secondary effects" of pornographic speech. As I have said elsewhere, however, in a case such as this our First Amendment traditions make "secondary effects" analysis quite unnecessary. The Constitution does not prevent those communities that wish to do so from regulating, or indeed entirely suppressing, the business of pandering sex.

☐ *Justice SOUTER, with whom Justice STEVENS and Justice GINSBURG join, and with whom Justice BREYER joins, dissenting.*

In 1977, the city of Los Angeles studied sections of the city with high and low concentrations of adult business establishments catering to the market for the erotic. The city found no certain correlation between the location of those establishments and depressed property values, but it did find some correlation between areas of higher concentrations of such business and higher crime rates. On that basis, Los Angeles followed the examples of other cities in adopting a zoning ordinance requiring dispersion of adult establishments. . . .

The city subsequently amended its ordinance to forbid clusters of such businesses at one address, as in a mall. The city has, in turn, taken a third step to apply this amendment to prohibit even a single proprietor from doing business in a traditional way that combines an adult bookstore, selling books, magazines, and videos, with an adult arcade, consisting of open viewing booths, where potential purchasers of videos can view them for a fee.

From a policy of dispersing adult establishments, the city has thus moved to a policy of dividing them in two. The justification claimed for this application of the new policy remains, however, the 1977 survey, as supplemented by the authority of one decided case on regulating adult arcades in another State. The case authority is not on point and the 1977 survey provides no support for the breakup policy. Its evidentiary insufficiency bears emphasis and is the principal reason that I respectfully dissent from the Court's judgment today.

This ordinance stands or falls on the results of what our cases speak of as intermediate scrutiny, generally contrasted with the demanding standard applied under the First Amendment to a content-based regulation of expression. The variants of middle-tier tests cover a grab-bag of restrictive statutes, with a corresponding variety of justifications. While spoken of as content neutral, these regulations are not uniformly distinct from the content-based regulations calling for scrutiny that is strict, and zoning of businesses based on their sales of expressive adult material receives mid-level scrutiny, even though it raises a risk of content-based restriction. It is worth being clear, then, on how close to a content basis adult business zoning can get, and why the application of a middle-tier standard to zoning regulation of adult bookstores calls for particular care.

Because content-based regulation applies to expression by very reason of what is said, it carries a high risk that expressive limits are imposed for the sake of suppressing a message that is disagreeable to listeners or readers, or the government. A restriction based on content survives only on a showing of necessity to serve a legitimate and compelling governmental interest, combined with least-restrictive narrow tailoring to serve it; since merely protecting listeners from offense at the message is not a legitimate interest of the government, see *Cohen v. California*, 403 U.S. 15 (1971), strict scrutiny leaves few survivors.

The comparatively softer intermediate scrutiny is reserved for regulations justified by something other than content of the message, such as a straightforward restriction going only to the time, place, or manner of speech or other expression. It is easy to see why review of such a regulation may be relatively relaxed. No one has to disagree with any message to find something wrong with a loudspeaker at three in the morning; the sentiment may not provoke, but being blasted out of a sound sleep does. In such a case, we ask simply whether the regulation is "narrowly tailored to serve a significant governmental interest, and . . . leave[s] open ample alternative channels for communication of the information." *Clark v. Community for Creative Non-Violence*, 468 U.S. 288 (1984). A middle-tier standard is also applied to limits on expression through action that is otherwise subject to regulation for non-expressive purposes, the best known example being the prohibition on destroying draft cards as an act of protest, *United States v. O'Brien*, 391 U.S. 367 (1968); here a regulation passes muster "if it furthers an important or substantial governmental interest . . . unrelated to the suppression of free expression" by a restriction "no greater than is essential to the furtherance of that interest." As mentioned already, yet another middle-tier variety is zoning restriction as a means of responding to the "secondary effects" of adult businesses, principally crime and declining property values in the neighborhood. *Renton v. Playtime Theatres, Inc.*, 475 U.S. 41 (1986).

Although this type of land-use restriction has even been called a variety of time, place, or manner regulation, equating a secondary-effects zoning regulation with a mere regulation of time, place, or manner jumps over an important difference between them. A restriction on loudspeakers has no obvious relationship to the substance of what is broadcast, while a zoning regulation of businesses in adult expression just as obviously does. And while it may be true that an adult business is burdened only because of its secondary effects, it is clearly burdened only if its expressive products have adult content. Thus, the Court has recognized that this kind of regulation, though called content neutral, occupies a kind of limbo between full-blown, content-based restrictions and regulations that apply without any reference to the substance of what is said.

It would in fact make sense to give this kind of zoning regulation a First Amendment label of its own, and if we called it content correlated, we would not only describe it for what it is, but keep alert to a risk of content-based regulation that it poses. The risk lies in the fact that when a law applies selectively only to speech of particular content, the more precisely the content is identified, the greater is the opportunity for government censorship. Adult speech refers not merely to sexually explicit content, but to speech reflecting a favorable view of being explicit about sex and a favorable view of the practices it depicts; a restriction on adult content is thus also a restriction turning on a particular viewpoint, of which the government may disapprove.

This risk of viewpoint discrimination is subject to a relatively simple safeguard, however. If combating secondary effects of property devaluation and crime is truly the reason for the regulation, it is possible to show by empirical evidence that the effects exist, that they are caused by the expressive activity subject to the zoning, and that the zoning can be expected either to ameliorate them or to enhance the capacity of the government to combat them (say, by concentrating them in one area), without suppressing the expressive activity itself. This capacity of zoning regulation to address the practical problems without eliminating the speech is, after all, the only possible excuse for speaking of secondary-effects zoning as akin to time, place, or manner regulations. . . .

The lesson is that the lesser scrutiny applied to content-correlated zoning restrictions is no excuse for a government's failure to provide a factual demonstration for claims it makes about secondary effects; on the contrary, this is what demands the demonstration. In this case, however, the government has not shown that bookstores containing viewing booths, isolated from other adult establishments, increase crime or produce other negative secondary effects in surrounding neighborhoods, and we are thus left without substantial justification for viewing the city's First Amendment restriction as content correlated but not simply content based. By the same token, the city has failed to show any causal relationship between the breakup policy and elimination or regulation of secondary effects. . . .

If we take the city's breakup policy at its face, enforcing it will mean that in every case two establishments will operate instead of the traditional one. Since the city presumably does not wish merely to multiply adult establishments, it makes sense to ask what offsetting gain the city may obtain from its new breakup policy. The answer may lie in the fact that two establishments in place of one will entail two business overheads in place of one: two monthly rents, two electricity bills, two payrolls. Every month business will be more expensive than it used to be, perhaps even twice as much. That sounds like a good strategy for driving out expressive adult businesses. It sounds, in other words, like a policy of content-based regulation.

I respectfully dissent.

Ashcroft v. Free Speech Coalition
535 U.S. 234, 122 S.CT. 1389 (2002)

In 1996 Congress enacted the Child Pornography Prevention Act (CPPA), making it a crime to create, distribute or possess "virtual child pornography" generated by computer images of young adults rather than actual children. The constitutionality of the law was challenged by the Free Speech Coalition—a coalition of artists, photographers, and adult entertainment businesses. A federal district court upheld its provisions but the Court of Appeals for the Ninth Circuit reversed and found that the CPPA violated the First Amendment. Attorney General John D. Ashcroft appealed that decision and the Supreme Court granted review.

The decision of the appellate court was affirmed in a vote of six and a half to two and a half. Justice Kennedy delivered the opinion for the Court. Justice Thomas filed a concurring opinion, indicating that a more narrowly drawn statute might pass constitutional muster. Chief Justice Rehnquist filed a dissenting opinion, which Justice Scalia joined. Justice O'Connor filed a separate opinion, in part concurring and in part dissenting.

☐ *Justice KENNEDY delivered the opinion of the Court.*

We consider in this case whether the Child Pornography Prevention Act of 1996 (CPPA) abridges the freedom of speech. . . . By prohibiting child pornography that does not depict an actual child, the statute goes beyond *New York v. Ferber*, 458 U.S. 747 (1982), which distinguished child pornography from other sexually explicit speech because of the State's interest in protecting the children exploited by the production process. As a general rule, pornography can be banned only if obscene, but under *Ferber*, pornography showing minors can be proscribed whether or not the images are obscene under the definition set forth in *Miller v. California*, 413 U.S. 15 (1973)....

The CPPA, however, is not directed at speech that is obscene; Congress has proscribed those materials through a separate statute. Like the law in *Ferber*, the CPPA seeks to reach beyond obscenity, and it makes no attempt to conform to the *Miller* standard. For instance, the statute would reach visual depictions, such as movies, even if they have redeeming social value.

The principal question to be resolved, then, is whether the CPPA is constitutional where it proscribes a significant universe of speech that is neither obscene under *Miller* nor child pornography under *Ferber*.

Before 1996, Congress defined child pornography as the type of depictions at issue in *Ferber*, images made using actual minors. The CPPA retains that prohibition at 18 U.S.C. Sec. 2256(8)(A) and adds three other prohibited categories of speech, of which the first, Sec. 2256(8)(B), and the third, Sec. 2256(8)(D), are at issue in this case. Section 2256(8)(B) prohibits "any visual depiction, including any photograph, film, video, picture, or computer or computer-generated image or picture" that "is, or appears to be, of a minor engaging in sexually explicit conduct." The prohibition on "any visual depiction" does not depend at all on how the image is produced. The section captures a range of depictions, sometimes called "virtual child pornography," which include computer-generated images, as well as images produced by more traditional means. For instance, the literal terms of the statute embrace a Renaissance painting depicting a scene from classical mythology, a "picture" that "appears to be of a minor engaging in sexually explicit conduct." The statute also prohibits Hollywood movies, filmed without any child actors, if a jury believes an actor "appears to be" a minor engaging in "actual or simulated ... sexual intercourse."

These images do not involve, let alone harm, any children in the production process; but Congress decided the materials threaten children in other, less direct, ways. Pedophiles might use the materials to encourage children to participate in sexual activity. Furthermore, pedophiles might "whet their own sexual appetites" with the pornographic images, "thereby increasing the creation and distribution of child pornography and the sexual abuse and exploitation of actual children." Under these rationales, harm flows from the content of the images, not from the means of their production. In addition, Congress identified another problem created by computer-generated images: Their existence can make it harder to prosecute pornographers who do use real minors. As imaging technology improves, Congress found, it becomes more difficult to prove that a particular picture was produced using actual children.

Section 2256(8)(C) prohibits a more common and lower tech means of creating virtual images, known as computer morphing. Rather than creating original images, pornographers can alter innocent pictures of real children so that the children appear to be engaged in sexual activity. Although morphed images may fall within the definition of virtual child pornography, they implicate the interests of real children and are in that sense closer to the images in *Ferber*. Respondents do not challenge this provision, and we do not consider it.

Respondents do challenge Sec. 2256(8)(D). Like the text of the "appears to be" provision, the sweep of this provision is quite broad. Section 2256(8)(D) defines child pornography to include any sexually explicit image that was "advertised, promoted, presented, described, or distributed in such a manner that conveys the impression" it depicts "a minor engaging in sexually explicit conduct." The statute is not so limited in its reach, however, as it punishes even those possessors who took no part in pandering. . . .

The CPPA's penalties are indeed severe. A first offender may be imprisoned for 15 years. A repeat offender faces a prison sentence of not less than 5 years and not more than 30 years in prison. While even minor punishments can chill protected speech, this case provides a textbook example of why we permit facial challenges to statutes that burden expression. With these severe penalties in force, few legitimate movie producers or book publishers, or few other speakers in any capacity, would risk distributing images in or near the uncertain reach of this law. . . .

Under *Miller v. California* the Government must prove that the work, taken as a whole, appeals to the prurient interest, is patently offensive in light of community standards, and lacks serious literary, artistic, political, or scientific value. The CPPA, however, extends to images that appear to depict a minor engaging in sexually explicit activity without regard to the *Miller* requirements. The materials need not appeal to the prurient interest. Any depiction of sexually explicit activity, no matter how it is presented, is proscribed. The CPPA applies to a picture in a psychology manual, as well as a movie depicting the horrors of sexual abuse. It is not necessary, moreover, that the image be patently offensive. Pictures of what appear to be 17-year-olds engaging in sexually explicit activity do not in every case contravene community standards.

The CPPA prohibits speech despite its serious literary, artistic, political, or scientific value. The statute proscribes the visual depiction of an idea—that of teenagers engaging in sexual activity—that is a fact of modern society and has been a theme in art and literature throughout the ages. Under the CPPA, images are prohibited so long as the persons appear to be under 18 years of age. This is higher than the legal age for marriage in many States, as well as the age at which persons may consent to sexual relations.

Both themes—teenage sexual activity and the sexual abuse of children—have inspired countless literary works. William Shakespeare created the most famous pair of teenage lovers, one of whom is just 13 years of age. See *Romeo and Juliet*, act I, sc. 2, l. 9 ("She hath not seen the change of fourteen years"). In the drama, Shakespeare portrays the relationship as something splendid and innocent, but not juvenile. The work has inspired no less than 40 motion pictures, some of which suggest that the teenagers consummated their relationship. Shakespeare may not have written sexually explicit scenes for the Elizabethan audience, but were modern directors to adopt a less conventional approach, that fact alone would not compel the conclusion that the work was obscene. . . .

In contrast to the speech in *Ferber*, speech that itself is the record of sexual abuse, the CPPA prohibits speech that records no crime and creates no victims by its production. Virtual child pornography is not "intrinsically related" to the sexual abuse of children, as were the materials in *Ferber*. While the Government asserts that the images can lead to actual instances of child abuse, the causal link is contingent and indirect. The harm does not necessarily follow from the speech, but depends upon some unquantified potential for subsequent criminal acts.

The Government says these indirect harms are sufficient because, as *Ferber* acknowledged, child pornography rarely can be valuable speech. This argument, however, suffers from two flaws. First, *Ferber's* judgment about child pornography was based upon how it was made, not on what it communicated. The case reaffirmed that where the speech is neither obscene nor the product of sexual abuse, it does not fall outside the protection of the First Amendment.

The second flaw in the Government's position is that *Ferber* did not hold that child pornography is by definition without value. On the contrary, the Court recognized some works in this category might have significant value, but relied on virtual images—the very images prohibited by the CPPA—as an alternative and permissible means of expression: "[I]f it were necessary for literary or artistic value, a person over the statutory age who perhaps looked younger could be utilized. Simulation outside of the prohibition of the statute could provide another alternative." *Ferber*, then, not only referred to the distinction between actual and virtual child pornography, it relied on it as a reason supporting its holding. *Ferber* provides no support for a statute that eliminates the distinction and makes the alternative mode criminal as well.

The CPPA, for reasons we have explored, is inconsistent with *Miller* and finds no support in *Ferber*. The Government seeks to justify its prohibitions in other ways. It argues that the CPPA is necessary because pedophiles may use virtual child pornography to seduce children. There are many things innocent in themselves, however, such as cartoons, video games, and candy, that might be used for immoral purposes, yet we would not expect those to be prohibited because they can be misused. The Government, of course, may punish adults who provide unsuitable materials to children, see *Ginsberg v. New York*, 390 U.S. 629 (1968), and it may enforce criminal penalties for unlawful solicitation. The precedents establish, however, that speech within the rights of adults to hear may not be silenced completely in an attempt to shield children from it. *Butler v. Michigan*, 352 U.S. 380 (1957).

Here, the Government wants to keep speech from children not to protect them from its content but to protect them from those who would commit other crimes. The principle, however, remains the same: The Government cannot ban speech fit for adults simply because it may fall into the hands of children. The evil in question depends upon the actor's unlawful conduct, conduct defined as criminal quite apart from any link to the speech in question. This establishes that the speech ban is not narrowly drawn. The objective is to prohibit illegal conduct, but this restriction goes well beyond that interest by restricting the speech available to law-abiding adults. . . .

In sum, Sec. 2256(8)(B) covers materials beyond the categories recognized in *Ferber* and *Miller*, and the reasons the Government offers in support of limiting the freedom of speech have no justification in our precedents or in the law of the First Amendment. The provision abridges the freedom to engage in a substantial amount of lawful speech. For this reason, it is overbroad and unconstitutional.

Respondents challenge Sec. 2256(8)(D) as well. This provision bans depictions of sexually explicit conduct that are "advertised, promoted, presented, described, or distributed in such a manner that conveys the impression that the material is or contains a visual depiction of a minor engaging in sexually explicit conduct." The parties treat the section as nearly identical to the provision prohibiting materials that appear to be child pornography. In the Government's view, the difference between the two is that "the 'conveys the impression' provision requires the jury to assess the material at issue in light of the manner in which it is promoted."

We disagree with this view. The CPPA prohibits sexually explicit materials that "conve[y] the impression" they depict minors. While that phrase may sound like the "appears to be" prohibition in Sec. 2256(8)(B), it requires little judgment about the content of the image. Under Sec. 2256(8)(D), the work must be sexually explicit, but otherwise the content is irrelevant. Even if a film contains no sexually explicit scenes involving minors, it could be treated as child pornography if the title and trailers convey the impression that the scenes would be found in the movie. The determination turns on how the speech is presented, not on what is depicted. While the legislative findings address at length the problems posed by materials that look like child pornography, they are silent on the evils posed by images simply pandered that way.

The Government does not offer a serious defense of this provision, and the other arguments it makes in support of the CPPA do not bear on Sec. 2256(8)(D). . . .

The CPPA does more than prohibit pandering. It prohibits possession of material described, or pandered, as child pornography by someone earlier in the distribution chain. The provision prohibits a sexually explicit film containing no youthful actors, just because it is placed in a box suggesting a prohibited movie. Possession is a crime even when the possessor knows the movie was mislabeled. The First Amendment requires a more precise restriction. For this reason, Sec. 2256(8)(D) is substantially overbroad and in violation of the First Amendment.

For the reasons we have set forth, the prohibitions of Sections 2256(8)(B) and 2256(8)(D) are overbroad and unconstitutional. . . .

☐ *CHIEF JUSTICE REHNQUIST, with whom Justice SCALIA joins in part, dissenting.*

Congress has a compelling interest in ensuring the ability to enforce prohibitions of actual child pornography, and we should defer to its findings that rapidly advancing technology soon will make it all but impossible to do so.

I also agree with Justice O'CONNOR that serious First Amendment concerns would arise were the Government ever to prosecute someone for simple distribution or possession of a film with literary or artistic value, such as "Traffic" or "American Beauty." I write separately, however, because the Child Pornography Prevention Act of 1996 (CPPA) need not be construed to reach such materials. . . .

Other than computer generated images that are virtually indistinguishable from real children engaged in sexually explicit conduct, the CPPA can be limited so as not to reach any material that was not already unprotected before the CPPA. The CPPA's definition of "sexually explicit conduct" is quite explicit in this regard. It makes clear that the statute only reaches "visual depictions." . . . I think the definition reaches only the sort of "hard core of child pornography" that we found without protection in *Ferber*. So construed, the CPPA bans visual depictions of youthful looking adult actors engaged in actual sexual activity; mere suggestions of sexual activity, such as youthful looking adult actors squirming under a blanket, are more akin to written descriptions than visual depictions, and thus fall outside the purview of the statute. . . .

To the extent the CPPA prohibits possession or distribution of materials that "convey the impression" of a child engaged in sexually explicit conduct, that prohibition can and should be limited to reach "the sordid business of pandering" which lies outside the bounds of First Amendment protection. *Ginsburg v. United States*, 383 U.S. 463 (1966). . . .

For these reasons, I would construe the CPPA in a manner consistent with the First Amendment, reverse the Court of Appeals' judgment, and uphold the statute in its entirety.

☐ *Justice O'CONNOR, with whom THE CHIEF JUSTICE and Justice SCALIA join, concurring in the judgment and dissenting in part.*

Because the Government may already prohibit obscenity without violating the First Amendment, see *Miller v. California* (1973), what the Government asks this Court to rule is that it may also prohibit youthful-adult and virtual-adult pornography that is merely indecent without violating that Amendment. Although such pornography looks like the material at issue in *New York v. Ferber*, no children are harmed in the process of creating such pornography. Therefore, *Ferber* does not support the Government's ban on youthful-adult and virtual-child pornography. . . .

I also agree with the Court's decision to strike down the CPPA's ban on material presented in a manner that "conveys the impression" that it contains pornographic depictions of actual children ("actual-child pornography"). The Government fails to explain how this ban serves any compelling state interest. . . .

Finally, I agree with the Court that the CPPA's ban on youthful-adult pornography is overbroad. . . .

I disagree with the Court, however, that the CPPA's prohibition of virtual-child pornography is overbroad. . . . Although Section 2256(8)(B) does not distinguish between youthful-adult and virtual-child pornography, the CPPA elsewhere draws a line between these two classes of speech. The statute provides an affirmative defense for those who produce, distribute, or receive pornographic images of individuals who are actually adults, Sec. 2252A(c), but not for those with pornographic images that are wholly computer generated. This is not surprising given that the legislative findings enacted by Congress contain no mention of youthful-adult pornography. Those findings focus explicitly only on actual-child pornography and virtual-child pornography. Drawing a line around, and striking just, the CPPA's ban on youthful-child pornography not only is consistent with Congress' understanding of the categories of speech encompassed by Section 2256(8)(B), but also preserves the CPPA's prohibition of the material that Congress found most dangerous to children.

In sum, I would strike down the CPPA's ban on material that "conveys the impression" that it contains actual-child pornography, but uphold the ban on pornographic depictions that "appea[r] to be" of minors so long as it is not applied to youthful-adult pornography.

D | *Commercial Speech*

In *Thompson v. Western States Medical Center* (2002) (excerpted below), the Court struck down a section of a federal statute that forbade advertising for "compound drugs," thereby continuing its trend toward extending greater and greater First Amendment protection for commercial speech. However, the justices split five to four, with the chief justice and Justices

Breyer, Stevens, and Ginsburg dissenting from Justice O'Connor's opinion for the Court.

Thompson v. Western States Medical Center
535 U.S. 357, 122 S.CT. 1497 (2002)

The pertinent facts are discussed by Justice O'Connor in her opinion for the Court. Justice Thomas filed a brief concurring opinion. Justice Breyer filed a dissent, which Chief Justice Rehnquist and Justices Stevens and Ginsburg joined.

☐ *Justice O'CONNOR delivered the opinion of the Court.*

Section 503A of the Food and Drug Administration Modernization Act of 1997 (FDAMA) exempts "compounded drugs" from the Food and Drug Administration's standard drug approval requirements as long as the providers of those drugs abide by several restrictions, including that they refrain from advertising or promoting particular compounded drugs. Respondents, a group of licensed pharmacies that specialize in compounding drugs, sought to enjoin enforcement of the subsections of the Act dealing with advertising and solicitation, arguing that those provisions violate the First Amendment's free speech guarantee. The District Court agreed with respondents and granted their motion for summary judgment, holding that the provisions do not meet the test for acceptable government regulation of commercial speech set forth in *Central Hudson Gas & Elec. Corp. v. Public Serv. Comm'n of N.Y.*, 447 U.S. 557 (1980)....The Court of Appeals for the Ninth Circuit affirmed....We conclude, as did the courts below, that Section 503A's provisions regarding advertisement and promotion amount to unconstitutional restrictions on commercial speech, and we therefore affirm....

The Federal Food, Drug, and Cosmetic Act of 1938 (FDCA) regulates drug manufacturing, marketing, and distribution. For approximately the first 50 years after the enactment of the FDCA, the FDA generally left regulation of compounding to the States. Pharmacists continued to provide patients with compounded drugs without applying for FDA approval of those drugs. The FDA eventually became concerned, however, that some pharmacists were manufacturing and selling drugs under the guise of compounding, thereby avoiding the FDCA's new drug requirements. In 1992, in response to this concern, the FDA issued a Compliance Policy Guide, which announced that ... it was FDA policy to permit pharmacists to compound drugs after receipt of a valid prescription for an individual patient or to compound drugs in "very limited quantities" before receipt of a valid prescription if they could document a history of receiving valid prescriptions "generated solely within an established professional practitioner–patient–pharmacy relationship" and if they maintained the prescription on file as required by state law. Compounding in such circumstances was permitted as long as the pharmacy's activities did not raise "the kinds of concerns normally associated with a manufacturer."

The Guide listed nine examples of activities that the FDA believed raised such concerns and that would therefore be considered by the agency in determining whether to bring an enforcement action. These activities included: "[s]oliciting business (e.g., promoting, advertising, or using salespersons) to compound specific drug products, product classes, or therapeutic classes of drug products"; "[c]ompounding, regularly, or in inordinate amounts, drug products that are commercially available . . . and that are essentially generic copies of commercially available, FDA–approved drug products"; using commercial scale manufacturing or testing equipment to compound drugs; offering compounded drugs at wholesale; and "[d]istributing inordinate amounts of compounded products out of state."

Congress turned portions of this policy into law when it enacted the FDAMA in 1997. The FDAMA, which amends the FDCA, exempts compounded drugs from the FDCA's "new drug" requirements and other requirements provided the drugs satisfy a number of restrictions. . . . [M]ost relevant for this litigation, the prescription must be "unsolicited," and the pharmacy, licensed pharmacist, or licensed physician compounding the drug may "not advertise or promote the compounding of any particular drug, class of drug, or type of drug." The pharmacy, licensed pharmacist, or licensed physician may, however, "advertise and promote the compounding service." . . .

Although commercial speech is protected by the First Amendment, not all regulation of such speech is unconstitutional. In *Central Hudson*, we articulated a test for determining whether a particular commercial speech regulation is constitutionally permissible. Under that test we ask as a threshold matter whether the commercial speech concerns unlawful activity or is misleading. If so, then the speech is not protected by the First Amendment. If the speech concerns lawful activity and is not misleading, however, we next ask "whether the asserted governmental interest is substantial." If it is, then we "determine whether the regulation directly advances the governmental interest asserted," and, finally, "whether it is not more extensive than is necessary to serve that interest." Each of these latter three inquiries must be answered in the affirmative for the regulation to be found constitutional. . . .

The Government does not attempt to defend the FDAMA's speech-related provisions under the first prong of the *Central Hudson* test; i.e., it does not argue that the prohibited advertisements would be about unlawful activity or would be misleading. Instead, the Government argues that the FDAMA satisfies the remaining three prongs of the *Central Hudson* test.

The Government asserts that three substantial interests underlie the FDAMA. The first is an interest in "preserv[ing] the effectiveness and integrity of the FDCA's new drug approval process and the protection of the public health that it provides." The second is an interest in "preserv[ing] the availability of compounded drugs for those individual patients who, for particularized medical reasons, cannot use commercially available products that have been approved by the FDA." Finally, the Government argues that "[a]chieving the proper balance between those two independently compelling but competing interests is itself a substantial governmental interest." . . .

The Government seems to believe that without advertising it would not be possible to market a drug on a large enough scale to make safety and efficacy testing economically feasible. The Government thus believes that conditioning an exemption from the FDA approval process on refraining from advertising is an ideal way to permit compounding and yet also guarantee that compounding is not conducted on such a scale as to undermine the

FDA approval process. Assuming it is true that drugs cannot be marketed on a large scale without advertising, the FDAMA's prohibition on advertising compounded drugs might indeed "directly advanc[e]" the Government's interests. Even assuming that it does, however, the Government has failed to demonstrate that the speech restrictions are "not more extensive than is necessary to serve [those] interest[s]." In previous cases addressing this final prong of the *Central Hudson* test, we have made clear that if the Government could achieve its interests in a manner that does not restrict speech, or that restricts less speech, the Government must do so.

Several non-speech-related means of drawing a line between compounding and large-scale manufacturing might be possible here. First, it seems that the Government could use the very factors the FDA relied on to distinguish compounding from manufacturing in its 1992 Compliance Policy Guide. For example, the Government could ban the use of "commercial scale manufacturing or testing equipment for compounding drug products." It could prohibit pharmacists from compounding more drugs in anticipation of receiving prescriptions than in response to prescriptions already received. It could prohibit pharmacists from "[o]ffering compounded drugs at wholesale to other state licensed persons or commercial entities for resale." Alternately, it could limit the amount of compounded drugs, either by volume or by numbers of prescriptions, that a given pharmacist or pharmacy sells out of State. . . .

The Government has not offered any reason why these possibilities, alone or in combination, would be insufficient to prevent compounding from occurring on such a scale as to undermine the new drug approval process. Indeed, there is no hint that the Government even considered these or any other alternatives. . . .

If the Government's failure to justify its decision to regulate speech were not enough to convince us that the FDAMA's advertising provisions were unconstitutional, the amount of beneficial speech prohibited by the FDAMA would be. Forbidding the advertisement of compounded drugs would affect pharmacists other than those interested in producing drugs on a large scale. It would prevent pharmacists with no interest in mass-producing medications, but who serve clienteles with special medical needs, from telling the doctors treating those clients about the alternative drugs available through compounding. For example, a pharmacist serving a children's hospital where many patients are unable to swallow pills would be prevented from telling the children's doctors about a new development in compounding that allowed a drug that was previously available only in pill form to be administered another way. Forbidding advertising of particular compounded drugs would also prohibit a pharmacist from posting a notice informing customers that if their children refuse to take medications because of the taste, the pharmacist could change the flavor, and giving examples of medications where flavoring is possible. The fact that the FDAMA would prohibit such seemingly useful speech even though doing so does not appear to directly further any asserted governmental objective confirms our belief that the prohibition is unconstitutional.

☐ *Justice BREYER, with whom THE CHIEF JUSTICE, Justice STEVENS, and Justice GINSBURG join, dissenting.*

In my view, the advertising restriction "directly advances" the statute's important safety objective. That objective, as the Court concedes, is to confine the sale of untested, compounded, drugs to where they are medically needed. But to do so the statute must exclude from the area of permitted drug sales both (1) those drugs that traditional drug manufacturers might supply after testing—typically drugs capable of being produced in large amounts, and (2) those compounded drugs sought by patients who may not clearly need them—including compounded drugs produced in small amounts.

The majority's discussion focuses upon the first exclusionary need, but it virtually ignores the second. It describes the statute's objective simply as drawing a "line" that will "distinguish compounded drugs produced on such a small scale that they could not undergo safety and efficacy testing from drugs produced and sold on a large enough scale that they could undergo such testing and therefore must do so." This description overlooks the need for a second line—a line that will distinguish (1) sales of compounded drugs to those who clearly need them from (2) sales of compounded drugs to those for whom a specially tailored but untested drug is a convenience but not a medical necessity. That is to say, the statute, in seeking to confine distribution of untested tailored drugs, must look both at the amount supplied (to help decide whether ordinary manufacturers might provide a tested alternative) and at the nature of demand (to help separate genuine need from simple convenience).

This second intermediate objective is logically related to Congress' primary end—the minimizing of safety risks. The statute's basic exemption from testing requirements inherently creates risks simply by placing untested drugs in the hands of the consumer. Where an individual has a specific medical need for a specially tailored drug those risks are likely offset. But where an untested drug is a convenience, not a necessity, that offset is unlikely to be present. . . .

I do not deny that the statute restricts the circulation of some truthful information. It prevents a pharmacist from including in an advertisement the information that "this pharmacy will compound Drug X." Nonetheless, this Court has not previously held that commercial advertising restrictions automatically violate the First Amendment. Rather, the Court has applied a more flexible test. It has examined the restriction's proportionality, the relation between restriction and objective, the fit between ends and means. In doing so, the Court has asked whether the regulation of commercial speech "directly advances" a "substantial" governmental objective and whether it is "more extensive than is necessary" to achieve those ends. It has done so because it has concluded that, from a constitutional perspective, commercial speech does not warrant application of the Court's strictest speech-protective tests. And it has reached this conclusion in part because restrictions on commercial speech do not often repress individual self-expression; they rarely interfere with the functioning of democratic political processes; and they often reflect a democratically determined governmental decision to regulate a commercial venture in order to protect, for example, the consumer, the public health, individual safety, or the environment. . . .

The Court, in my view, gives insufficient weight to the Government's regulatory rationale, and too readily assumes the existence of practical alternatives. It thereby applies the commercial speech doctrine too strictly. . . . For these reasons, I dissent.

F | *Regulating the Broadcast and Cable Media, and the Internet*

For a second time the Court affirmed a lower court order enjoining the enforcement of the Child Online Protection Act (COPA) of 1998. In *Ashcroft v. American Civil Liberties Union* (2004) (excerpted below), a bare majority concluded that the COPA's criminal penalties were not the least restrictive means of preventing harm to minors and limiting their access to obscene materials on the Internet.

However, in *United States v. American Library Association* (excerpted below), a plurality of the Court upheld the Children's Internet Protection Act of 2001, which requires public libraries that receive federal funding to install pornography filters on all computers providing Internet access. Writing for the Court, Chief Justice Rehnquist held that the limitations on access to the Internet were no greater for library patrons than those on access to books that for whatever reason librarians chose not to acquire. The law also authorizes, but does not require, librarians to unblock Internet sites at the request of adult users. Two justices—Justices Kennedy and Breyer—in concurring opinions indicated that the law might still not survive First Amendment challenges if it proved unduly burdensome on adult library patrons' access to the Internet. Justices Stevens, Souter, and Ginsburg dissented.

Ashcroft v. American Civil Liberties Union
124 S.CT. 2783 (2004)

Following the Supreme Court's invalidation of the Communications Decency Act (CDA) of 1996 in *Reno v. American Civil Liberties Union*, 521 U.S. 844 (1997) (excerpted in Vol. 2, Ch. 5), in 1998 Congress enacted the Child Online Protection Act (COPA), prohibiting any person from "knowingly and with knowledge of the character of the material, in interstate or foreign commerce by means of the World Wide Web, making any communication for commercial purposes that is available to any minor and that includes any material that is harmful to minors." Compared with the CDA, Congress limited COPA's scope in three ways. First, while the CDA applied to communications over the Internet as a whole, including e-mail messages, COPA applies only to material displayed on the web. Second, unlike the CDA, COPA covers only communications made "for commercial purposes." And third, whereas the

CDA prohibited "indecent" and "patently offensive" communications, the COPA restricts only the narrower category of "material that is harmful to minors."

Drawing on the three-part test for obscenity set forth in *Miller v. California*, 413 U.S. 15 (1973) (excerpted in Vol. 2, Ch. 5), COPA defines "material that is harmful to minors" as "any communication, picture, image, graphic image file, article, recording, writing, or other matter of any kind that is obscene or that (A) the average person, applying contemporary community standards, would find, taking the material as a whole and with respect to minors, is designed to appeal to, or is designed to pander to, the prurient interest; (B) depicts, describes, or represents, in a manner patently offensive with respect to minors, an actual or simulated sexual act or sexual contact, an actual or simulated normal or perverted sexual act, or a lewd exhibition of the genitals or postpubescent female breast; and (C) taken as a whole, lacks serious literary, artistic, political, or scientific value for minors." A civil penalty of up to $50,000 may be imposed for each violation of the statute, and criminal penalties of up to six months in prison.

One month before COPA was scheduled to go into effect, the American Civil Liberties Union (ACLU) challenged the constitutionality of the act. A federal district court granted a motion for a preliminary injunction, barring the enforcement of the act. Subsequently, the district court concluded that the ACLU was likely to establish at trial that COPA could not withstand strict scrutiny because, among other reasons, it had not been shown to be the least restrictive means of preventing minors from accessing harmful materials. Attorney General John Ashcroft appealed that decision and the Court of Appeals for the Third Circuit affirmed the lower court. On appeal, in *Ashcroft v. American Civil Liberties Union*, 535 U.S. 564 (2002) (*Ashcroft I*), the Court held that the law's use of "community standards" to define what material in cyberspace is "harmful to minors" did not necessarily violate the First Amendment. However, the Court also allowed the law to remain enjoined from going into effect until questions about its impact on free speech were resolved. On the remand, the appellate court again affirmed the lower court and found that the COPA was not narrowly tailored and was not the least restrictive means of preventing minors from using the Internet to obtain access to harmful materials. Ashcroft appealed that decision and the Supreme Court granted review.

The appellate court's decision was affirmed by a five-to-four vote. Justice Kennedy delivered the opinion for the Court, holding that the appellate court correctly affirmed the order enjoining enforcement of the statute. Justice Stevens filed a concurring opinion. Justices Scalia and Breyer filed dissenting opinions; the latter's dissent was joined by Chief Justice Rehnquist and Justice O'Connor.

☐ *Justice KENNEDY delivered the opinion of the Court.*

Content-based prohibitions, enforced by severe criminal penalties, have the constant potential to be a repressive force in the lives and thoughts of a free people. To guard against that threat the Constitution demands that content-based restrictions on speech be presumed invalid, *R. A. V. v. St. Paul*, 505 U.S. 377 (1992), and that the Government bear the burden of showing their constitutionality. *United States v. Playboy Entertainment Group, Inc.*, 529 U.S. 803 (2000). This is true even when Congress twice has attempted to find a constitutional means to restrict, and punish, the speech in question. . . .

The Government has failed, at this point, to rebut the plaintiffs' contention that there are plausible, less restrictive alternatives to the statute. Substantial practical considerations, furthermore, argue in favor of upholding the injunction and allowing the case to proceed to trial. For those reasons, we affirm the decision of the Court of Appeals upholding the preliminary injunction, and we remand the case so that it may be returned to the District Court for trial on the issues presented.

[T]he District Court concluded that respondents were likely to prevail. That conclusion was not an abuse of discretion, because on this record there are a number of plausible, less restrictive alternatives to the statute.

The primary alternative considered by the District Court was blocking and filtering software. Blocking and filtering software is an alternative that is less restrictive than COPA, and, in addition, likely more effective as a means of restricting children's access to materials harmful to them. The District Court, in granting the preliminary injunction, did so primarily because the plaintiffs had proposed that filters are a less restrictive alternative to COPA and the Government had not shown it would be likely to disprove the plaintiffs' contention at trial.

Filters are less restrictive than COPA. They impose selective restrictions on speech at the receiving end, not universal restrictions at the source. Under a filtering regime, adults without children may gain access to speech they have a right to see without having to identify themselves or provide their credit card information. Even adults with children may obtain access to the same speech on the same terms simply by turning off the filter on their home computers. Above all, promoting the use of filters does not condemn as criminal any category of speech, and so the potential chilling effect is eliminated, or at least much diminished. All of these things are true, moreover, regardless of how broadly or narrowly the definitions in COPA are construed.

Filters also may well be more effective than COPA. First, a filter can prevent minors from seeing all pornography, not just pornography posted to the Web from America. [F]ilters also may be more effective because they can be applied to all forms of Internet communication, including e-mail, not just communications available via the World Wide Web.

That filtering software may well be more effective than COPA is confirmed by the findings of the Commission on Child Online Protection, a blue-ribbon commission created by Congress in COPA itself. . . .

There are also important practical reasons to let the injunction stand pending a full trial on the merits. First, the potential harms from reversing the injunction outweigh those of leaving it in place by mistake. Where a prosecution is a likely possibility, yet only an affirmative defense is available, speakers may self-censor rather than risk the perils of trial. There is a potential for extraordinary harm and a serious chill upon protected speech.

The harm done from letting the injunction stand pending a trial on the merits, in contrast, will not be extensive. No prosecutions have yet been undertaken under the law, so none will be disrupted if the injunction stands. Further, if the injunction is upheld, the Government in the interim can enforce obscenity laws already on the books.

Second, there are substantial factual disputes remaining in the case. As mentioned above, there is a serious gap in the evidence as to the effectiveness of filtering software. For us to assume, without proof, that filters are less effective than COPA would usurp the District Court's factfinding role. . . .

Third, and on a related point, the factual record does not reflect current technological reality—a serious flaw in any case involving the Internet. The technology of the Internet evolves at a rapid pace. Yet the factfindings of the District Court were entered in February 1999, over five years ago. Since then, certain facts about the Internet are known to have changed. It is reasonable to assume that other technological developments important to the First Amendment analysis have also occurred during that time. More and better filtering alternatives may exist than when the District Court entered its findings. Indeed, we know that after the District Court entered its fact findings, a congressionally appointed commission issued a report that found that filters are more effective than verification screens. . . .

On a final point, it is important to note that this opinion does not hold that Congress is incapable of enacting any regulation of the Internet designed to prevent minors from gaining access to harmful materials. The parties, because of the conclusion of the Court of Appeals that the statute's definitions rendered it unconstitutional, did not devote their attention to the question whether further evidence might be introduced on the relative restrictiveness and effectiveness of alternatives to the statute. On remand, however, the parties will be able to introduce further evidence on this point. This opinion does not foreclose the District Court from concluding, upon a proper showing by the Government that meets the Government's constitutional burden as defined in this opinion, that COPA is the least restrictive alternative available to accomplish Congress' goal.

On this record, the Government has not shown that the less restrictive alternatives proposed by respondents should be disregarded. Those alternatives, indeed, may be more effective than the provisions of COPA. The District Court did not abuse its discretion when it entered the preliminary injunction. The judgment of the Court of Appeals is affirmed, and the case is remanded for proceedings consistent with this opinion.

It is so ordered.

□ *Justice SCALIA, dissenting.*

I agree with Justice BREYER's conclusion that the Child Online Protection Act (COPA) is constitutional. Both the Court and Justice BREYER err, however, in subjecting COPA to strict scrutiny. Nothing in the First Amendment entitles the type of material covered by COPA to that exacting standard of review. "We have recognized that commercial entities which engage in 'the sordid business of pandering' by 'deliberately emphasiz[ing] the sexually provocative aspects of [their nonobscene products], in order to catch the salaciously disposed,' engage in constitutionally unprotected behavior." *United States v. Playboy Entertainment Group, Inc.*, 529 U.S. 803 (2000) (Scalia, J., dissenting) [quoting *Ginzburg v. United States*, 383 U.S. 463 (1966)].

There is no doubt that the commercial pornography covered by COPA fits this description. The statute applies only to a person who, "as a regular course of such person's trade or business, with the objective of earning a profit," and "with knowledge of the character of the material" communicates material that depicts certain specified sexual acts and that "is designed to appeal to, or is designed to pander to, the prurient interest." Since this business could, consistent with the First Amendment, be banned entirely, COPA's lesser restrictions raise no constitutional concern.

□ *Justice BREYER, with whom THE CHIEF JUSTICE and Justice O'CONNOR join, dissenting.*

[M]y examination of (1) the burdens the Act imposes on protected expression, (2) the Act's ability to further a compelling interest, and (3) the proposed "less restrictive alternatives" convinces me that the Court is wrong. I cannot accept its conclusion that Congress could have accomplished its statutory objective—protecting children from commercial pornography on the Internet–in other, less restrictive ways.

The Act's definitions limit the material it regulates to material that does not enjoy First Amendment protection, namely legally obscene material, and very little more. . . .

[T]he statute, read literally, insofar as it extends beyond the legally obscene, could reach only borderline cases. And to take the words of the statute literally is consistent with Congress' avowed objective in enacting this law; namely, putting material produced by professional pornographers behind screens that will verify the age of the viewer. . . .

The Act does not censor the material it covers. Rather, it requires providers of the "harmful to minors" material to restrict minors' access to it by verifying age. They can do so by inserting screens that verify age using a credit card, adult personal identification number, or other similar technology. In this way, the Act requires creation of an Internet screen that minors, but not adults, will find difficult to bypass.

I recognize that the screening requirement imposes some burden on adults who seek access to the regulated material, as well as on its providers. The cost is, in part, monetary. The parties agreed that a Web site could store card numbers or passwords at between 15 and 20 cents per number. . . .

In addition to the monetary cost, and despite strict requirements that identifying information be kept confidential, the identification requirements inherent in age-screening may lead some users to fear embarrassment. Both monetary costs and potential embarrassment can deter potential viewers and, in that sense, the statute's requirements may restrict access to a site. But this Court has held that in the context of congressional efforts to protect children, restrictions of this kind do not automatically violate the Constitution. And the Court has approved their use. See, e.g., *United States v. American Library Assn., Inc.*, 539 U.S. 194 (2003).

In sum, the Act at most imposes a modest additional burden on adult access to legally obscene material, perhaps imposing a similar burden on access to some protected borderline obscene material as well.

I turn next to the question of "compelling interest," that of protecting minors from exposure to commercial pornography. No one denies that such an interest is "compelling." Rather, the question here is whether the Act, given its restrictions on adult access, significantly advances that interest. In other words, is the game worth the candle?

The majority argues that it is not, because of the existence of "blocking and filtering software." The majority refers to the presence of that software as a "less restrictive alternative." But that is a misnomer—a misnomer that may lead the reader to believe that all we need do is look to see if the blocking and filtering software is less restrictive; and to believe that, because in one sense it is (one can turn off the software), that is the end of the constitutional matter.

But such reasoning has no place here. Conceptually speaking, the presence of filtering software is not an alternative legislative approach to the problem of protecting children from exposure to commercial pornography. Rather, it is part of the status quo, i.e., the backdrop against which Congress enacted the present statute. It is always true, by definition, that the status quo is less restrictive than a new regulatory law. It is always less restrictive to do nothing than to do something. But "doing nothing" does not address the problem Congress sought to address—namely that, despite the availability of filtering software, children were still being exposed to harmful material on the Internet. . . .

Filtering software, as presently available, does not solve the "child protection" problem. It suffers from four serious inadequacies that prompted Congress to pass legislation instead of relying on its voluntary use. First, its filtering is faulty, allowing some pornographic material to pass through without hindrance. . . .

Second, filtering software costs money. Not every family has the $40 or so necessary to install it. By way of contrast, age screening costs less.

Third, filtering software depends upon parents willing to decide where their children will surf the Web and able to enforce that decision. As to millions of American families, that is not a reasonable possibility. More than 28 million school age children have both parents or their sole parent in the work force, at least 5 million children are left alone at home without supervision each week, and many of those children will spend afternoons and evenings with friends who may well have access to computers and more lenient parents.

Fourth, software blocking lacks precision, with the result that those who wish to use it to screen out pornography find that it blocks a great deal of material that is valuable. . . .

In sum, a "filtering software status quo" means filtering that underblocks, imposes a cost upon each family that uses it, fails to screen outside the home, and lacks precision. Thus, Congress could reasonably conclude that a system that relies entirely upon the use of such software is not an effective system. And a law that adds to that system an age-verification screen requirement significantly increases the system's efficacy. That is to say, at a modest additional cost to those adults who wish to obtain access to a screened program, that law will bring about better, more precise blocking, both inside and outside the home. . . .

My conclusion is that the Act, as properly interpreted, risks imposition of minor burdens on some protected material—burdens that adults wishing to view the material may overcome at modest cost. At the same time, it significantly helps to achieve a compelling congressional goal, protecting children from exposure to commercial pornography. There is no serious, practically available "less restrictive" way similarly to further this compelling interest. Hence the Act is constitutional. . . . For these reasons, I dissent.

United States v. American Library Association
539 U.S. 126, 123 S.CT. 2297 (2003)

Congress authorized federal funding for public libraries to acquire and to provide access to the Internet through an E-rate program under the Telecommunications Act of 1996 and the Library Services and Technology Act (LSTA). Subsequently, Congress was lobbied to enact the Children's Internet Protection Act (CIPA) of 2001. Under that law, public libraries may not receive federal funding for Internet access unless they install software to block obscene or pornographic images and prevent minors from assessing such materials. The statute authorizes, but does not require, librarians to unblock Internet sites at the request of adult users. It also neither specifies what kinds of filters libraries should install nor provides standards and procedures for unblocking Internet sites at the request of adult users. The American Library Association and a number of other organizations and individuals challenged the constitutionality of the law. A federal district court ruled that the law ran afoul of the First Amendment and blocked its enforcement. The government appealed.

The lower court's decision was reversed by a six-to-three vote. Chief Justice Rehnquist delivered the opinion of the Court, which only Justices O'Connor, Scalia, and Thomas joined. Justices Kennedy and Breyer filed opinions concurring in the judgment. Justices Stevens and Souter filed dissenting opinions, which Justice Ginsburg joined.

☐ *CHIEF JUSTICE REHNQUIST announced the judgment of the Court and delivered an opinion, in which Justice O'CONNOR, Justice SCALIA, and Justice THOMAS joined.*

By connecting to the Internet, public libraries provide patrons with a vast amount of valuable information. But there is also an enormous amount of pornography on the Internet, much of which is easily obtained. The accessibility of this material has created serious problems for libraries, which have found that patrons of all ages, including minors, regularly search for online pornography. Some patrons also expose others to pornographic images by leaving them displayed on Internet terminals or printed at library printers.

Upon discovering these problems, Congress became concerned that the E-rate and LSTA programs were facilitating access to illegal and harmful pornography. Congress learned that adults "us[e] library computers to access pornography that is then exposed to staff, passersby, and children," and that "minors acces[s] child and adult pornography in libraries."

But Congress also learned that filtering software that blocks access to pornographic Web sites could provide a reasonably effective way to prevent such uses of library resources. By 2000, before Congress enacted CIPA, almost 17% of public libraries used such software on at least some of their Internet terminals, and 7% had filters on all of them. A library can set such software to block categories of material, such as "Pornography" or "Violence." When a patron tries to view a site that falls within such a category, a screen appears indicating that the site is blocked. But a filter set to block pornography may sometimes block other sites that present neither obscene nor pornographic material, but that nevertheless trigger the filter. To minimize this problem, a library can set its software to prevent the blocking of material that falls into categories like "Education," "History," and "Medical." A library may also add or delete specific sites from a blocking category, and anyone can ask companies that furnish filtering software to unblock particular sites. Responding to this information, Congress enacted CIPA. . . .

Congress has wide latitude to attach conditions to the receipt of federal assistance in order to further its policy objectives. *South Dakota v. Dole*, 483 U.S. 203 (1987). But Congress may not "induce" the recipient "to engage in activities that would themselves be unconstitutional." To determine whether libraries would violate the First Amendment by employing the filtering software that CIPA requires, we must first examine the role of libraries in our society.

Public libraries pursue the worthy missions of facilitating learning and cultural enrichment. To this end, libraries collect only those materials deemed to have "requisite and appropriate quality."

We have held in two analogous contexts that the government has broad discretion to make content-based judgments in deciding what private speech to make available to the public. In *Arkansas Ed. Television Comm'n v. Forbes*, 523 U.S. 666 (1998), we held that public forum principles do not generally apply to a public television station's editorial judgments regarding the private speech it presents to its viewers. Recognizing a broad right of public access "would [also] risk implicating the courts in judgments that should be left to the exercise of journalistic discretion."

Similarly, in *National Endowment for Arts v. Finley*, 524 U.S. 569 (1998), we upheld an art funding program that required the National Endowment for the Arts (NEA) to use content-based criteria in making funding decisions. We explained that "[a]ny content-based considerations that may be taken into account in the grant-making process are a consequence of the nature of arts funding."

The principles underlying *Forbes* and *Finley* also apply to a public library's exercise of judgment in selecting the material it provides to its patrons. Just as forum analysis and heightened judicial scrutiny are incompatible with the role of public television stations and the role of the NEA, they are also incompatible with the discretion that public libraries must have to fulfill their traditional missions. Public library staffs necessarily consider content in making collection decisions and enjoy broad discretion in making them.

The public forum principles on which the District Court relied are out of place in the context of this case. Internet access in public libraries is neither a "traditional" nor a "designated" public forum. First, this resource—which did not exist until quite recently—has not "immemorially been held in trust for the use of the public and, time out of mind, . . . been used for purposes of assembly, communication of thoughts between citizens, and discussing public questions."

Nor does Internet access in a public library satisfy our definition of a "designated public forum." To create such a forum, the government must make an affirmative choice to open up its property for use as a public forum.

The situation here is very different. A public library does not acquire Internet terminals in order to create a public forum for Web publishers to express themselves, any more than it collects books in order to provide a public forum for the authors of books to speak. It provides Internet access, not to "encourage a diversity of views from private speakers," but for the same reasons it offers other library resources: to facilitate research, learning, and recreational pursuits by furnishing materials of requisite and appropriate quality. . . .

Moreover, because of the vast quantity of material on the Internet and the rapid pace at which it changes, libraries cannot possibly segregate, item by item, all the Internet material that is appropriate for inclusion from all that is not. While a library could limit its Internet collection to just those sites it found worthwhile, it could do so only at the cost of excluding an enormous amount of valuable information that it lacks the capacity to review. Given that tradeoff, it is entirely reasonable for public libraries to reject that approach and instead exclude certain categories of content, without making individualized judgments that everything they do make available has requisite and appropriate quality. . . .

Because public libraries' use of Internet filtering software does not violate their patrons' First Amendment rights, CIPA does not induce libraries to violate the Constitution, and is a valid exercise of Congress' spending power. Nor does CIPA impose an unconstitutional condition on public libraries.

☐ *Justice KENNEDY, concurring in the judgment.*

If on the request of an adult user, a librarian will unblock filtered material or disable the Internet software filter without significant delay, there is little to this case. The Government represents this is indeed the fact. . . .

If some libraries do not have the capacity to unblock specific Web sites or to disable the filter or if it is shown that an adult user's election to view constitutionally protected Internet material is burdened in some other substantial way, that would be the subject for an as-applied challenge, not the facial challenge made in this case.

There are, of course, substantial Government interests at stake here. The interest in protecting young library users from material inappropriate for minors is legitimate, and even compelling, as all Members of the Court appear to agree. Given this interest, and the failure to show that the ability of adult library users to have access to the material is burdened in any significant degree, the statute is not unconstitutional on its face. For these reasons, I concur in the judgment of the Court.

☐ *Justice STEVENS, dissenting.*

The unchallenged findings of fact made by the District Court reveal fundamental defects in the filtering software that is now available or that will be available in the foreseeable future. Because the software relies on key words or phrases to block undesirable sites, it does not have the capacity to exclude a precisely defined category of images. Given the quantity and ever-changing character of Web sites offering free sexually explicit material, it is inevitable that a substantial amount of such material will never be blocked. Because of this "underblocking," the statute will provide parents with a false sense of security without really solving the problem that motivated its enactment. Conversely, the software's reliance on words to identify undesirable sites necessarily results in the blocking of thousands of pages that "contain content that is completely innocuous for both adults and minors, and that no rational person could conclude matches the filtering companies' category definitions, such as 'pornography' or 'sex.'" In my judgment, a statutory blunderbuss that mandates this vast amount of "overblocking" abridges the freedom of speech protected by the First Amendment. . . .

The plurality incorrectly argues that the statute does not impose "an unconstitutional condition on public libraries." On the contrary, it impermissibly conditions the receipt of Government funding on the restriction of significant First Amendment rights. . . .

☐ *Justice SOUTER, with whom Justice GINSBURG joins, dissenting.*

Like the other Members of the Court, I have no doubt about the legitimacy of governmental efforts to put a barrier between child patrons of public libraries and the raw offerings on the Internet otherwise available to them there, and if the only First Amendment interests raised here were those of children, I would uphold application of the Act. We have said that the governmental interest in "shielding" children from exposure to indecent material is "compelling," *Reno v. American Civil Liberties Union*, 521 U.S. 844 (1997), and I do not think that the awkwardness a child might feel on asking for an unblocked terminal is any such burden as to affect constitutionality. . . .

The question for me, then, is whether a local library could itself constitutionally impose these restrictions on the content otherwise available to an adult patron through an Internet connection, at a library terminal provided for public use. The answer is no. A library that chose to block an adult's Internet access to material harmful to children (and whatever else the undiscriminating filter might interrupt) would be imposing a content-based restriction on communication of material in the library's control that an adult could otherwise lawfully see. This would simply be censorship. True, the censorship would not necessarily extend to every adult, for an intending Internet user might convince a librarian that he was a true researcher or had a "lawful purpose" to obtain everything the library's terminal could provide. But as to those who did not qualify for discretionary unblocking, the censorship would be complete and, like all censorship by an agency of the Government, presumptively invalid owing to strict scrutiny in implementing the Free Speech Clause of the First Amendment. . . .

H | *Symbolic Speech and Speech-Plus-Conduct*

In its 2001–2002 term the Court upheld Chicago's ordinance requiring permits for public assemblies in *Thomas v. Chicago Park District*, 534 U.S. 316 (2002). The ordinance requires obtaining a permit to "conduct a public assembly, parade, picnic, or other event involving more than fifty individuals," or to engage in any activity "creat[ing] or emit[ting] any

Amplified Sound." The Court of Appeals for the Seventh Circuit rejected the petitioner's argument that the ordinance was unconstitutionally vague and a prior restraint on free speech. The Supreme Court affirmed that the ordinance was a content-neutral time, place, and manner regulation of the use of public forums and was "subject to effective judicial review."

Virginia v. Black

538 U.S. 343, 123 S.Ct. 1536 (2003)

In 1998, Barry Elton Black led a Ku Klux Klan rally at which a 25-foot cross was burned on private property with the owner's permission, but which was clearly visible to nearby homeowners and motorists on a state road. He was convicted, under Virginia's 50-year-old law making cross burning a crime, and fined $2,500. Also in 1998, Richard J. Elliott and Jonathan O'Mara burned a cross on the yard of James Jubilee, an African American, because they were angry with him. Both were convicted and sentenced to 90 days in jail and fined $2,500. On appeal in 2001, the Virginia Supreme Court overturned their convictions and struck down the state's law in holding that it ran afoul of the First Amendment's guarantee for freedom of expression. The state appealed and the Supreme Court granted *certiorari*.

Justice O'Connor's opinion for the Court commanded only a plurality, but by a vote of six to three the Court held that a properly drafted law punishing cross burning would survive a First Amendment challenge. Justice O'Connor's opinion, joined by Chief Justice Rehnquist and Justices Stevens and Breyer, held that states may make it a crime to burn a cross because it is "a particularly virulent form of intimidation." Justice Scalia, in a separate opinion in part concurring and dissenting, and Justice Thomas, in a dissenting opinion, agreed. However, Justice O'Connor also ruled that Virginia's law was unconstitutional because a section of the law dealing with jury instructions permitting an inference of intent to intimidate invited juries to ignore "all of the contextual factors that are necessary to decide whether a particular cross burning [was] intended to intimidate" instead of to express a political message. Justice Scalia disagreed with that part of her analysis and holding in contending that under the statute a jury could be properly instructed and the inference of intimidation rebutted. In his dissent, Justice Thomas contended that the plurality went too far and that cross burning could never receive First Amendment protection because its sole message was one of terror and lawlessness. Justice Souter, joined by Justices Kennedy and

Ginsburg, filed another separate opinion in part concurring and dissenting. These three justices agreed that Virginia's law was unconstitutional, but maintained that the First Amendment forbids all content-based regulations of speech. Cross burning, in their view, was inherently symbolic and might convey not only a message of terror but also of political ideology. Accordingly, they would have held that any law punishing cross burning could not survive First Amendment scrutiny.

☐ *Justice O'CONNOR announced the judgment of the Court and delivered the opinion of the Court with respect to Parts I, II, and III, and an opinion with respect to Parts IV and V, in which THE CHIEF JUSTICE, Justice STEVENS, and Justice BREYER join.*

In this case we consider whether the Commonwealth of Virginia's statute banning cross burning with "an intent to intimidate a person or group of persons" violates the First Amendment. We conclude that while a State, consistent with the First Amendment, may ban cross burning carried out with the intent to intimidate, the provision in the Virginia statute treating any cross burning as prima facie evidence of intent to intimidate renders the statute unconstitutional in its current form. . . .

■ **II**

Cross burning originated in the 14th century as a means for Scottish tribes to signal each other. . . . Cross burning in this country, however, long ago became unmoored from its Scottish ancestry. Burning a cross in the United States is inextricably intertwined with the history of the Ku Klux Klan.

The first Ku Klux Klan began in Pulaski, Tennessee, in the spring of 1866. Although the Ku Klux Klan started as a social club, it soon changed into something far different. The Klan fought Reconstruction and the corresponding drive to allow freed blacks to participate in the political process. Soon the Klan imposed "a veritable reign of terror" throughout the South. The Klan employed tactics such as whipping, threatening to burn people at the stake, and murder. The Klan's victims included blacks, southern whites who disagreed with the Klan and "carpetbagger" northern whites.

The activities of the Ku Klux Klan prompted legislative action at the national level. . . . Congress passed what is now known as the Ku Klux Klan Act. President Grant used these new powers to suppress the Klan in South Carolina, the effect of which severely curtailed the Klan in other States as well. By the end of Reconstruction in 1877, the first Klan no longer existed.

The genesis of the second Klan began in 1905, with the publication of Thomas Dixon's *The Clansmen: An Historical Romance of the Ku Klux Klan.* Dixon's book was a sympathetic portrait of the first Klan, depicting the Klan as a group of heroes "saving" the South from blacks and the "horrors" of Reconstruction. Although the first Klan never actually practiced cross burning, Dixon's book depicted the Klan burning crosses to celebrate the execution of former slaves. Cross burning thereby became associated with the first Ku Klux Klan. When D. W. Griffith turned Dixon's book into the movie *The Birth of a Nation* in 1915, the association between cross burning and the Klan became indelible. In addition to the cross burnings in the movie, a poster advertising the film displayed a hooded Klansman riding a hooded horse, with his left hand holding the reins of the horse and his right hand holding a burning cross above his head. Soon thereafter, in November 1915, the second Klan began.

From the inception of the second Klan, cross burnings have been used to communicate both threats of violence and messages of shared ideology. The first initiation ceremony occurred on Stone Mountain near Atlanta, Georgia. While a 40-foot cross burned on the mountain, the Klan members took their oaths of loyalty. This cross burning was the second recorded instance in the United States. The first known cross burning in the country had occurred a little over one month before the Klan initiation, when a Georgia mob celebrated the lynching of Leo Frank by burning a "gigantic cross" on Stone Mountain that was "visible throughout" Atlanta. . . .

The Klan continued to use cross burnings to intimidate after World War II. . . . The decision of this Court in *Brown v. Board of Education*, 347 U.S. 483 (1954), along with the civil rights movement of the 1950s and 1960s, sparked another outbreak of Klan violence. These acts of violence included bombings, beatings, shootings, stabbings, and mutilations. Members of the Klan burned crosses on the lawns of those associated with the civil rights movement, assaulted the Freedom Riders, bombed churches, and murdered blacks as well as whites whom the Klan viewed as sympathetic toward the civil rights movement.

Throughout the history of the Klan, cross burnings have also remained potent symbols of shared group identity and ideology. The burning cross became a symbol of the Klan itself and a central feature of Klan gatherings. . . .

To this day, regardless of whether the message is a political one or whether the message is also meant to intimidate, the burning of a cross is a "symbol of hate." And while cross burning sometimes carries no intimidating message, at other times the intimidating message is the only message conveyed. For example, when a cross burning is directed at a particular person not affiliated with the Klan, the burning cross often serves as a message of intimidation, designed to inspire in the victim a fear of bodily harm. Moreover, the history of violence associated with the Klan shows that the possibility of injury or death is not just hypothetical. The person who burns a cross directed at a particular person often is making a serious threat, meant to coerce the victim to comply with the Klan's wishes unless the victim is willing to risk the wrath of the Klan. Indeed, as the cases of respondents Elliott and O'Mara indicate, individuals without Klan affiliation who wish to threaten or menace another person sometimes use cross burning because of this association between a burning cross and violence.

In sum, while a burning cross does not inevitably convey a message of intimidation, often the cross burner intends that the recipients of the message fear for their lives. And when a cross burning is used to intimidate, few if any messages are more powerful.

■ III

The First Amendment affords protection to symbolic or expressive conduct as well as to actual speech. See, e.g., *R. A. V. v. City of St. Paul*, 505 U.S. [377 (1992)]; *Texas v. Johnson*, [491 U.S. 397 (1989)]; *United States v. O'Brien*, 391 U.S. 367 (1968); *Tinker v. Des Moines Independent Community School Dist.*, 393 U.S. 503 (1969).

The protections afforded by the First Amendment, however, are not absolute and we have long recognized that the government may regulate certain categories of expression consistent with the Constitution. See, e.g., *Chaplinsky v. New Hampshire,* 315 U.S. 568 (1942) ("There are certain well-defined and narrowly limited classes of speech, the prevention and punishment of which has never been thought to raise any Constitutional problem").

We have consequently held that fighting words—"those personally abusive epithets which, when addressed to the ordinary citizen, are, as a matter of common knowledge, inherently likely to provoke violent reaction"—are generally proscribable under the First Amendment. *Cohen v. California,* 403 U.S. 15 (1971). Furthermore, "the constitutional guarantees of free speech and free press do not permit a State to forbid or proscribe advocacy of the use of force or of law violation except where such advocacy is directed to inciting or producing imminent lawless action and is likely to incite or produce such action." *Brandenburg v. Ohio,* 395 U.S. 444 (1969). And the First Amendment also permits a State to ban a "true threat." *Watts v. United States,* 394 U.S. 705 (1969); accord, *R. A. V.* ("[T]hreats of violence are outside the First Amendment").

"True threats" encompass those statements where the speaker means to communicate a serious expression of an intent to commit an act of unlawful violence to a particular individual or group of individuals. The speaker need not actually intend to carry out the threat. Rather, a prohibition on true threats "protect[s] individuals from the fear of violence" and "from the disruption that fear engenders," in addition to protecting people "from the possibility that the threatened violence will occur." Intimidation in the constitutionally proscribable sense of the word is a type of true threat, where a speaker directs a threat to a person or group of persons with the intent of placing the victim in fear of bodily harm or death. . . .

The fact that cross burning is symbolic expression, however, does not resolve the constitutional question. The Supreme Court of Virginia relied upon *R. A. V.* to conclude that once a statute discriminates on the basis of this type of content, the law is unconstitutional. We disagree.

In *R. A. V.,* we held that a local ordinance that banned certain symbolic conduct, including cross burning, when done with the knowledge that such conduct would " 'arouse anger, alarm or resentment in others on the basis of race, color, creed, religion or gender' " was unconstitutional. We held that the ordinance did not pass constitutional muster because it discriminated on the basis of content by targeting only those individuals who "provoke violence" on a basis specified in the law.

We did not hold in *R. A. V.* that the First Amendment prohibits all forms of content-based discrimination within a proscribable area of speech. Rather, we specifically stated that some types of content discrimination did not violate the First Amendment. Indeed, we noted that it would be constitutional to ban only a particular type of threat: "[T]he Federal Government can criminalize only those threats of violence that are directed against the President . . . since the reasons why threats of violence are outside the First Amendment . . . have special force when applied to the person of the President." And a State may "choose to prohibit only that obscenity which is the most patently offensive in its prurience—i.e., that which involves the most lascivious displays of sexual activity." Consequently, while the holding of *R. A. V.* does not permit a State to ban only obscenity based on "offensive political messages," or "only those threats against the President that mention his policy on aid to inner cities" the First Amendment permits content discrimination "based on the very reasons why the particular class of speech at issue . . . is proscribable."

Similarly, Virginia's statute does not run afoul of the First Amendment insofar as it bans cross burning with intent to intimidate. Unlike the statute at issue in *R. A. V.*, the Virginia statute does not single out for opprobrium only that speech directed toward "one of the specified disfavored topics." It does not matter whether an individual burns a cross with intent to intimidate because of the victim's race, gender, or religion, or because of the victim's "political affiliation, union membership, or homosexuality." . . .

The First Amendment permits Virginia to outlaw cross burnings done with the intent to intimidate because burning a cross is a particularly virulent form of intimidation. Instead of prohibiting all intimidating messages, Virginia may choose to regulate this subset of intimidating messages in light of cross burning's long and pernicious history as a signal of impending violence. Thus, just as a State may regulate only that obscenity which is the most obscene due to its prurient content, so too may a State choose to prohibit only those forms of intimidation that are most likely to inspire fear of bodily harm. A ban on cross burning carried out with the intent to intimidate is fully consistent with our holding in *R. A. V.* and is proscribable under the First Amendment.

■ **IV**

The Supreme Court of Virginia ruled in the alternative that Virginia's cross-burning statute was unconstitutionally overbroad due to its provision stating that "[a]ny such burning of a cross shall be prima facie evidence of an intent to intimidate a person or group of persons." . . . In this Court, as in the Supreme Court of Virginia, respondents do not argue that the prima facie evidence provision is unconstitutional as applied to any one of them. Rather, they contend that the provision is unconstitutional on its face. . . .

As construed by the jury instruction, the prima facie provision strips away the very reason why a State may ban cross burning with the intent to intimidate. The prima facie evidence provision permits a jury to convict in every cross-burning case in which defendants exercise their constitutional right not to put on a defense. And even where a defendant like Black presents a defense, the prima facie evidence provision makes it more likely that the jury will find an intent to intimidate regardless of the particular facts of the case. The provision permits the Commonwealth to arrest, prosecute, and convict a person based solely on the fact of cross burning itself. . . .

As the history of cross burning indicates, a burning cross is not always intended to intimidate. Rather, sometimes the cross burning is a statement of ideology, a symbol of group solidarity. . . . Thus, "[b]urning a cross at a political rally would almost certainly be protected expression." *R. A. V.* . . .

The prima facie provision makes no effort to distinguish among these different types of cross burnings. It does not distinguish between a cross burning done with the purpose of creating anger or resentment and a cross burning done with the purpose of threatening or intimidating a victim. It does not distinguish between a cross burning at a public rally or a cross burning on a neighbor's lawn. It does not treat the cross burning directed at an individual differently from the cross burning directed at a group of like-minded believers. It allows a jury to treat a cross burning on the property of another with the owner's acquiescence in the same manner as a cross burning on the property of another without the owner's permission. To this extent I agree with Justice

SOUTER that the prima facie evidence provision can "skew jury deliberations toward conviction in cases where the evidence of intent to intimidate is relatively weak and arguably consistent with a solely ideological reason for burning." . . .

For these reasons, the prima facie evidence provision, as interpreted through the jury instruction and as applied in Barry Black's case, is unconstitutional on its face. . . . Unlike Justice SCALIA, we refuse to speculate on whether any interpretation of the prima facie evidence provision would satisfy the First Amendment. Rather, all we hold is that because of the interpretation of the prima facie evidence provision given by the jury instruction, the provision makes the statute facially invalid at this point. . . .

■ V

With respect to Barry Black, we agree with the Supreme Court of Virginia that his conviction cannot stand, and we affirm the judgment of the Supreme Court of Virginia. With respect to Elliott and O'Mara, we vacate the judgment of the Supreme Court of Virginia, and remand the case for further proceedings. It is so ordered.

□ *Justice STEVENS, concurring.*

Cross burning with "an intent to intimidate" unquestionably qualifies as the kind of threat that is unprotected by the First Amendment. For the reasons stated in the separate opinions that Justice WHITE and I wrote in *R. A. V.* that simple proposition provides a sufficient basis for upholding the basic prohibition in the Virginia statute even though it does not cover other types of threatening expressive conduct. With this observation, I join Justice O'CONNOR's opinion.

□ *Justice THOMAS, dissenting.*

Although I agree with the majority's conclusion that it is constitutionally permissible to "ban . . . cross burning carried out with intent to intimidate," I believe that the majority errs in imputing an expressive component to the activity in question. In my view, whatever expressive value cross burning has, the legislature simply wrote it out by banning only intimidating conduct undertaken by a particular means. A conclusion that the statute prohibiting cross burning with intent to intimidate sweeps beyond a prohibition on certain conduct into the zone of expression overlooks not only the words of the statute but also reality. . . .

[T]his statute prohibits only conduct, not expression. And, just as one cannot burn down someone's house to make a political point and then seek refuge in the First Amendment, those who hate cannot terrorize and intimidate to make their point. In light of my conclusion that the statute here addresses only conduct, there is no need to analyze it under any of our First Amendment tests.

Even assuming that the statute implicates the First Amendment, in my view, the fact that the statute permits a jury to draw an inference of intent to intimidate from the cross burning itself presents no constitutional problems. Therein lies my primary disagreement with the plurality. . . .

Because the prima facie clause here is an inference, not an irrebuttable presumption, there is all the more basis under our Due Process precedents to sustain this statute. . . .

Moreover, even in the First Amendment context, the Court has upheld such regulations where conduct that initially appears culpable, ultimately results in dismissed charges. A regulation of pornography is one such example. While possession of child pornography is illegal, *New York v. Ferber*, 458 U.S. 747 (1982), possession of adult pornography, as long as it is not obscene, is allowed, *Miller v. California*, 413 U.S. 15 (1973). As a result, those pornographers trafficking in images of adults who look like minors, may be not only deterred but also arrested and prosecuted for possessing what a jury might find to be legal materials. This "chilling" effect has not, however, been a cause for grave concern with respect to overbreadth of such statutes among the members of this Court. . . .

Because I would uphold the validity of this statute, I respectfully dissent.

☐ *Justice SCALIA, with whom Justice THOMAS joins, concurring in part, concurring in the judgment in part, and dissenting in part.*

I agree with the Court that, under our decision in *R. A. V.*, a State may, without infringing the First Amendment, prohibit cross burning carried out with the intent to intimidate. Accordingly, I join Parts I–III of the Court's opinion. I also agree that we should vacate and remand the judgment of the Virginia Supreme Court so that that Court can have an opportunity authoritatively to construe the prima-facie-evidence provision of Section 18.2-423. I write separately, however, to describe what I believe to be the correct interpretation of Sec. 18.2-423, and to explain why I believe there is no justification for the plurality's apparent decision to invalidate that provision on its face.

In order to determine whether this component of the statute violates the Constitution, it is necessary, first, to establish precisely what the presentation of prima facie evidence accomplishes. . . . [P]resentation of evidence that a defendant burned a cross in public view is automatically sufficient, on its own, to support an inference that the defendant intended to intimidate only until the defendant comes forward with some evidence in rebuttal.

The question presented, then, is whether, given this understanding of the term "prima facie evidence," the cross-burning statute is constitutional. The Virginia Supreme Court answered that question in the negative. It stated that "[Sec.] 18.2-423 sweeps within its ambit for arrest and prosecution, both protected and unprotected speech." "The enhanced probability of prosecution under the statute chills the expression of protected speech sufficiently to render the statute overbroad."

This approach toward overbreadth analysis is unprecedented. We have never held that the mere threat that individuals who engage in protected conduct will be subject to arrest and prosecution suffices to render a statute overbroad. Rather, our overbreadth jurisprudence has consistently focused on whether the prohibitory terms of a particular statute extend to protected conduct; that is, we have inquired whether individuals who engage in protected conduct can be convicted under a statute, not whether they might be subject to arrest and prosecution. . . .

In deeming Sec. 18.2-423 facially invalid, the plurality presumably means to rely on some species of overbreadth doctrine. But it must be a rare species indeed. . . . The class of persons that the plurality contemplates could impermissibly be convicted under Sec. 18.2-423 includes only those individuals who (1) burn a cross in public view, (2) do not intend to intimidate, (3) are nonetheless charged and prosecuted, and (4) refuse to present a defense. ("The prima facie evidence provision permits a jury to convict in every cross-burning case in which defendants exercise their constitutional right not to put on a defense.")

Conceding (quite generously, in my view) that this class of persons exists, it cannot possibly give rise to a viable facial challenge, not even with the aid of our First Amendment overbreadth doctrine.

I believe the prima-facie-evidence provision in Virginia's cross-burning statute is constitutionally unproblematic. . . .

□ *Justice SOUTER, with whom Justice KENNEDY and Justice GINSBURG join, concurring in the judgment in part and dissenting in part.*

I agree with the majority that the Virginia statute makes a content-based distinction within the category of punishable intimidating or threatening expression, the very type of distinction we considered in *R.A.V.* I disagree that any exception should save Virginia's law from unconstitutionality under the holding in *R.A.V.* or any acceptable variation of it.

As the majority points out, the burning cross can broadcast threat and ideology together, ideology alone, or threat alone, as was apparently the choice of respondents Elliott and O'Mara.

The issue is whether the statutory prohibition restricted to this symbol falls within one of the exceptions to *R.A.V.'s* general condemnation of limited content-based proscription within a broader category of expression proscribable generally. Because of the burning cross's extraordinary force as a method of intimidation, the *R.A.V.* exception most likely to cover the statute is the first of the three mentioned there, which the *R.A.V.* opinion called an exception for content discrimination on a basis that "consists entirely of the very reason the entire class of speech at issue is proscribable." *R.A.V.* This is the exception the majority speaks of here as covering statutes prohibiting "particularly virulent" proscribable expression.

I do not think that the Virginia statute qualifies for this virulence exception as *R.A.V.* explained it. The statute fits poorly with the illustrative examples given in *R.A.V.*, none of which involves communication generally associated with a particular message, and in fact, the majority's discussion of a special virulence exception here moves that exception toward a more flexible conception than the version in *R.A.V.* I will reserve judgment on that doctrinal development, for even on a pragmatic conception of *R.A.V.* and its exceptions the Virginia statute could not pass muster, the most obvious hurdle being the statute's prima facie evidence provision. That provision is essential to understanding why the statute's tendency to suppress a message disqualifies it from any rescue by exception from *R.A.V.'s* general rule. . . .

[N]o content-based statute should survive even under a pragmatic recasting of *R.A.V.* without a high probability that no "official suppression of ideas is afoot," *R.A.V.* I believe the prima facie evidence provision stands in the way of any finding of such a high probability here. . . .

As I see the likely significance of the evidence provision, its primary effect is to skew jury deliberations toward conviction in cases where the evidence of intent to intimidate is relatively weak and arguably consistent with a solely ideological reason for burning. To understand how the provision may work, recall that the symbolic act of burning a cross, without more, is consistent with both intent to intimidate and intent to make an ideological statement free of any aim to threaten. One can tell the intimidating instance from the wholly ideological one only by reference to some further circumstance. In the real world, of course, and in real-world prosecutions, there will always be further circumstances, and the factfinder will always learn something more than the isolated fact of cross burning. Sometimes those circumstances will show an intent to intimidate, but sometimes they will be at least equivocal, as in cases where a white supremacist group burns a cross at an initiation ceremony or political rally visible to the public. In such a case, if the fact finder is aware of the prima facie evidence provision, as the jury was in respondent Black's case, the provision will have the practical effect of tilting the jury's thinking in favor of the prosecution. What is significant is not that the provision permits a fact finder's conclusion that the defendant acted with proscribable and punishable intent without any further indication, because some such indication will almost always be presented. What is significant is that the provision will encourage a fact finder to err on the side of a finding of intent to intimidate when the evidence of circumstances fails to point with any clarity either to the criminal intent or to the permissible one. . . . The provision will thus tend to draw nonthreatening ideological expression within the ambit of the prohibition of intimidating expression, as Justice O'CONNOR notes.

To the extent the prima facie evidence provision skews prosecutions, then, it skews the statute toward suppressing ideas. Thus, the appropriate way to consider the statute's prima facie evidence term, in my view, is not as if it were an overbroad statutory definition amenable to severance or a narrowing construction. The question here is not the permissible scope of an arguably overbroad statute, but the claim of a clearly content-based statute to an exception from the general prohibition of content-based proscriptions, an exception that is not warranted if the statute's terms show that suppression of ideas may be afoot. Accordingly, the way to look at the prima facie evidence provision is to consider it for any indication of what is afoot. And if we look at the provision for this purpose, it has a very obvious significance as a mechanism for bringing within the statute's prohibition some expression that is doubtfully threatening though certainly distasteful. . . .

I conclude that the statute under which all three of the respondents were prosecuted violates the First Amendment, since the statute's content-based distinction was invalid at the time of the charged activities, regardless of whether the prima facie evidence provision was given any effect in any respondent's individual case. In my view, severance of the prima facie evidence provision now could not eliminate the unconstitutionality of the whole statute at the time of the respondents' conduct. I would therefore affirm the judgment of the Supreme Court of Virginia vacating the respondents' convictions and dismissing the indictments. Accordingly, I concur in the Court's judgment as to respondent Black and dissent as to respondents Elliott and O'Mara.

6

FREEDOM FROM AND
OF RELIGION

I n a controversial ruling in *Zelman v. Simmons-Harris* (2002)
(excerpted below in Section A) a bare majority of the Court
upheld a school voucher program, permitting children to attend
private religious schools, over (dis)establishment objections. Opponents of vouchers have challenged the constitutionality of such
programs under state constitutions that in thirty-eight states expressly forbid public financing for religious institutions; most of
these provisions were adopted in the late nineteenth century as
so-called Blaine amendments, named after House of Representatives speaker James G. Blaine who championed a similar though
unsuccessful federal constitutional amendment to bar support
for Catholic schools. Although avoiding ruling on the constitutionality of Blaine amendments in *Locke v. Davey* (2004) (excerpted below in Section B), the Court held that a student
awarded a scholarship who wanted to earn a degree in theology
could be barred from using it for that purpose under Washington state's constitutional bar against public expenditures for religion over his objections that that provision violated the First
Amendment guarantee for the free exercise of religion. Writing
for the Court, Chief Justice Rehnquist distinguished *Zelman*
and other (dis)establishment clause rulings permitting indirect
aid for religious schools, whether through vouchers, computer
software, or scholarships, on the ground that those programs

directly benefited students and turned on individual student choices. Thus, in *Witters v. Washington Department of Services for the Blind*, 474 U.S. 481 (1986), the Court held that the (dis)establishment clause was not violated by permitting Larry Witters to use a state scholarship to pursue biblical studies. But Witters never received the scholarship because on remand state courts held that the state constitution imposed a more strict separation of government from religion than the federal constitution. When Joshua Davey subsequently argued that the state's constitutional provision barring his use of a scholarship to pursue a pastoral degree violated the First Amendment free exercise clause in *Locke v. Davey*, the Court ruled that the free exercise clause does not compel what the (dis)establishment clause would permit.

In sum, in *Locke v. Davey* the Court attempted to reconcile the tensions between competing (dis)establishment and free exercise claims and to clarify the contours of the latter guarantee. On the one hand, under *Oregon v. Smith*, 494 U.S. 872 (1990) (excerpted in Vol. 2, Ch. 5), religious minorities are not exempt under the free exercise clause from otherwise neutral and generally applicable laws. On the other hand, under *Church of the Lukumi Babalu Aye v. City Hialeah*, 508 U.S. 520 (1993) (excerpted in Vol. 2, Ch. 5), the free exercise clause protects religious minorities from overt discrimination and legislation that specifically targets them and burdens their religious freedom by banning or imposing penalties for their practices. Under *Locke*, however, the free exercise clause does not override state provisions barring governmental aid to religion and compel such support, even though such aid would be permissible under the First Amendment (dis)establishment clause. In *Locke*, Justices Scalia and Thomas dissented and objected to the majority's permitting states to discriminate against religion.

Finally, the Court avoided the heated controversy over whether requiring school children to recite the Pledge of Allegiance violates the First Amendment by denying standing to raise the issue in *Elk Grove Unified School District* (2004) (excerpted here in Vol. 1, Ch. 2). Writing for the Court, Justice Stevens held that Michael A. Newdow, who challenged the policy on behalf of his daughter, though he was not her legal custodian, lacked "prudential standing" to bring the suit. In other words, when legal claims are based on domestic relations law, a field largely left to state law, "the prudent course is for the federal court to stay its hand rather than reach out to resolve a weighty question of federal constitutional law." But in separate concurring opinions Chief Justice Rehnquist and Justices O'Connor and Thomas would have granted standing and rejected Newdow's First Amendment claims, though for different reasons. Chief Justice Rehnquist contended that *Lee v. Weisman* (excerpted in Vol. 2, Ch. 6), which invalidated school-sponsored prayer at graduation ceremonies, could be distinguished and that the words "under God" in the Pledge are "not endorsement of any religion." Justice O'Connor agreed; however, she deemed teacher-led recitations of "under God" as simply "ceremonial deism." By contrast, Justice Thomas would have upheld the school district's policy because *Lee v. Weisman* and other prior decisions applying the (dis)establishment clause to the states were wrongly decided and should be overruled. Justice Scalia recused himself because in off-the-bench remarks he had criticized the lower court for ruling that the First Amendment had been violated.

A | *The (Dis)Establishment of Religion*

Zelman v. Simmons-Harris
536 U.S. 639, 122 S.Ct. 2460 (2002)

In 1995, Cleveland, Ohio's low-income inner-city schools were declared to be in crisis and placed under state control. Subsequently, Ohio adopted a "Pilot Project Scholarship Program," providing school vouchers of up to $2,250 to send inner-city children to schools outside the Cleveland school district. About 96 percent of the money went to religious schools. A group of taxpayers challenged the constitutionality of the program for violating the First Amendment's separation of government from religion. A federal district held the voucher program unconstitutional and the Court of Appeals for the Sixth Circuit affirmed that decision.

The appellate court's decision was reversed on a vote of five to four. Chief Justice Rehnquist delivered the opinion of the Court. Justices

O'Connor and Thomas issued concurring opinions. Justices Stevens, Breyer, and Souter filed dissenting opinions, and Justice Ginsburg joined the latter's dissent.

☐ *CHIEF JUSTICE REHNQUIST delivered the opinion of the Court.*

The Establishment Clause of the First Amendment, applied to the States through the Fourteenth Amendment, prevents a State from enacting laws that have the "purpose" or "effect" of advancing or inhibiting religion. *Agostini v. Felton,* 521 U.S. 203 (1997). There is no dispute that the program challenged here was enacted for the valid secular purpose of providing educational assistance to poor children in a demonstrably failing public school system. Thus, the question presented is whether the Ohio program nonetheless has the forbidden "effect" of advancing or inhibiting religion.

To answer that question, our decisions have drawn a consistent distinction between government programs that provide aid directly to religious schools, *Mitchell v. Helms,* 530 U.S. 793 (2000); *Agostini; Rosenberger v. Rector and Visitors of Univ. of Va.,* 515 U.S. 819 (1995), and programs of true private choice, in which government aid reaches religious schools only as a result of the genuine and independent choices of private individuals, *Mueller v. Allen,* 463 U.S. 388 (1983); *Witters v. Washington Dept. of Servs. for Blind,* 474 U.S. 481 (1986); *Zobrest v. Catalina Foothills School Dist.,* 509 U.S. 1 (1993). While our jurisprudence with respect to the constitutionality of direct aid programs has "changed significantly" over the past two decades, our jurisprudence with respect to true private choice programs has remained consistent and unbroken. Three times we have confronted Establishment Clause challenges to neutral government programs that provide aid directly to a broad class of individuals, who, in turn, direct the aid to religious schools or institutions of their own choosing. Three times we have rejected such challenges.

In *Mueller,* we rejected an Establishment Clause challenge to a Minnesota program authorizing tax deductions for various educational expenses, including private school tuition costs, even though the great majority of the program's beneficiaries (96%) were parents of children in religious schools. . . .

In *Witters,* we used identical reasoning to reject an Establishment Clause challenge to a vocational scholarship program that provided tuition aid to a student studying at a religious institution to become a pastor. . . .

Finally, in *Zobrest,* we applied *Mueller* and *Witters* to reject an Establishment Clause challenge to a federal program that permitted sign-language interpreters to assist deaf children enrolled in religious schools. Reviewing our earlier decisions, we stated that "government programs that neutrally provide benefits to a broad class of citizens defined without reference to religion are not readily subject to an Establishment Clause challenge." Looking once again to the challenged program as a whole, we observed that the program "distributes benefits neutrally to any child qualifying as 'disabled.' " Its "primary beneficiaries," we said, were "disabled children, not sectarian schools." . . .

Mueller, Witters, and *Zobrest* thus make clear that where a government aid program is neutral with respect to religion, and provides assistance directly to a broad class of citizens who, in turn, direct government aid to religious schools wholly as a result of their own genuine and independent private choice, the program is not readily subject to challenge under the Establishment Clause. A program that shares these features permits government aid to reach religious institutions only by way of the deliberate choices of numerous individual recipients. The incidental advancement of a religious mission, or the perceived endorsement of a religious message, is reasonably attributable to the individual recipient, not to the government, whose role ends with the disbursement of benefits.

We believe that the program challenged here is a program of true private choice, consistent with *Mueller, Witters,* and *Zobrest,* and thus constitutional. . . .

Respondents suggest that even without a financial incentive for parents to choose a religious school, the program creates a "public perception that the State is endorsing religious practices and beliefs." But we have repeatedly recognized that no reasonable observer would think a neutral program of private choice, where state aid reaches religious schools solely as a result of the numerous independent decisions of private individuals, carries with it the imprimatur of government endorsement. The argument is particularly misplaced here since "the reasonable observer in the endorsement inquiry must be deemed aware" of the "history and context" underlying a challenged program. *Good News Club v. Milford Central School,* 533 U.S. 98 (2001). Any objective observer familiar with the full history and context of the Ohio program would reasonably view it as one aspect of a broader undertaking to assist poor children in failed schools, not as an endorsement of religious schooling in general. . . .

Respondents and Justice SOUTER claim that even if we do not focus on the number of participating schools that are religious schools, we should attach constitutional significance to the fact that 96% of scholarship recipients have enrolled in religious schools. They claim that this alone proves parents lack genuine choice, even if no parent has ever said so. We need not consider this argument in detail, since it was flatly rejected in *Mueller,* where we found it irrelevant that 96% of parents taking deductions for tuition expenses paid tuition at religious schools. Indeed, we have recently found it irrelevant even to the constitutionality of a direct aid program that a vast majority of program benefits went to religious schools. . . .

Respondents finally claim that we should look to *Committee for Public Ed. & Religious Liberty v. Nyquist,* 413 U.S. 756 (1973), to decide these cases. We disagree for two reasons. First, the program in *Nyquist* was quite different from the program challenged here. *Nyquist* involved a New York program that gave a package of benefits exclusively to private schools and the parents of private school enrollees. Although the program was enacted for ostensibly secular purposes, we found that its "function" was "unmistakably to provide desired financial support for nonpublic, sectarian institutions." Its genesis, we said, was that private religious schools faced "increasingly grave fiscal problems." The program thus provided direct money grants to religious schools.

Second, were there any doubt that the program challenged in *Nyquist* is far removed from the program challenged here, we expressly reserved judgment with respect to "a case involving some form of public assistance (e.g., scholarships) made available generally without regard to the sectarian-nonsectarian, or public-nonpublic nature of the institution benefited." That, of course, is the very question now before us, and it has since been answered, first in *Mueller.* To the extent the scope of *Nyquist* has remained an open question in light of these later decisions, we now hold that *Nyquist* does not govern neutral educational assistance programs that, like the program here, offer aid directly to a broad class of individual recipients defined without regard to religion.

In sum, the Ohio program is entirely neutral with respect to religion. It provides benefits directly to a wide spectrum of individuals, defined only by financial need and residence in a particular school district. It permits such individuals to exercise genuine choice among options public and private, secular and religious. The program is therefore a program of true private choice. In keeping with an unbroken line of decisions rejecting challenges to similar programs, we hold that the program does not offend the Establishment Clause. The judgment of the Court of Appeals is reversed. It is so ordered.

☐ *Justice O'CONNOR, concurring.*

While I join the Court's opinion, I write separately for two reasons. First, although the Court takes an important step, I do not believe that today's decision, when considered in light of other long-standing government programs that impact religious organizations and our prior Establishment Clause jurisprudence, marks a dramatic break from the past. Second, given the emphasis the Court places on verifying that parents of voucher students in religious schools have exercised "true private choice," I think it is worth elaborating on the Court's conclusion that this inquiry should consider all reasonable educational alternatives to religious schools that are available to parents. To do otherwise is to ignore how the educational system in Cleveland actually functions.

These cases are different from prior indirect aid cases in part because a significant portion of the funds appropriated for the voucher program reach religious schools without restrictions on the use of these funds. The share of public resources that reach religious schools is not, however, as significant as respondents suggest. Data from the 1999–2000 school year indicate that 82 percent of schools participating in the voucher program were religious and that 96 percent of participating students enrolled in religious schools (46 of 56 private schools in the program are religiously affiliated; 3,637 of 3,765 voucher students attend religious private schools), but these data are incomplete. These statistics do not take into account all of the reasonable educational choices that may be available to students in Cleveland public schools. When one considers the option to attend community schools, the percentage of students enrolled in religious schools falls to 62.1 percent. If magnet schools are included in the mix, this percentage falls to 16.5 percent.

Even these numbers do not paint a complete picture. The Cleveland program provides voucher applicants from low-income families with up to $2,250 in tuition assistance and provides the remaining applicants with up to $1,875 in tuition assistance. In contrast, the State provides community schools $4,518 per pupil and magnet schools, on average, $7,097 per pupil. Even if one assumes that all voucher students came from low-income families and that each voucher student used up the entire $2,250 voucher, at most $8.2 million of public funds flowed to religious schools under the voucher program in 1999–2000. Although just over one-half as many students attended community schools as religious private schools on the state fisc, the State spent over $1 million more—$9.4 million—on students in community schools than on students in religious private schools because per-pupil aid to community schools is more than double the per-pupil aid to private schools under the voucher program. Moreover, the amount spent on religious private schools is minor compared to the $114.8 million the State spent on students in the Cleveland magnet schools.

Although $8.2 million is no small sum, it pales in comparison to the amount of funds that federal, state, and local governments already provide religious institutions. Religious organizations may qualify for exemptions from the federal corporate income tax; the corporate income tax in many States; and property taxes in all 50 States; and clergy qualify for a federal tax break on income used for housing expenses. In addition, the Federal Government provides individuals, corporations, trusts, and estates a tax deduction for charitable contributions to qualified religious groups. See §§170, 642(c). Finally, the Federal Government and certain state governments provide tax credits for educational expenses, many of which are spent on education at religious schools. . . .

Based on the reasoning in the Court's opinion, which is consistent with the realities of the Cleveland educational system, I am persuaded that the Cleveland voucher program affords parents of eligible children genuine nonreligious options and is consistent with the Establishment Clause.

☐ *Justice THOMAS, concurring.*

Frederick Douglass once said that "[e]ducation . . . means emancipation. It means light and liberty. It means the uplifting of the soul of man into the glorious light of truth, the light by which men can only be made free." Today many of our inner-city public schools deny emancipation to urban minority students. Despite this Court's observation nearly 50 years ago in *Brown v. Board of Education* that "it is doubtful that any child may reasonably be expected to succeed in life if he is denied the opportunity of an education," urban children have been forced into a system that continually fails them. These cases present an example of such failures. Besieged by escalating financial problems and declining academic achievement, the Cleveland City School District was in the midst of an academic emergency when Ohio enacted its scholarship program.

The dissents and respondents wish to invoke the Establishment Clause of the First Amendment, as incorporated through the Fourteenth, to constrain a State's neutral efforts to provide greater educational opportunity for underprivileged minority students. Today's decision properly upholds the program as constitutional, and I join it in full. . . .

☐ *Justice STEVENS, dissenting.*

Is a law that authorizes the use of public funds to pay for the indoctrination of thousands of grammar school children in particular religious faiths a "law respecting an establishment of religion" within the meaning of the First Amendment? In answering that question, I think we should ignore three factual matters that are discussed at length by my colleagues.

First, the severe educational crisis that confronted the Cleveland City School District when Ohio enacted its voucher program is not a matter that should affect our appraisal of its constitutionality. . . .

Second, the wide range of choices that have been made available to students within the public school system has no bearing on the question whether the State may pay the tuition for students who wish to reject public education entirely and attend private schools that will provide them with a sectarian education. The fact that the vast majority of the voucher recipients who have entirely rejected public education receive religious indoctrination at state expense does, however, support the claim that the law is one "respecting an establishment of religion." The State may choose to divide up its public schools into a dozen different options and label them magnet schools, community schools, or whatever else it decides to call them, but the State is still required to provide a public education and it is the State's decision to fund private school education over and above its traditional obligation that is at issue in these cases.

Third, the voluntary character of the private choice to prefer a parochial education over an education in the public school system seems to me quite irrelevant to the question whether the government's choice to pay for religious indoctrination is constitutionally permissible. Today, however, the Court seems to have decided that the mere fact that a family that cannot afford a private education wants its children educated in a parochial school is a sufficient justification for this use of public funds.

For the reasons stated by Justice SOUTER and Justice BREYER, I am convinced that the Court's decision is profoundly misguided. Admittedly, in reaching that conclusion I have been influenced by my understanding of the impact of religious strife on the decisions of our forbears to migrate to this continent, and on the decisions of neighbors in the Balkans, Northern Ireland, and the Middle East to mistrust one another. Whenever we remove a brick from the wall that was designed to separate religion and government, we increase the risk of religious strife and weaken the foundation of our democracy.

I respectfully dissent.

☐ *Justice BREYER, with whom Justice STEVENS and Justice SOUTER join, dissenting.*

I join Justice SOUTER's opinion, and I agree substantially with Justice STEVENS. I write separately, however, to emphasize the risk that publicly financed voucher programs pose in terms of religiously based social conflict. I do so because I believe that the Establishment Clause concern for protecting the Nation's social fabric from religious conflict poses an overriding obstacle to the implementation of this well-intentioned school voucher program. And by explaining the nature of the concern, I hope to demonstrate why, in my view, "parental choice" cannot significantly alleviate the constitutional problem. . . .

I do not believe that the "parental choice" aspect of the voucher program sufficiently offsets the concerns I have mentioned. Parental choice cannot help the taxpayer who does not want to finance the religious education of children. It will not always help the parent who may see little real choice between inadequate nonsectarian public education and adequate education at a school whose religious teachings are contrary to his own. It will not satisfy religious minorities unable to participate because they are too few in number to support the creation of their own private schools. It will not satisfy groups whose religious beliefs preclude them from participating in a government-sponsored program, and who may well feel ignored as government funds primarily support the education of children in the doctrines of the dominant religions. And it does little to ameliorate the entanglement problems or the related problems of social division. Consequently, the fact that the parent may choose which school can cash the government's voucher check does not alleviate the Establishment Clause concerns associated with voucher programs.

The Court, in effect, turns the clock back. It adopts, under the name of "neutrality," an interpretation of the Establishment Clause that this Court rejected more than half a century ago. In its view, the parental choice that offers each religious group a kind of equal opportunity to secure government funding overcomes the Establishment Clause concern for social concord. An earlier Court found that "equal opportunity" principle insufficient; it read the

Clause as insisting upon greater separation of church and state, at least in respect to primary education. See *Nyquist*. In a society composed of many different religious creeds, I fear that this present departure from the Court's earlier understanding risks creating a form of religiously based conflict potentially harmful to the Nation's social fabric. Because I believe the Establishment Clause was written in part to avoid this kind of conflict, and for reasons set forth by Justice SOUTER and Justice STEVENS, I respectfully dissent.

☐ *Justice SOUTER, with whom Justice STEVENS, Justice GINSBURG, and Justice BREYER join, dissenting.*

The applicability of the Establishment Clause to public funding of benefits to religious schools was settled in *Everson v. Board of Ed. of Ewing*, 330 U.S. 1 (1947), which inaugurated the modern era of establishment doctrine. The Court stated the principle in words from which there was no dissent: "No tax in any amount, large or small, can be levied to support any religious activities or institutions, whatever they may be called, or whatever form they may adopt to teach or practice religion." The Court has never in so many words repudiated this statement, let alone, in so many words, overruled *Everson*. . . .

How can a Court consistently leave *Everson* on the books and approve the Ohio vouchers? The answer is that it cannot. It is only by ignoring *Everson* that the majority can claim to rest on traditional law in its invocation of neutral aid provisions and private choice to sanction the Ohio law. It is, moreover, only by ignoring the meaning of neutrality and private choice themselves that the majority can even pretend to rest today's decision on those criteria.

The majority's statements of Establishment Clause doctrine cannot be appreciated without some historical perspective on the Court's announced limitations on government aid to religious education, and its repeated repudiation of limits previously set. . . .

Viewed with the necessary generality, the cases can be categorized in three groups. In the period from 1947 to 1968, the basic principle of no aid to religion through school benefits was unquestioned. Thereafter for some 15 years, the Court termed its efforts as attempts to draw a line against aid that would be divertible to support the religious, as distinct from the secular, activity of an institutional beneficiary. Then, starting in 1983, concern with divertibility was gradually lost in favor of approving aid in amounts unlikely to afford substantial benefits to religious schools, when offered evenhandedly without regard to a recipient's religious character, and when channeled to a religious institution only by the genuinely free choice of some private individual. Now, the three stages are succeeded by a fourth, in which the substantial character of government aid is held to have no constitutional significance, and the espoused criteria of neutrality in offering aid, and private choice in directing it, are shown to be nothing but examples of verbal formalism. . . .

Although it has taken half a century since *Everson* to reach the majority's twin standards of neutrality and free choice, the facts show that, in the majority's hands, even these criteria cannot convincingly legitimize the Ohio scheme.

Consider first the criterion of neutrality. As recently as two Terms ago, a majority of the Court recognized that neutrality conceived of as evenhandedness toward aid recipients had never been treated as alone sufficient to satisfy the Establishment Clause, *Mitchell [v. Helms]*. But at least in its limited significance, formal neutrality seemed to serve some purpose. Today, however, the majority employs the neutrality criterion in a way that renders it impossible to understand.

Neutrality in this sense refers, of course, to evenhandedness in setting eligibility as between potential religious and secular recipients of public money. Thus, for example, the aid scheme in *Witters* provided an eligible recipient with a scholarship to be used at any institution within a practically unlimited universe of schools; it did not tend to provide more or less aid depending on which one the scholarship recipient chose, and there was no indication that the maximum scholarship amount would be insufficient at secular schools. Neither did any condition of *Zobrest*'s interpreter's subsidy favor religious education.

In order to apply the neutrality test, then, it makes sense to focus on a category of aid that may be directed to religious as well as secular schools, and ask whether the scheme favors a religious direction. Here, one would ask whether the voucher provisions, allowing for as much as $2,250 toward private school tuition (or a grant to a public school in an adjacent district), were written in a way that skewed the scheme toward benefiting religious schools.

This, however, is not what the majority asks. The majority looks not to the provisions for tuition vouchers, but to every provision for educational opportunity: "The program permits the participation of all schools within the district [as well as public schools in adjacent districts], religious or nonreligious." The majority then finds confirmation that "participation of all schools" satisfies neutrality by noting that the better part of total state educational expenditure goes to public schools, thus showing there is no favor of religion.

The illogic is patent. If regular, public schools (which can get no voucher payments) "participate" in a voucher scheme with schools that can, and public expenditure is still predominantly on public schools, then the majority's reasoning would find neutrality in a scheme of vouchers available for private tuition in districts with no secular private schools at all. "Neutrality" as the majority employs the term is, literally, verbal and nothing more. This, indeed, is the only way the majority can gloss over the very nonneutral feature of the total scheme covering "all schools": public tutors may receive from the State no more than $324 per child to support extra tutoring (that is, the State's 90% of a total amount of $360), whereas the tuition voucher schools (which turn out to be mostly religious) can receive up to $2,250.

Why the majority does not simply accept the fact that the challenge here is to the more generous voucher scheme and judge its neutrality in relation to religious use of voucher money seems very odd. It seems odd, that is, until one recognizes that comparable schools for applying the criterion of neutrality are also the comparable schools for applying the other majority criterion, whether the immediate recipients of voucher aid have a genuinely free choice of religious and secular schools to receive the voucher money. And in applying this second criterion, the consideration of "all schools" is ostensibly helpful to the majority position.

The majority addresses the issue of choice the same way it addresses neutrality, by asking whether recipients or potential recipients of voucher aid have a choice of public schools among secular alternatives to religious schools. Again, however, the majority asks the wrong question and misapplies the criterion. The majority has confused choice in spending scholarships with choice from the entire menu of possible educational placements, most of them open to anyone willing to attend a public school. I say "confused" because the majority's new use of the choice criterion, which it frames negatively as "whether

Ohio is coercing parents into sending their children to religious schools" ignores the reason for having a private choice enquiry in the first place. Cases since *Mueller* have found private choice relevant under a rule that aid to religious schools can be permissible so long as it first passes through the hands of students or parents. The majority's view that all educational choices are comparable for purposes of choice thus ignores the whole point of the choice test: it is a criterion for deciding whether indirect aid to a religious school is legitimate because it passes through private hands that can spend or use the aid in a secular school. The question is whether the private hand is genuinely free to send the money in either a secular direction or a religious one. The majority now has transformed this question about private choice in channeling aid into a question about selecting from examples of state spending (on education) including direct spending on magnet and community public schools that goes through no private hands and could never reach a religious school under any circumstance. When the choice test is transformed from where to spend the money to where to go to school, it is cut loose from its very purpose.

Defining choice as choice in spending the money or channeling the aid is, moreover, necessary if the choice criterion is to function as a limiting principle at all. If "choice" is present whenever there is any educational alternative to the religious school to which vouchers can be endorsed, then there will always be a choice and the voucher can always be constitutional, even in a system in which there is not a single private secular school as an alternative to the religious school. And because it is unlikely that any participating private religious school will enroll more pupils than the generally available public system, it will be easy to generate numbers suggesting that aid to religion is not the significant intent or effect of the voucher scheme.

That is, in fact, just the kind of rhetorical argument that the majority accepts in these cases. In addition to secular private schools (129 students), the majority considers public schools with tuition assistance (roughly 1,400 students), magnet schools (13,000 students), and community schools (1,900 students), and concludes that fewer than 20% of pupils receive state vouchers to attend religious schools. . . .

If, contrary to the majority, we ask the right question about genuine choice to use the vouchers, the answer shows that something is influencing choices in a way that aims the money in a religious direction: of 56 private schools in the district participating in the voucher program (only 53 of which accepted voucher students in 1999–2000), 46 of them are religious; 96.6% of all voucher recipients go to religious schools, only 3.4% to nonreligious ones. Unfortunately for the majority position, there is no explanation for this that suggests the religious direction results simply from free choices by parents. One answer to these statistics, for example, which would be consistent with the genuine choice claimed to be operating, might be that 96.6% of families choosing to avail themselves of vouchers choose to educate their children in schools of their own religion. This would not, in my view, render the scheme constitutional, but it would speak to the majority's choice criterion. Evidence shows, however, that almost two out of three families using vouchers to send their children to religious schools did not embrace the religion of those schools. The families made it clear they had not chosen the schools because they wished their children to be proselytized in a religion not their own, or in any religion, but because of educational opportunity.

Even so, the fact that some 2,270 students chose to apply their vouchers to schools of other religions might be consistent with true choice if the students "chose" their religious schools over a wide array of private nonreligious options, or if it could be shown generally that Ohio's program had no effect on educational choices and thus no impermissible effect of advancing religious education. But both possibilities are contrary to fact. First, even if all existing nonreligious private schools in Cleveland were willing to accept large numbers of voucher students, only a few more than the 129 currently enrolled in such schools would be able to attend, as the total enrollment at all nonreligious private schools in Cleveland for kindergarten through eighth grade is only 510 children, and there is no indication that these schools have many open seats. Second, the $2,500 cap that the program places on tuition for participating low-income pupils has the effect of curtailing the participation of nonreligious schools: "nonreligious schools with higher tuition (about $4,000) stated that they could afford to accommodate just a few voucher students." By comparison, the average tuition at participating Catholic schools in Cleveland in 1999–2000 was $1,592, almost $1,000 below the cap.

Of course, the obvious fix would be to increase the value of vouchers so that existing nonreligious private and non-Catholic religious schools would be able to enroll more voucher students, and to provide incentives for educators to create new such schools given that few presently exist. Private choice, if as robust as that available to the seminarian in *Witters*, would then be "true private choice" under the majority's criterion. But it is simply unrealistic to presume that parents of elementary and middle schoolchildren in Cleveland will have a range of secular and religious choices even arguably comparable to the statewide program for vocational and higher education in *Witters*. And to get to that hypothetical point would require that such massive financial support be made available to religion as to disserve every objective of the Establishment Clause even more than the present scheme does.

There is, in any case, no way to interpret the 96.6% of current voucher money going to religious schools as reflecting a free and genuine choice by the families that apply for vouchers. The 96.6% reflects, instead, the fact that too few nonreligious school desks are available and few but religious schools can afford to accept more than a handful of voucher students. And contrary to the majority's assertion, public schools in adjacent districts hardly have a financial incentive to participate in the Ohio voucher program, and none has. For the overwhelming number of children in the voucher scheme, the only alternative to the public schools is religious. And it is entirely irrelevant that the State did not deliberately design the network of private schools for the sake of channeling money into religious institutions. The criterion is one of genuinely free choice on the part of the private individuals who choose, and a Hobson's choice is not a choice, whatever the reason for being Hobsonian.

I do not dissent merely because the majority has misapplied its own law, for even if I assumed arguendo that the majority's formal criteria were satisfied on the facts, today's conclusion would be profoundly at odds with the Constitution. Proof of this is clear on two levels. The first is circumstantial, in the now discarded symptom of violation, the substantial dimension of the aid. The second is direct, in the defiance of every objective supposed to be served by the bar against establishment.

The scale of the aid to religious schools approved today is unprecedented, both in the number of dollars and in the proportion of systemic school expenditure supported. Each measure has received attention in previous cases. On one hand, the sheer quantity of aid, when delivered to a class of religious primary and secondary schools, was suspect on the theory that the greater the aid, the greater its proportion to a religious school's existing expenditures, and the greater the likelihood that public money was supporting religious as well as secular instruction. . . . On the other hand, the Court has found the gross amount unhelpful for Establishment Clause analysis when the aid afforded a benefit solely to one individual, however substantial as to him, but only an incidental benefit to the religious school at which the individual chose to spend the State's money. When neither the design nor the implementation of an aid scheme channels a series of individual students' subsidies toward religious recipients, the relevant beneficiaries for establishment purposes, the Establishment Clause is unlikely to be implicated. The majority's reliance on the observations of five Members of the Court in *Witters* as to the irrelevance of substantiality of aid in that case is therefore beside the point in the matter before us, which involves considerable sums of public funds systematically distributed through thousands of students attending religious elementary and middle schools in the city of Cleveland. . . .

It is virtually superfluous to point out that every objective underlying the prohibition of religious establishment is betrayed by this scheme, but something has to be said about the enormity of the violation. I anticipated these objectives earlier in discussing *Everson*, which cataloged them, the first being respect for freedom of conscience. Jefferson described it as the idea that no one "shall be compelled to . . . support any religious worship, place, or ministry whatsoever," A Bill for Establishing Religious Freedom.

As for the second objective, to save religion from its own corruption, Madison wrote of the "experience . . . that ecclesiastical establishments, instead of maintaining the purity and efficacy of Religion, have had a contrary operation." Memorial and Remonstrance. . . .

The risk is already being realized. In Ohio, for example, a condition of receiving government money under the program is that participating religious schools may not "discriminate on the basis of . . . religion," which means the school may not give admission preferences to children who are members of the patron faith; children of a parish are generally consigned to the same admission lotteries as non-believers. . . .

For perspective on this foot-in-the-door of religious regulation, it is well to remember that the money has barely begun to flow. Prior examples of aid, whether grants through individuals or in-kind assistance, were never significant enough to alter the basic fiscal structure of religious schools; state aid was welcome, but not indispensable. . . .

When government aid goes up, so does reliance on it; the only thing likely to go down is independence. . . .

Justice BREYER has addressed this issue in his own dissenting opinion, which I join, and here it is enough to say that the intensity of the expectable friction can be gauged by realizing that the scramble for money will energize not only contending sectarians, but taxpayers who take their liberty of conscience seriously. Religious teaching at taxpayer expense simply cannot be cordoned from taxpayer politics, and every major religion currently espouses social positions that provoke intense opposition. . . .

My own course as a judge on the Court cannot, however, simply be to hope that the political branches will save us from the consequences of the majority's decision. *Everson's* statement is still the touchstone of sound law, even though the reality is that in the matter of educational aid the Establishment Clause has largely been read away. True, the majority has not approved vouchers for religious schools alone, or aid earmarked for religious instruction. But no scheme so clumsy will ever get before us, and in the cases that we may see, like these, the Establishment Clause is largely silenced. I do not have the option to leave it silent, and I hope that a future Court will reconsider today's dramatic departure from basic Establishment Clause principle.

Elk Grove Unified School District v. Newdow
124 S.CT. 2301 (2004)

This case is excerpted here in Volume One, Chapter 2 (reprise).

B | *Free Exercise of Religion*

Locke v. Davey
124 S.CT. 1307 (2004)

Washington created a Promise Scholarship Program to assist academically gifted students, from low-income families, with postsecondary education expenses of up to $1,125 per year. In accord with the state constitution, students could not use such a scholarship to pursue a degree in theology. Article I, Section 11, of the state constitution goes beyond the First Amendment in providing that "No public money or property shall be appropriated for or applied to any religious worship, exercise or instruction, or the support of any religious establishment."

Joshua Davey was awarded a Promise Scholarship and chose to attend Northwest College, a church-affiliated institution, in order to pursue a double major in pastoral ministries and business administration. But he was told that he could not use his scholarship to pursue a pastoral degree, and he sued Governor Gary Locke and other state officials. Davey argued that the denial of the scholarship violated the First Amendment's Free Exercise. A federal district court rejected Davey's claims, but the Court of Appeals for the Ninth Circuit reversed, concluding that the state had singled out religion for unfavorable treatment and its exclusion of theology majors ran afoul of the ruling in *Church of Lukumi Babalu Aye, Inc. v. Hialeah*, 508 U. S. 520 (1993) (excerpted in Vol. 2, Ch. 5), as well as declared the program unconstitutional. Locke appealed that decision to the Supreme Court.

The appellate court's decision was reversed by a seven-to-two vote. Chief Justice Rehnquist delivered the opinion for the Court. Justices Scalia and Thomas each delivered dissenting opinions.

☐ *CHIEF JUSTICE REHNQUIST delivered the opinion of the Court.*

The Religion Clauses of the First Amendment . . . are frequently in tension. Yet we have long said that "there is room for play in the joints" between them. *Walz v. Tax Comm'n of City of New York*, 397 U. S. 664 (1970). In other words, there are some state actions permitted by the Establishment Clause but not required by the Free Exercise Clause.

This case involves that "play in the joints" described above. Under our Establishment Clause precedent, the link between government funds and religious training is broken by the independent and private choice of recipients. See *Zelman v. Simmons-Harris*, 536 U. S. 639 (2002); *Zobrest v. Catalina Foothills School Dist.*, 509 U. S. 1 (1993); *Witters v. Washington Dept. of Servs. for Blind*, 474 U. S. 481 (1986); *Mueller v. Allen*, 463 U. S. 388 (1983). As such, there is no doubt that the State could, consistent with the Federal Constitution, permit Promise Scholars to pursue a degree in devotional theology, *Witters*, and the State does not contend otherwise. The question before us, however, is whether Washington, pursuant to its own constitution, which has been authoritatively interpreted as prohibiting even indirectly funding religious instruction that will prepare students for the ministry, see *Witters v. State Comm'n for the Blind*, 112 Wash. 2d 363 (1989), can deny them such funding without violating the Free Exercise Clause.

Davey urges us to answer that question in the negative. He contends that under the rule we enunciated in *Church of Lukumi Babalu Aye, Inc. v. Hialeah* the program is presumptively unconstitutional because it is not facially neutral with respect to religion. We reject his claim of presumptive unconstitutionality, however; to do otherwise would extend the *Lukumi* line of cases well beyond not only their facts but their reasoning. In *Lukumi*, the city of Hialeah made it a crime to engage in certain kinds of animal slaughter. . . . In the present case, the State's disfavor of religion (if it can be called that) is of a far milder kind. It imposes neither criminal nor civil sanctions on any type of religious service or rite. And it does not require students to choose between their religious beliefs and receiving a government benefit. *Sherbert v. Verner*, 374 U.S. 398 (1963). The State has merely chosen not to fund a distinct category of instruction. . . .

Even though the differently worded Washington Constitution draws a more stringent line than that drawn by the United States Constitution, the interest it seeks to further is scarcely novel. . . . Most States that sought to avoid an establishment of religion around the time of the founding placed in their constitutions formal prohibitions against using tax funds to support the ministry [citing the constitutions of Georgia, Pennsylvania, Delaware, Kentucky, Vermont, Tennessee, and Ohio]. The plain text of these constitutional provisions prohibited any tax dollars from supporting the clergy. We have found nothing to indicate, as Justice SCALIA contends, that these provisions would not have applied so long as the State equally supported other professions or if the amount at stake was *de minimis*. That early state constitutions saw no problem in explicitly excluding only the ministry from receiving state dollars reinforces our conclusion that religious instruction is of a different ilk.

Far from evincing the hostility toward religion which was manifest in *Lukumi*, we believe that the entirety of the Promise Scholarship Program goes a long way toward including religion in its benefits. The program permits students to attend pervasively religious schools, so long as they are accredited. As Northwest advertises, its "concept of education is distinctly Christian in the evangelical sense." . . .

In short, we find neither in the history or text of Article I, Sec. 11 of the Washington Constitution, nor in the operation of the Promise Scholarship Program, anything that suggests animus towards religion. Given the historic and substantial state interest at issue, we therefore cannot conclude that the denial of funding for vocational religious instruction alone is inherently constitutionally suspect. . . .

The judgment of the Court of Appeals is therefore reversed.

☐ *Justice SCALIA, with whom Justice THOMAS joins, dissenting.*

In *Church of Lukumi Babalu Aye, Inc. v. Hialeah*, 508 U. S. 520 (1993), the majority opinion held that "[a] law burdening religious practice that is not neutral . . . must undergo the most rigorous of scrutiny," and that "the minimum requirement of neutrality is that a law not discriminate on its face." [That decision is] irreconcilable with today's decision, which sustains a public benefits program that facially discriminates against religion.

We articulated the principle that governs this case more than 50 years ago in *Everson v. Board of Ed. of Ewing*, 330 U. S. 1 (1947). . . . When the State makes a public benefit generally available, that benefit becomes part of the baseline against which burdens on religion are measured; and when the State withholds that benefit from some individuals solely on the basis of religion, it violates the Free Exercise Clause no less than if it had imposed a special tax.

That is precisely what the State of Washington has done here. It has created a generally available public benefit, whose receipt is conditioned only on academic performance, income, and attendance at an accredited school. It has then carved out a solitary course of study for exclusion: theology. No field of study but religion is singled out for disfavor in this fashion. Davey . . . seeks only equal treatment—the right to direct his scholarship to his chosen course of study, a right every other Promise Scholar enjoys.

The Court's reference to historical "popular uprisings against procuring taxpayer funds to support church leaders" is therefore quite misplaced. That history involved not the inclusion of religious ministers in public benefits programs like the one at issue here, but laws that singled them out for financial aid. One can concede the Framers' hostility to funding the clergy specifically, but that says nothing about whether the clergy had to be excluded from benefits the State made available to all. No one would seriously contend, for example, that the Framers would have barred ministers from using public roads on their way to church.

The Court does not dispute that the Free Exercise Clause places some constraints on public benefits programs, but finds none here, based on a principle of " 'play in the joints.' " I use the term "principle" loosely, for that is not so much a legal principle as a refusal to apply any principle when faced with competing constitutional directives. There is nothing anomalous about constitutional commands that abut. A municipality hiring public contractors may not discriminate against blacks or in favor of them; it cannot discriminate a little bit each way and then plead "play in the joints" when hauled into court. If the Religion Clauses demand neutrality, we must enforce them, in hard cases as well as easy ones. . . .

In any case, the State already has all the play in the joints it needs. There are any number of ways it could respect both its unusually sensitive concern for the conscience of its taxpayers and the Federal Free Exercise Clause. It could make the scholarships redeemable only at public universities (where it sets the curriculum), or only for select courses of study. Either option would replace a program that facially discriminates against religion with one that just happens not to subsidize it. The State could also simply abandon the scholarship program altogether. If that seems a dear price to pay for freedom of conscience, it is only because the State has defined that freedom so broadly that it would be offended by a program with such an incidental, indirect religious effect.

What is the nature of the State's asserted interest here? [T]he interest to which the Court defers is not fear of a conceivable Establishment Clause violation, budget constraints, avoidance of endorsement, or substantive neutrality—none of these. It is a pure philosophical preference: the State's opinion that it would violate taxpayers' freedom of conscience not to discriminate against candidates for the ministry. This sort of protection of "freedom of conscience" has no logical limit and can justify the singling out of religion for exclusion from public programs in virtually any context. . . .

The Court has not approached other forms of discrimination this way. When we declared racial segregation unconstitutional, we did not ask whether the State had originally adopted the regime, not out of "animus" against blacks, but because of a well-meaning but misguided belief that the races would be better off apart. It was sufficient to note the current effect of segregation on racial minorities. Similarly, the Court does not excuse statutes that facially discriminate against women just because they are the vestigial product of a well-intentioned view of women's appropriate social role. . . .

It may be that Washington's original purpose in excluding the clergy from public benefits was benign, [b]ut those singled out for disfavor can be forgiven for suspecting more invidious forces at work. Let there be no doubt: This case is about discrimination against a religious minority. Most citizens of this country identify themselves as professing some religious belief, but the State's policy poses no obstacle to practitioners of only a tepid, civic version of faith. Those the statutory exclusion actually affects—those whose belief in their religion is so strong that they dedicate their study and their lives to its ministry—are a far narrower set. One need not delve too far into modern popular culture to perceive a trendy disdain for deep religious conviction. In an era when the Court is so quick to come to the aid of other disfavored groups, see, *Romer v. Evans*, 517 U. S. 620 (1996), its indifference in this case, which involves a form of discrimination to which the Constitution actually speaks, is exceptional. . . . I respectfully dissent.

7

THE FOURTH AMENDMENT
GUARANTEE AGAINST
UNREASONABLE SEARCHES
AND SEIZURES

A | *Requirements for a Warrant and*
  | *Reasonable Searches and Seizures*

The Court reaffirmed the core principle that a warrant must describe the items to be seized in *Groh v. Ramirez*, 124 S.Ct. 1284 (2004), when holding that a search warrant violated the Fourth Amendment as it failed to identify the items to be seized and described the defendant's house only as the place to be searched. Writing for the Court, Justice Stevens reminded law enforcement officers, who have had greater freedom to conduct searches under the USA PATRIOT Act: "Given that the particularity requirement is set forth in the text of the Constitution, no reasonable officer could believe that a warrant that plainly did not comply with that requirement was valid."

In its 2004–2005 term, the Court will consider, in *Devenpeck v. Alford* (No. 03-710), whether after stopping a suspicious car an officer had probable cause to arrest the driver for a "closely related" offense and whether, under the Privacy Act, a suspect may secretly tape a conversation that occurs during a routine traffic stop. Tony Alford stopped to help some stranded motorists and left when Joi Haner, a Washington state trooper, arrived. The motorists informed Haner that Alford's headlights were flashing and they believed he was a police officer. Haner became concerned that Alford was pretending to be an officer and pulled him over to question him about the lights. Alford claimed an alarm system had been installed earlier in the day and he did not know how to work it properly. However, Haner noticed that Alford had an amateur radio broadcasting the communications of the sheriff's office, a microphone, a portable police scanner, and handcuffs. A little later, Gerald Devenpeck, a patrol sergeant, arrived and, during his questioning of Alford, noticed that Alford was recording the conversation. He ordered Haner to remove Alford from the car and informed Alford he was under arrest for making an illegal tape recording. Alford countered that the Privacy Act did not apply to police officers working in their official capacity. Nonetheless, he was arrested and spent the night in jail. Subsequently, Alford sued the officers, alleging that his arrest, incarceration, and prosecution violated the Fourth Amendment right against unreasonable seizures. In a federal district court, a jury found in favor of the officers and Alford appealed. The U.S. Court of Appeals for the Ninth Circuit reversed, ruling that the officers did not have probable cause to justify an arrest for violating the Privacy Act or other offenses unrelated to the tape recording, and that the Privacy Act prohibits recording of private conversations only and a traffic stop is not a private encounter.

B | *Exceptions to the Warrant Requirement*

The Court reaffirmed three earlier interrelated rulings, bearing on searches of citizens in public places, that the "consent" of a passenger on a bus to a request by an officer to a pat-down search for contraband, *Minnesota v. Dickerson*, 508 U.S. 366 (1993) (excerpted in Vol. 2, Ch. 7), "presupposes an innocent person" would consent, *Florida v. Bostick*, 501 U.S. 429 (1991), and that the officers are not required to inform citizens of their right to refuse, *Ohio v. Robinette*, 519 U.S. 33 (1996). Here three law enforcement officers boarded a bus in Tallahassee, Florida, which was bound for Detroit, Michigan. One sat in the driver's seat, another in the back of the bus, and the third questioned passengers. Two young men wearing jackets and baggy pants, in the summer, were questioned and consented to pat-downs, which revealed plastic bags of cocaine under their clothing. Writing for the Court in *United States v. Drayton*, 536 U.S. 194 (2002), Justice Kennedy observed:

Law enforcement officers do not violate the Fourth Amendment's prohibition of unreasonable seizures merely by approaching individuals on the street or in other public places and putting questions to them if they are willing to listen. Even when law enforcement officers have no basis for suspecting a particular individual, they may pose questions, ask for identification, and request consent to search luggage—provided they do not induce cooperation by coercive means. See *Florida v. Bostick*, 501 U.S. [429 (1991)]. If a reasonable person would feel free to terminate the encounter, then he or she has not been seized.

The Court has addressed on a previous occasion the specific question of drug interdiction efforts on buses. In *Bostick*, two police officers requested a bus passenger's consent to a search of his luggage. The passenger agreed, and the resulting search revealed cocaine in his suitcase. . . .

Bostick first made it clear that for the most part per se rules are inappropriate in the Fourth Amendment context. The proper inquiry necessitates a consideration of "all the circumstances surrounding the encounter." The Court noted next that the traditional rule, which states that a seizure does not occur so long as a reasonable person would feel free "to disregard the police and go about his business," *California v. Hodari D.*, 499 U.S. 621 (1991), is not an accurate measure of the coercive effect of a bus encounter. A passenger may not want to get off a bus if there is a risk it will depart before the opportunity to reboard. A bus rider's movements are confined in this sense, but this is the natural result of choosing to take the bus; it says nothing about whether the police conduct is coercive. The proper inquiry "is whether a reasonable person would feel free to decline the officers' requests or otherwise terminate the encounter." Finally, the Court rejected Bostick's argument that he must have been seized because no reasonable person would consent to a search of luggage containing drugs. The reasonable person test, the Court explained, is objective and "presupposes an innocent person."

Justice Souter dissented and was joined by Justices Stevens and Ginsburg.

The Court reaffirmed its view that police have flexibility, because of potential physical harm and the risk that suspects may destroy evidence, when announcing their presence and entry into the home of suspected drug dealers, in *United States v. Banks*, 124 U.S. 521 (2003). Writing for a unanimous Court, Justice Souter held that the reasonableness of a forced entry under the "knock and announce" rule depends on the "totality of the circumstances," not how long police wait; here, police entered a house 15–20 seconds after announcing. The Court reaffirmed its view that police have flexibility, because of their presence.

In *Kaupp v. Texas*, 538 U.S. 626 (2003), the Court reaffirmed the central principle that an illegal search and seizure, without probable cause, precludes the admission as evidence of incriminating statements made by the accused prior to arrest and reaffirmed the contours of "consent" to a search. However, in *Hiibel v. Sixth Judicial District of Nevada* (2004) (excerpted below) a bare majority held an individual may be arrested for not identifying himself during a *Terry* stop by police.

Hiibel v. Sixth Judicial District of Nevada
124 S.Ct. 2451 (2004)

The Humboldt County, Nevada, sheriff's department received a call reporting a man assaulting a woman in a red and silver GMC truck on Grass Valley Road. Deputy sheriff Lee Dove was dispatched, and when he arrived, he found the truck parked. A man was standing by the truck, and a young woman was sitting inside it. Dove approached the man and explained that he was investigating a fight. The man appeared intoxicated and Dove asked him if he had any identification. The man asked why the officer wanted to see identification. Dove responded that he was conducting an investigation and wanted to find out who the man was and what he was doing there. After continued refusals to comply with the request to show the officer identification, the man began to taunt Dove by placing his hands behind his back and asking Dove to arrest him. Dove asked for identification eleven times and finally arrested the man, Larry Dudley Hiibel. Hiibel was charged with resisting arrest and obstructing a public officer in discharging his legal duties in violation of state law. At his trial Hiibel claimed unsuccessfully that the state law violated the Fourth and Fifth Amendments. On appeal the state supreme court affirmed the lower court, and Hiibel appealed to the U.S. Supreme Court.

The state supreme court's decision was affirmed by a five-to-four vote. The opinion for the Court was delivered by Justice Kennedy. Justices Stevens and Breyer filed dissenting opinions; Justices Souter and Ginsburg joined the latter's dissent.

□ *Justice KENNEDY delivered the opinion of the Court.*

The petitioner was arrested and convicted for refusing to identify himself during a stop allowed by *Terry v. Ohio*, 392 U.S. 1 (1968). He challenges his conviction under the Fourth and Fifth Amendments to the United States Constitution, applicable to the States through the Fourteenth Amendment. . . .

Stop and identify statutes often combine elements of traditional vagrancy laws with provisions intended to regulate police behavior in the course of investigatory stops. The statutes vary from State to State, but all permit an officer to ask or require a suspect to disclose his identity. . . .

Stop and identify statutes have their roots in early English vagrancy laws that required suspected vagrants to face arrest unless they gave "a good Account of themselves," a power that itself reflected common-law rights of private persons to "arrest any suspicious night-walker, and detain him till he give a good account of himself. . . ." 2 W. Hawkins, *Pleas of the Crown* (6th ed. 1787). In recent decades, the Court has found constitutional infirmity in traditional vagrancy laws. In *Papachristou v. Jacksonville*, 405 U.S. 156 (1972), the Court held that a traditional vagrancy law was void for vagueness. Its broad scope and imprecise terms denied proper notice to potential offenders and permitted police officers to exercise unfettered discretion in the enforcement of the law.

The Court has recognized similar constitutional limitations on the scope and operation of stop and identify statutes. In *Brown v. Texas*, 443 U.S. 47 (1979), the Court invalidated a conviction for violating a Texas stop and identify statute on Fourth Amendment grounds. The Court ruled that the initial stop was not based on specific, objective facts establishing reasonable suspicion to believe the suspect was involved in criminal activity. Absent that factual basis for detaining the defendant, the Court held, the risk of "arbitrary and abusive police practices" was too great and the stop was impermissible. Four Terms later, the Court invalidated a modified stop and identify statute on vagueness grounds. The California law in *Kolender* [*v. Lawson*, 461 U.S. 352 (1983),] required a suspect to give an officer "'credible and reliable'" identification when asked to identify himself. The Court held that the statute was void because it provided no standard for determining what a suspect must do to comply with it, resulting in "'virtually unrestrained power to arrest and charge persons with a violation.'"

The present case begins where our prior cases left off. Here there is no question that the initial stop was based on reasonable suspicion, satisfying the Fourth Amendment requirements noted in *Brown*. Further, the petitioner has not alleged that the statute is unconstitutionally vague, as in *Kolender*. Here the Nevada statute is narrower and more precise. The statute in *Kolender* had been interpreted to require a suspect to give the officer "credible and reliable" identification. In contrast, the Nevada Supreme Court has interpreted [the state law] to require only that a suspect disclose his name. As we understand it, the statute does not require a suspect to give the officer a driver's license or any other document. Provided that the suspect either states his name or communicates it to the officer by other means—a choice, we assume, that the suspect may make—the statute is satisfied and no violation occurs.

Hiibel argues that his conviction cannot stand because the officer's conduct violated his Fourth Amendment rights. We disagree.

Asking questions is an essential part of police investigations. In the ordinary course a police officer is free to ask a person for identification without implicating the Fourth Amendment. Beginning with *Terry v. Ohio*, 392 U.S. 1 (1968), the Court has recognized that a law enforcement officer's reasonable suspicion that a person may be involved in criminal activity permits the officer to stop the person for a brief time and take additional steps to investigate further. To ensure that the resulting seizure is constitutionally reasonable, a *Terry* stop must be limited. The officer's action must be "'justified at its inception, and reasonably related in scope to the circumstances which justified the interference in the first place.'" . . .

Obtaining a suspect's name in the course of a *Terry* stop serves important government interests. Knowledge of identity may inform an officer that a suspect is wanted for another offense, or has a record of violence or mental disorder. On the other hand, knowing identity may help clear a suspect and allow the police to concentrate their efforts elsewhere. Identity may prove particularly important in cases such as this, where the police are investigating what appears to be a domestic assault. Officers called to investigate domestic disputes need to know whom they are dealing with in order to assess the situation, the threat to their own safety, and possible danger to the potential victim. . . .

The principles of *Terry* permit a State to require a suspect to disclose his name in the course of a *Terry* stop. The reasonableness of a seizure under the Fourth Amendment is determined "by balancing its intrusion on the individual's Fourth Amendment interests against its promotion of legitimate government interests." *Delaware v. Prouse*, 440 U.S. 648 (1979). The Nevada statute satisfies that standard. The request for identity has an immediate relation to the purpose, rationale, and practical demands of a *Terry* stop. The threat of criminal sanction helps ensure that the request for identity does not become a legal nullity. On the other hand, the Nevada statute does not alter the nature of the stop itself: it does not change its duration, or its location. . . .

Petitioner further contends that his conviction violates the Fifth Amendment's prohibition on compelled self-incrimination. . . .

The Fifth Amendment prohibits only compelled testimony that is incriminating. A claim of Fifth Amendment privilege must establish "'reasonable ground to apprehend danger to the witness from his being compelled to answer. . . . [T]he danger to be apprehended must be real and appreciable, with reference to the ordinary operation of law in the ordinary course of things—not a danger of an imaginary and unsubstantial character, having reference to some extraordinary and barely possible contingency, so improbable that no reasonable man would suffer it to influence his conduct.'"(quoting *Queen v. Boyes*, 1 Best & S. 311 1861). . . .

In this case petitioner's refusal to disclose his name was not based on any articulated real and appreciable fear that his name would be used to incriminate him, or that it "would furnish a link in the chain of evidence needed to prosecute" him. As best we can tell, petitioner refused to identify himself only because he thought his name was none of the officer's business. Even today, petitioner does not explain how the disclosure of his name could have been used against him in a criminal case. While we recognize petitioner's strong belief that he should not have to disclose his identity, the Fifth Amendment does not override the Nevada Legislature's judgment to the contrary absent a reasonable belief that the disclosure would tend to incriminate him.

The narrow scope of the disclosure requirement is also important. One's identity is, by definition, unique; yet it is, in another sense, a universal characteristic. Answering a request to disclose a name is likely to be so insignificant in the scheme of things as to be incriminating only in unusual circumstances. Even witnesses who plan to invoke the Fifth Amendment privilege answer when their names are called to take the stand. Still, a case may arise where there is a substantial allegation that furnishing identity at the time of a stop would have given the police a link in the chain of evidence needed to convict the individual of a separate offense. In that case, the court can then consider whether the privilege applies, and, if the Fifth Amendment has been violated, what remedy must follow. We need not resolve those questions here.

☐ *Justice STEVENS, dissenting.*

Under the Nevada law, [r]efusal to identify oneself upon request is punishable as a crime. Presumably the statute does not require the detainee to answer any other question because the Nevada Legislature realized that the Fifth Amendment prohibits compelling the target of a criminal investigation to make any other statement. In my judgment, the broad constitutional right to remain silent, which derives from the Fifth Amendment's guarantee that "[n]o person . . . shall be compelled in any criminal case to be a witness against himself," is not as circumscribed as the Court suggests, and does not admit even of the narrow exception defined by the Nevada statute. . . .

It is a "settled principle" that "the police have the right to request citizens to answer voluntarily questions concerning unsolved crimes," but "they have no right to compel them to answer." *Davis v. Mississipi*, 394 U.S. 721 (1969). The protections of the Fifth Amendment are directed squarely toward those who are the focus of the government's investigative and prosecutorial powers. In a criminal trial, the indicted defendant has an unqualified right to refuse to testify and may not be punished for invoking that right. The unindicted target of a grand jury investigation enjoys the same constitutional protection even if he has been served with a subpoena. So does an arrested suspect during custodial interrogation in a police station. *Miranda* [*v. Arizona*, 384 U.S. 436 (1966)].

There is no reason why the subject of police interrogation based on mere suspicion, rather than probable cause, should have any lesser protection. Indeed, we have said that the Fifth Amendment's protections apply with equal force in the context of *Terry* stops, where an officer's inquiry "must be 'reasonably related in scope to the justification for [the stop's] initiation.'" *Berkemer v. McCarty*, 468 U.S. 420 (1984). Given our statements to the effect that citizens are not required to respond to police officers' questions during a *Terry* stop, it is no surprise that petitioner assumed, as have we, that he had a right not to disclose his identity.

The Court correctly observes that a communication does not enjoy the Fifth Amendment privilege unless it is testimonial. Although the Court declines to resolve this question, I think it clear that this case concerns a testimonial communication. Recognizing that whether a communication is testimonial is sometimes a "difficult question," we have stated generally that "[i]t is the 'extortion of information from the accused,' the attempt to force him 'to disclose the contents of his own mind,' that implicates the Self-Incrimination Clause." While "[t]he vast majority of verbal statements thus will be testimonial and, to that extent at least, will fall within the privilege," certain acts and physical evidence fall outside the privilege. . . .

Considered in light of these precedents, the compelled statement at issue in this case is clearly testimonial. . . . Surely police questioning during a *Terry* stop qualifies as an interrogation, and it follows that responses to such questions are testimonial in nature. . . .

A person's identity obviously bears informational and incriminating worth, "even if the [name] itself is not inculpatory." A name can provide the key to a broad array of information about the person, particularly in the hands of a police officer with access to a range of law enforcement databases. And that information, in turn, can be tremendously useful in a criminal prosecution. It is therefore quite wrong to suggest that a person's identity provides a link in the chain to incriminating evidence "only in unusual circumstances."

The officer in this case told petitioner, in the Court's words, that "he was conducting an investigation and needed to see some identification." As the target of that investigation, petitioner, in my view, acted well within his rights when he opted to stand mute. Accordingly, I respectfully dissent.

☐ *Justice BREYER, with whom Justice SOUTER and Justice GINSBURG join, dissenting.*

In *Terry v. Ohio*, 392 U.S. 1 (1968), the Court considered whether police, in the absence of probable cause, can stop, question, or frisk an individual at all.

The Court recognized that the Fourth Amendment protects the " 'right of every individual to the possession and control of his own person.' "...About 10 years later, the Court, in *Brown v. Texas*, 443 U.S. 47 (1979), held that police lacked "any reasonable suspicion" to detain the particular petitioner and require him to identify himself...Then, five years later, the Court wrote that an "officer may ask the [*Terry*] detainee a moderate number of questions to determine his identity and to try to obtain information confirming or dispelling the officer's suspicions. But the detainee is not obliged to respond." *Berkemer v. McCarty*, 468 U.S. 420 (1984). See also *Illinois v. Wardlow*, 528 U.S. 119 (2000) (stating that allowing officers to stop and question a fleeing person "is quite consistent with the individual's right to go about his business or to stay put and remain silent in the face of police questioning")....

There is no good reason now to reject this generation-old statement of the law. There are sound reasons rooted in Fifth Amendment considerations for adhering to this Fourth Amendment legal condition circumscribing police authority to stop an individual against his will. Administrative considerations also militate against change. Can a State, in addition to requiring a stopped individual to answer "What's your name?" also require an answer to "What's your license number?" or "Where do you live?" Can a police officer, who must know how to make a *Terry* stop, keep track of the constitutional answers? After all, answers to any of these questions may, or may not, incriminate, depending upon the circumstances.

Indeed, as the majority points out, a name itself—even if it is not "Killer Bill" or "Rough 'em up Harry"—will sometimes provide the police with "a link in the chain of evidence needed to convict the individual of a separate offense." The majority reserves judgment about whether compulsion is permissible in such instances. How then is a police officer in the midst of a *Terry* stop to distinguish between the majority's ordinary case and this special case where the majority reserves judgment?

The majority presents no evidence that the rule enunciated by Justice WHITE and then by the *Berkemer* Court, which for nearly a generation has set forth a settled *Terry*-stop condition, has significantly interfered with law enforcement. Nor has the majority presented any other convincing justification for change. I would not begin to erode a clear rule with special exceptions. I consequently dissent.

C | *The Special Problems of Automobiles in a Mobile Society*

In its 2003 term the Court limited its earlier ruling in *Indianapolis v. Edmond*, 531 U.S. 32 (2000), which held that police may not search cars at checkpoints for drugs solely in order to advance a state's "general interest in crime control," in contrast with sobriety checkpoints. In *Illinois v. Lidster* (excerpted below), the Court distinguished and limited *Edmond* in upholding "informational checkpoints" that aim to obtain information pertaining to a criminal activity—in this case, the identity of the driver involved in a hit-and-run accident. The decision has broad implications in sanctioning such checkpoints, which have become increasingly common in police investigations for missing persons and individuals suspected of criminal activities.

The Court also reaffirmed and extended its ruling in *New York v. Belton*, 453 U.S. 454 (1981), holding that when police make a custodial arrest of a driver, they may search the car as a contemporaneous incident of the arrest. In *Thorton v. United States*, 124 S.Ct. 2127 (2004), Chief Justice Rehnquist held that under *Belton* police could permissibly search the passenger compartment of a car after the driver got out and a pat-down search revealed drugs in his pocket, for which he was arrested. A subsequent search of the car revealed a handgun under the driver's seat, for which Thorton, the driver, was also prosecuted. Justices Stevens and Souter dissented.

In its 2004–2005 term, the Court will consider the application of the test in *Terry v. Ohio* (1968) (excerpted in Vol. 2, Ch. 7) to the search of an automobile stopped for a traffic violation, after which a police dog indicated that marijuana was in the trunk, leading police to search the car. Roy Caballes was stopped for speeding by an Illinois state trooper. Caballes told the officer he was traveling cross country, although he had no visible luggage, and appeared nervous, in spite of the officer's assuring him that he would just receive a traffic ticket. Another trooper arrived with a canine who sniffed around the car for the scent of illegal drugs and alerted the troopers to the scent of marijuana in the trunk. The trunk was searched and drugs were found. At trial, Caballes's attorney moved to suppress the drugs but was denied. An appellate court affirmed Caballes's conviction, holding that "the police did not need reasonable articulate suspicion to justify the canine sniff." But the Supreme Court of Illinois reversed and applied the *Terry v. Ohio* test, which requires the officers' actions to be justified and reasonably related to the reason for the stop in the first place. That court found the search of the trunk to exceed the scope of a traffic stop because there was not enough evidence that drugs would be found to justify the canine sniff. The state appealed that decision.

Illinois v. Lidster
124 S.CT. 885 (2004)

Shortly after midnight in Lombard, Illinois, a seventy-year-old bicyclist was killed in a hit-and-run accident. A week later, at about the same time and same place, police set up a highway checkpoint. Drivers were stopped, asked whether they had witnessed the incident, and given a flyer requesting assistance in identifying the vehicle and driver. As Robert Lidster approached the checkpoint, his van swerved, nearly hitting an officer, and subsequently he failed a sobriety test. Following his arrest and conviction for driving under the influence of alcohol, his attorney challenged the lawfulness of the arrest and conviction on the ground that the informational checkpoint stop violated the Fourth Amendment. The trial court dismissed the challenge, but the Illinois state supreme court disagreed and held that under *Indianapolis v. Edmond*, 431 U.S. 32 (2000), such informational checkpoint stops lack individual suspicion and, hence, run afoul of the Fourth Amendment.

The state supreme court's decision was reversed by a vote of six to three. Justice Breyer announced the judment of the Court. Justice Stevens, joined by Justices Souter and Ginsburg, filed an opinion in part concurring and dissenting.

☐ *Justice BREYER delivered the opinion of the Court.*

This Fourth Amendment case focuses upon a highway checkpoint where police stopped motorists to ask them for information about a recent hit-and-run accident. We hold that the police stops were reasonable, hence, constitutional.

The Illinois Supreme Court basically held that our decision in [*Indianapolis v.*] *Edmond*, [531 U.S. 32 (2000)] governs the outcome of this case. We do not agree. *Edmond* involved a checkpoint at which police stopped vehicles to look for evidence of drug crimes committed by occupants of those vehicles. After stopping a vehicle at the checkpoint, police would examine (from outside the vehicle) the vehicle's interior; they would walk a drug-sniffing dog around the exterior; and, if they found sufficient evidence of drug (or other) crimes, they would arrest the vehicle's occupants. We found that police had set up this checkpoint primarily for general "crime control" purposes, i.e., "to detect evidence of ordinary criminal wrongdoing." We noted that the stop was made without individualized suspicion. And we held that the Fourth Amendment forbids such a stop, in the absence of special circumstances.

The checkpoint stop here differs significantly from that in *Edmond*. The stop's primary law enforcement purpose was not to determine whether a vehicle's occupants were committing a crime, but to ask vehicle occupants, as members of the public, for their help in providing information about a crime in all likelihood committed by others. The police expected the information elicited to help them apprehend, not the vehicle's occupants, but other individuals. . . .

We concede that *Edmond* describes the law enforcement objective there in question as a "general interest in crime control," but it specifies that the phrase "general interest in crime control" does not refer to every "law enforcement" objective. We must read this and related general language in *Edmond* as we often read general language in judicial opinions—as referring in context to circumstances similar to the circumstances then before the Court and not referring to quite different circumstances that the Court was not then considering.

Neither do we believe, *Edmond* aside, that the Fourth Amendment would have us apply an *Edmond*-type rule of automatic unconstitutionality to brief, information-seeking highway stops of the kind now before us. For one thing, the fact that such stops normally lack individualized suspicion cannot by itself determine the constitutional outcome. The Fourth Amendment does not treat a motorist's car as his castle. And special law enforcement concerns will sometimes justify highway stops without individualized suspicion. See *Michigan Dept. of State Police v. Sitz*, 496 U. S. 444 (1990) (sobriety checkpoint); [*United States v.*] *Martinez-Fuerte*, [428 U.S. 543 (1976)] (Border Patrol checkpoint). Moreover, unlike *Edmond*, the context here (seeking information from the public) is one in which, by definition, the concept of individualized suspicion has little role to play. Like certain other forms of police activity, say, crowd control or public safety, an information-seeking stop is not the kind of event that involves suspicion, or lack of suspicion, of the relevant individual.

For another thing, information-seeking highway stops are less likely to provoke anxiety or to prove intrusive. The stops are likely brief. The police are not likely to ask questions designed to elicit self-incriminating information. . . .

Finally, we do not believe that an *Edmond*-type rule is needed to prevent an unreasonable proliferation of police checkpoints. Practical considerations—namely, limited police resources and community hostility to related traffic tie-ups—seem likely to inhibit any such proliferation. And, of course, the Fourth Amendment's normal insistence that the stop be reasonable in context will still provide an important legal limitation on police use of this kind of information-seeking checkpoint. . . .

We hold that the stop was constitutional. . . . The relevant public concern was grave. Police were investigating a crime that had resulted in a human death. . . . The stop advanced this grave public concern to a significant degree. Most importantly, the stops interfered only minimally with liberty of the sort the Fourth Amendment seeks to protect. Viewed objectively, each stop required only a brief wait in line—a very few minutes at most. . . . Viewed subjectively, the contact provided little reason for anxiety or alarm. The police stopped all vehicles systematically. And there is no allegation here that the police acted in a discriminatory or otherwise unlawful manner while questioning motorists during stops.

For these reasons we conclude that the checkpoint stop was constitutional.

☐ *Justice STEVENS, with whom Justice SOUTER and Justice GINSBURG join, concurring in part and dissenting in part.*

There is a valid and important distinction between seizing a person to determine whether she has committed a crime and seizing a person to ask whether she has any information about an unknown person who committed a crime a week earlier. I therefore join [p]arts of the Court's opinion explaining why our decision in *Indianapolis v. Edmond* is not controlling in this case. However, I find the issue . . . closer than the Court does and believe it would be wise to remand the case to the Illinois state courts to address that issue in the first instance.

In contrast to pedestrians, who are free to keep walking when they encounter police officers handing out flyers or seeking information, motorists who confront a roadblock are required to stop, and to remain stopped for as long as the officers choose to detain them. Such a seizure may seem relatively innocuous to some, but annoying to others who are forced to wait for several minutes when the line of cars is lengthened—for example, by a surge of vehicles leaving a factory at the end of a shift. Still other drivers may find an unpublicized roadblock at midnight on a Saturday somewhat alarming.

On the other side of the equation, the likelihood that questioning a random sample of drivers will yield useful information about a hit-and-run accident that occurred a week earlier is speculative at best. To be sure, the sample in this case was not entirely random: The record reveals that the police knew that the victim had finished work at the Post Office shortly before the fatal accident, and hoped that other employees of the Post Office or the nearby industrial park might work on similar schedules and, thus, have been driving the same route at the same time the previous week. That is a plausible theory, but there is no evidence in the record that the police did anything to confirm that the nearby businesses in fact had shift changes at or near midnight on Saturdays, or that they had reason to believe that a roadblock would be more effective than, say, placing flyers on the employees' cars.

In short, [w]e should be especially reluctant to abandon our role as a court of review in a case in which the constitutional inquiry requires analysis of local conditions and practices more familiar to judges closer to the scene. I would therefore remand the case to the Illinois courts to undertake the initial analysis of the issue that the Court resolves in . . . its opinion. To that extent, I respectfully dissent.

■ THE DEVELOPMENT OF LAW

Automobiles and Border Patrol Searches

CASE	VOTE	RULING
United States v. Arvizu, 534 U.S. 161 (2002)	9:0	Writing for the Court, Chief Justice Rehnquist held that under *Terry v. Ohio,* 392 U.S. 1 (1968),

based on "the totality of the circumstances" an experienced border patrol officer had "reasonable suspicion" to stop on an unpaved road in a remote area of Arizona an otherwise innocuous automobile, which in turn led to a search that uncovered over 100 pounds of marijuana.

United States v. Flores-Montano, 124 S.Ct. 1582 (2004)	9:0	International border customs officers may, without reasonable suspicion, search, remove, disassemble, and reassemble a vehicle's gas tank, in order to search for drugs or

other contraband. Writing for the Court, Chief Justice Rehnquist held that the government's interests in protecting the border is at its "zenith" at international borders and paramount to any privacy interests in an automobile.

D | *Other Governmental Searches in the Administrative State*

Board of Education of Independent School District No. 92 of Pottawatomie City v. Earls
536 U.S. 822, 122 S.CT. 2559 (2002)

Following the Court's upholding of random drug testing of high school athletes, in *Vernonia School District No. 47J v. Acton*, 515 U.S. 646 (1995) (excerpted in Vol. 2, Ch. 7), in 1998 the school district of Tecumseh, Oklahoma, a rural community about 40 miles from Oklahoma City, adopted a policy of requiring all middle and high school students who participate in any extracurricular activities to consent to random drug testing. Lindsay Earls, a member of the choir and the marching band, challenged the constitutionality of the policy for violating the Fourth Amendment guarantee against unreasonable searches and seizures. A federal district court rejected her claim, but the Court of Appeals for the Tenth Circuit reversed and the school board appealed.

The appellate court's decision was reversed by a five-to-four vote. Justice Thomas delivered the opinion of the Court. Justice Breyer filed a concurring opinion. Justices O'Connor and Ginsburg filed dissenting opinions, which Justices Stevens and Souter joined.

☐ *Justice THOMAS delivered the opinion of the Court.*

The Fourth Amendment to the United States Constitution protects "[t]he right of the people to be secure in their persons, houses, papers, and effects, against unreasonable searches and seizures." Searches by public school officials, such as the collection of urine samples, implicate Fourth Amendment interests. See *Vernonia; New Jersey v. T. L. O.*, 469 U.S. 325 (1985). We must therefore review the School District's Policy for "reasonableness," which is the touchstone of the constitutionality of a governmental search.

In the criminal context, reasonableness usually requires a showing of probable cause. See, e.g., *Skinner v. Railway Labor Executives' Assn.*, 489 U.S. 602 (1989). The probable-cause standard, however, "is peculiarly related to criminal investigations" and may be unsuited to determining the reasonableness of administrative searches where the "Government seeks to prevent the development of hazardous conditions." *Treasury Employees v. Von Raab*, 489 U.S. 656 (1989).

Given that the School District's Policy is not in any way related to the conduct of criminal investigations, respondents do not contend that the School District requires probable cause before testing students for drug use. Respondents instead argue that drug testing must be based at least on some level of individualized suspicion. It is true that we generally determine the reasonableness of a search by balancing the nature of the intrusion on the individual's privacy against the promotion of legitimate governmental interests. But we have long held that "the Fourth Amendment imposes no irreducible requirement of [individualized] suspicion." *United States v. Martinez-Fuerte*, 428 U.S. 543 (1976).

Significantly, this Court has previously held that "special needs" inhere in the public school context. While schoolchildren do not shed their constitutional rights when they enter the schoolhouse, see *Tinker v. Des Moines Independent Community School Dist.*, 393 U.S. 503 (1969), "Fourth Amendment rights . . . are different in public schools than elsewhere; the 'reasonableness' inquiry cannot disregard the schools' custodial and tutelary responsibility for children." *Vernonia.* In particular, a finding of individualized suspicion may not be necessary when a school conducts drug testing.

In *Vernonia*, this Court held that the suspicionless drug testing of athletes was constitutional. Applying the principles of *Vernonia* to the somewhat different facts of this case, we conclude that Tecumseh's Policy is also constitutional.

We first consider the nature of the privacy interest allegedly compromised by the drug testing. . . . A student's privacy interest is limited in a public school environment where the State is responsible for maintaining discipline, health, and safety. Schoolchildren are routinely required to submit to physical examinations and vaccinations against disease. Securing order in the school environment sometimes requires that students be subjected to greater controls than those appropriate for adults.

Respondents argue that because children participating in nonathletic extracurricular activities are not subject to regular physicals and communal undress, they have a stronger expectation of privacy than the athletes tested in *Vernonia*. This distinction, however, was not essential to our decision in *Vernonia*, which depended primarily upon the school's custodial responsibility and authority.

In any event, students who participate in competitive extracurricular activities voluntarily subject themselves to many of the same intrusions on their privacy as do athletes. Some of these clubs and activities require occasional off-campus travel and communal undress. All of them have their own rules and requirements for participating students that do not apply to the student body as a whole.

Next, we consider the character of the intrusion imposed by the Policy. Urination is "an excretory function traditionally shielded by great privacy." *Skinner.* But the "degree of intrusion" on one's privacy caused by collecting a urine sample "depends upon the manner in which production of the urine sample is monitored." *Vernonia.*

Under the Policy, a faculty monitor waits outside the closed restroom stall for the student to produce a sample and must "listen for the normal sounds of urination in order to guard against tampered specimens and to insure an accurate chain of custody." The monitor then pours the sample into two bottles that are sealed and placed into a mailing pouch along with a consent form signed by the student. This procedure is virtually identical to that reviewed in *Vernonia*, except that it additionally protects privacy by allowing male students to produce their samples behind a closed stall. Given that we considered the method of collection in *Vernonia* a "negligible" intrusion, the method here is even less problematic. . . .

Finally, this Court must consider the nature and immediacy of the government's concerns and the efficacy of the Policy in meeting them. This Court has already articulated in detail the importance of the governmental concern in preventing drug use by schoolchildren. The drug abuse problem among our Nation's youth has hardly abated since *Vernonia* was decided in 1995. In fact, evidence suggests that it has only grown worse. As in *Vernonia*, "the necessity for the State to act is magnified by the fact that this evil is being visited not just upon individuals at large, but upon children for whom it has undertaken a special responsibility of care and direction." The health and safety risks identified in *Vernonia* apply with equal force to Tecumseh's children. Indeed, the nationwide drug epidemic makes the war against drugs a pressing concern in every school. . . .

Given the nationwide epidemic of drug use, and the evidence of increased drug use in Tecumseh schools, it was entirely reasonable for the School District to enact this particular drug testing policy. We reject the Court of Appeals' novel test that "any district seeking to impose a random suspicion-less drug testing policy as a condition to participation in a school activity must demonstrate that there is some identifiable drug abuse problem among a sufficient number of those subject to the testing, such that testing that group of students will actually redress its drug problem." Among other problems, it would be difficult to administer such a test. As we cannot articulate a threshold level of drug use that would suffice to justify a drug testing program for schoolchildren, we refuse to fashion what would in effect be a constitutional quantum of drug use necessary to show a "drug problem." . . .

We also reject respondents' argument that drug testing must presumptively be based upon an individualized reasonable suspicion of wrongdoing because such a testing regime would be less intrusive. In this context, the Fourth Amendment does not require a finding of individualized suspicion. And we decline to impose such a requirement on schools attempting to prevent and detect drug use by students. Moreover, we question whether testing based on individualized suspicion in fact would be less intrusive. Such a regime would place an additional burden on public school teachers who are already tasked with the difficult job of maintaining order and discipline. A program of individualized suspicion might unfairly target members of unpopular groups. The fear of lawsuits resulting from such targeted searches may chill enforcement of the program, rendering it ineffective in combating drug use.

Finally, we find that testing students who participate in extracurricular activities is a reasonably effective means of addressing the School District's legitimate concerns in preventing, deterring, and detecting drug use. . . . Accordingly, we reverse the judgment of the Court of Appeals. It is so ordered.

☐ *Justice O'CONNOR, with whom Justice SOUTER joins, dissenting.*

I dissented in *Vernonia School Dist. 47J v. Acton,* 515 U.S. 646 (1995), and continue to believe that case was wrongly decided. Because *Vernonia* is now this Court's precedent, and because I agree that petitioners' program fails even under the balancing approach adopted in that case, I join Justice GINSBURG's dissent.

☐ *Justice GINSBURG, with whom Justice STEVENS, Justice O'CONNOR, and Justice SOUTER join, dissenting.*

This case presents circumstances dispositively different from those of *Vernonia.* True, as the Court stresses, Tecumseh students participating in competitive extracurricular activities other than athletics share two relevant characteristics with the athletes of *Vernonia*. First, both groups attend public schools. "[O]ur decision in *Vernonia*," the Court states, "depended primarily upon the school's custodial responsibility and authority." Concern for student health and safety is basic to the school's caretaking, and it is undeniable that "drug use carries a variety of health risks for children, including death from overdose."

Those risks, however, are present for all schoolchildren. *Vernonia* cannot be read to endorse invasive and suspicionless drug testing of all students upon any evidence of drug use, solely because drugs jeopardize the life and health of those who use them. Many children, like many adults, engage in dangerous activities on their own time; that the children are enrolled in school scarcely allows government to monitor all such activities. If a student has a reasonable subjective expectation of privacy in the personal items she brings to school, surely she has a similar expectation regarding the chemical composition of her urine. Had the *Vernonia* Court agreed that public school attendance, in and of itself, permitted the State to test each student's blood or urine for drugs, the opinion in *Vernonia* could have saved many words.

The second commonality to which the Court points is the voluntary character of both interscholastic athletics and other competitive extracurricular activities. "By choosing to 'go out for the team,' [school athletes] voluntarily subject themselves to a degree of regulation even higher than that imposed on students generally." Comparably, the Court today observes, "students who participate in competitive extracurricular activities voluntarily subject themselves to" additional rules not applicable to other students. . . .

The comparison is enlightening. While extracurricular activities are "voluntary" in the sense that they are not required for graduation, they are part of the school's educational program; for that reason, the petitioner (hereinafter School District) is justified in expending public resources to make them available. Participation in such activities is a key component of school life, essential in reality for students applying to college, and, for all participants, a significant contributor to the breadth and quality of the educational experience.

Voluntary participation in athletics has a distinctly different dimension: Schools regulate student athletes discretely because competitive school sports by their nature require communal undress and, more important, expose students to physical risks that schools have a duty to mitigate. For the very reason that schools cannot offer a program of competitive athletics without intimately affecting the privacy of students, *Vernonia* reasonably analogized school athletes to "adults who choose to participate in a closely regulated industry." Industries fall within the closely regulated category when the nature of their activities requires substantial government oversight. Interscholastic athletics similarly require close safety and health regulation; a school's choir, band, and academic team do not.

In short, *Vernonia* applied, it did not repudiate, the principle that "the legality of a search of a student should depend simply on the reasonableness, under all the circumstances, of the search." *T. L. O.* Enrollment in a public school, and election to participate in school activities beyond the bare minimum that the curriculum requires, are indeed factors relevant to reasonableness, but they do not on their own justify intrusive, suspicionless searches. *Vernonia*, accordingly, did not rest upon these factors; instead, the Court performed what today's majority aptly describes as a "fact-specific balancing." Balancing of that order, applied to the facts now before the Court, should yield a result other than the one the Court announces today. . . .

Nationwide, students who participate in extracurricular activities are significantly less likely to develop substance abuse problems than are their less-involved peers. Even if students might be deterred from drug use in order to preserve their extracurricular eligibility, it is at least as likely that other students might forgo their extracurricular involvement in order to avoid detection of their drug use. Tecumseh's policy thus falls short doubly if deterrence is its aim: It invades the privacy of students who need deterrence least, and risks steering students at greatest risk for substance abuse away from extracurricular involvement that potentially may palliate drug problems.

To summarize, this case resembles *Vernonia* only in that the School Districts in both cases conditioned engagement in activities outside the obligatory curriculum on random subjection to urinalysis. The defining characteristics of the two programs, however, are entirely dissimilar. The *Vernonia* district sought to test a subpopulation of students distinguished by their reduced expectation of privacy, their special susceptibility to drug-related injury, and their heavy involvement with drug use. The Tecumseh district seeks to test a much larger population associated with none of these factors. It does so, moreover, without carefully safeguarding student confidentiality and without regard to the program's untoward effects. A program so sweeping is not sheltered by *Vernonia*; its unreasonable reach renders it impermissible under the Fourth Amendment. . . . For the reasons stated, I would affirm the judgment of the Tenth Circuit declaring the testing policy at issue unconstitutional.

8

THE FIFTH AMENDMENT GUARANTEE AGAINST SELF-ACCUSATION

A | Coerced Confessions and Police Interrogations

Although the Fifth Amendment guarantee against self-incrimination applies beyond criminal investigations, for example, before congressional investigating committees, in *Chavez v. Martinez*, 358 U.S. 760 (2003), the Court ruled that violations of *Miranda* (excerpted in Vol. 2, Ch. 8) do not run afoul of the constitutional protection against self-incrimination in civil cases. Writing for the Court, Justice Thomas held that "a violation of the constitutional right against self-incrimination occurs only if one has been compelled to be a witness against himself in a criminal case." Oliverio Martinez had sought civil damage in a suit against Ben Chavez, a police officer who repeatedly questioned him without advising him of his *Miranda* rights and over his objections and begging to be left alone. At the time, Martinez was in the hospital being treated for a police shooting that left him blind and paralyzed. Martinez's statements were never introduced in a criminal case against him and Justice Thomas held that "the absence of a 'criminal case' in which Martinez was compelled to be a 'witness' against himself defeats his Fifth Amendment claim." Justices Stevens and Ginsburg joined a dissent by Justice Kennedy, who vigorously disagreed: "Our cases and our legal tradition establish that the self-incrimination clause is a substantive constraint on the conduct of the government, not merely an evidentiary rule governing the work of the courts."

In two sharply divided rulings on *Miranda*, the Court held, on the one hand, in *Missouri v. Seibert* (2004) (excerpted below), that the practice of police first questioning suspects without reading them their *Miranda* rights and obtaining confessions and, then, giving them the *Miranda* warnings and again obtaining incriminating statements is unconstitutional. Such mid-interrogation warnings are invalid under *Miranda*; the first confession must be excluded because the suspect was not read the *Miranda* rights, and the second must be excluded because it was obtained by police using the first confession. On the other hand, *United States v. Patane* (2004) (excerpted below) held that, notwithstanding the ruling in *Dickerson v. United States*, 530 U.S. 428 (2000) (excerpted in Vol. 2, Ch. 8), holding that *Miranda* was a constitutional decision, the *Miranda* warnings are merely prophylactic rules and if a suspect during police questioning without being given the *Miranda* warnings makes statements that lead police to incriminating physical evidence, that evidence may be used at trial and its introduction does not violate the Fifth Amendment. In short, the plurality held that the failure to provide *Miranda* warnings is not itself a constitutional violation and there was no reason to fashion a "fruit of the poisonous tree" doctrine in order to deter un-*Mirandized* police questioning.

A bare majority also ruled, in *Hiibel v. Sixth Judicial District of Nevada* (2004) (excerpted here in Vol. 2, Ch. 7), that the Fifth Amendment is not violated by statutes that permit police to arrest individuals who refuse to identify themselves.

Missouri v. Seibert
124 S.CT. 2601 (2004)

Patrice Seibert's twelve-year-old son Jonathan had cerebral palsy, and when he died in his sleep she feared charges of neglect because of bedsores on his body. In her presence, two of her teenage sons and two of their friends devised a plan to conceal the facts surrounding Jonathan's death by incinerating his body in the course of burning the family's mobile home, in which they planned to leave Donald Rector, a mentally ill teenager living with the family, to avoid any appearance that Jonathan was unattended. Seibert's son Darian and a friend set the fire, and Donald died. Five days later, the police woke Seibert at 3 A.M. at a hospital where Darian was being treated for burns. When arresting her, officer Kevin Clinton followed instructions from officer Richard Hanrahan not to give *Miranda* warnings. After Seibert had been taken to the police station and left alone in an interview room for fifteen to twenty minutes, Hanrahan questioned her without *Miranda* warnings for about a half an hour, squeezing her arm and repeating "Donald was also to die in his sleep." After Seibert finally admitted she knew Donald was meant to die in the fire, she was given a twenty-minute coffee and cigarette break. Hanrahan then turned on a tape recorder, gave Seibert the *Miranda* warnings, and obtained a signed waiver of rights from her. He resumed the questioning with "Ok, 'trice, we've been talking for a little while about what happened on Wednesday the twelfth, haven't we?," and confronted her with her prewarning statements:

Hanrahan: "Now, in discussion you told us, you told us that there was a[n] understanding about Donald."
Seibert: "Yes."
Hanrahan: "Did that take place earlier that morning?"
Seibert: "Yes."
Hanrahan: "And what was the understanding about Donald?"
Seibert: "If they could get him out of the trailer, to take him out of the trailer."
Hanrahan: "And if they couldn't?"
Seibert: "I, I never even thought about it. I just figured they would."
Hanrahan: "'Trice, didn't you tell me that he was supposed to die in his sleep?"
Seibert: "If that would happen, 'cause he was on that new medicine, you know . . ."
Hanrahan: "The Prozac? And it makes him sleepy. So he was supposed to die in his sleep?"
Seibert: "Yes."

After being charged with first-degree murder, Seibert sought to exclude both her prewarning and postwarning statements. At the suppression hearing, Hanrahan testified that he made a "conscious decision" to withhold *Miranda* warnings, thus resorting to an interrogation technique he had been taught: question first, then give the warnings, and then repeat the question "until I get the answer that she's already provided once." He acknowledged that Seibert's ultimate statement was "largely a repeat of information . . . obtained" prior to the warning.

The trial court suppressed the prewarning statement but admitted the responses given after the *Miranda* recitation. A jury convicted Seibert of second-degree murder. On appeal, the Missouri Court of Appeals affirmed, treating the case as indistinguishable from *Oregon v. Elstad*, 470 U.S. 298 (1985). The Supreme Court of Missouri reversed, holding that "[i]n the circumstances here, where the interrogation was nearly continuous, . . . the second statement, clearly the product of the invalid first statement, should have been suppressed." The court distinguished *Elstad* on the ground that warnings had not intentionally been withheld there. The state appealed and the Supreme Court granted review.

The state supreme court's decision was affirmed by a five-to-four vote. Justice Souter delivered the opinion for the Court, Justices Kennedy and Breyer filed concurring opinions. Justice O'Connor filed a dissenting opinion, which Chief Justice Rehnquist and Justices Scalia and Thomas joined.

☐ *Justice SOUTER announced the judgment of the Court and delivered an opinion, in which Justice STEVENS, Justice GINSBURG, and Justice BREYER join.*

This case tests a police protocol for custodial interrogation that calls for giving no warnings of the rights to silence and counsel until interrogation has produced a confession. Although such a statement is generally inadmissible, since taken in violation of *Miranda v. Arizona*, 384 U. S 436 (1966), the interrogating officer follows it with *Miranda* warnings and then leads the suspect to cover the same ground a second time. The question here is the admissibility of the repeated statement. Because this midstream recitation of warnings after interrogation and unwarned confession could not effectively comply with *Miranda*'s constitutional requirement, we hold that a statement repeated after a warning in such circumstances is inadmissible. . . .

"In criminal trials, in the courts of the United States, wherever a question arises whether a confession is incompetent because not voluntary, the issue is controlled by that portion of the Fifth Amendment . . . commanding that no person 'shall be compelled in any criminal case to be a witness against himself.'" *Bram v. United States*, 168 U.S. 532 (1897). A parallel rule governing the admissibility of confessions in state courts emerged from the Due Process Clause of the Fourteenth Amendment, see *Brown v. Mississippi*, 297 U.S. 278 (1936), which governed state cases until we concluded in *Malloy v. Hogan*, 378 U.S. 1 (1964), that "[t]he Fourteenth Amendment secures against state invasion the same privilege that the Fifth Amendment guarantees against federal infringement—the right of a person to remain silent unless he chooses to speak in the unfettered exercise of his own will, and to suffer no penalty . . . for such silence." In unifying the Fifth and Fourteenth Amendment voluntariness tests, *Malloy* "made clear what had already become apparent—that the substantive and procedural safeguards surrounding admissibility of confessions in state cases had become exceedingly exacting, reflecting all the policies embedded in the privilege" against self-incrimination.

In *Miranda*, we explained that the "voluntariness doctrine in the state cases . . . encompasses all interrogation practices which are likely to exert such pressure upon an individual as to disable him from making a free and rational choice." We appreciated the difficulty of judicial enquiry post hoc into the circumstances of a police interrogation, *Dickerson v. United States*, 530 U.S. 428 (2000), and recognized that "the coercion inherent in custodial interrogation blurs the line between voluntary and involuntary statements, and thus heightens the risk" that the privilege against self-incrimination will not be observed. Hence our concern that the "traditional totality-of-the-circumstances" test posed an "unacceptably great" risk that involuntary custodial confessions would escape detection.

Accordingly, "to reduce the risk of a coerced confession and to implement the Self-Incrimination Clause," this Court in *Miranda* concluded that "the accused must be adequately and effectively apprised of his rights and the exercise of those rights must be fully honored." *Miranda* conditioned the admissibility at trial of any custodial confession on warning a suspect of his rights: failure to give the prescribed warnings and obtain a waiver of rights before custodial questioning generally requires exclusion of any statements obtained. Conversely, giving the warnings and getting a waiver has generally produced a virtual ticket of admissibility; maintaining that a statement is involuntary even though given after warnings and voluntary waiver of rights requires unusual stamina, and litigation over voluntariness tends to end with the finding of a valid waiver. To point out the obvious, this common consequence would not be common at all were it not that *Miranda* warnings are customarily given under circumstances allowing for a real choice between talking and remaining silent. . . .

The technique of interrogating in successive, unwarned, and warned phases raises a new challenge to *Miranda*. Although we have no statistics on the frequency of this practice, it is not confined to Rolla, Missouri. An officer of that police department testified that the strategy of withholding *Miranda* warnings until after interrogating and drawing out a confession was promoted not only by his own department, but by a national police training organization and other departments in which he had worked. Consistently with the officer's testimony, the Police Law Institute, for example, instructs that "officers may conduct a two-stage interrogation. . . . At any point during the pre-*Miranda* interrogation, usually after arrestees have confessed, officers may then read the *Miranda* warnings and ask for a waiver. If the arrestees waive their *Miranda* rights, officers will be able to repeat any subsequent incriminating statements later in court. The upshot of all this advice is a question-first practice of some popularity, as one can see from the reported cases describing its use, sometimes in obedience to departmental policy.

When a confession so obtained is offered and challenged, attention must be paid to the conflicting objects of *Miranda* and question-first. *Miranda* addressed "interrogation practices . . . likely . . . to disable [an individual] from making a free and rational choice" about speaking, and held that a suspect must be "adequately and effectively" advised of the choice the Constitution guarantees. The object of question-first is to render *Miranda* warnings ineffective by waiting for a particularly opportune time to give them, after the suspect has already confessed. . . .

By any objective measure, applied to circumstances exemplified here, it is likely that if the interrogators employ the technique of withholding warnings until after interrogation succeeds in eliciting a confession, the warnings will be ineffective in preparing the suspect for successive interrogation, close in time and similar in content. After all, the reason that question-first is catching on is as obvious as its manifest purpose, which is to get a confession the suspect would not make if he understood his rights at the outset; the sensible underlying assumption is that with one confession in hand before the warnings, the interrogator can count on getting its duplicate, with trifling additional trouble. Upon hearing warnings only in the aftermath of interrogation and just after making a confession, a suspect would hardly think he had a genuine right to remain silent, let alone persist in so believing once the police began to lead him over the same ground again. . . .

Strategists dedicated to draining the substance out of *Miranda* cannot accomplish by training instructions what Dickerson held Congress could not do by statute. Because the question-first tactic effectively threatens to thwart *Miranda*'s purpose of reducing the risk that a coerced confession would be admitted, and because the facts here do not reasonably support a conclusion that the warnings given could have served their purpose, Seibert's post-warning statements are inadmissible. The judgment of the Supreme Court of Missouri is affirmed.

☐ *Justice O'CONNOR, with whom THE CHIEF JUSTICE, Justice SCALIA, and Justice THOMAS join, dissenting.*

On two preliminary questions I am in full agreement with the plurality. First, the plurality appropriately follows *Elstad* in concluding that Seibert's statement cannot be held inadmissible under a "fruit of the poisonous tree" theory. Second, the plurality correctly declines to focus its analysis on the subjective intent of the interrogating officer. . . .

The plurality's adherence to *Elstad*, and mine to the plurality, end there. . . . I would analyze the two-step interrogation procedure under the voluntariness standards central to the Fifth Amendment and reiterated in *Elstad*. *Elstad* commands that if Seibert's first statement is shown to have been involuntary, the court must examine whether the taint dissipated through the passing of time or a change in circumstances. In addition, Seibert's second statement should be suppressed if she showed that it was involuntary despite the *Miranda* warnings. . . . .

I respectfully dissent.

United States v. Patane

124 S.Ct. 2620 (2004)

Samuel Francis Patane was arrested for harassing his ex-girlfriend, Linda O'Donnell, and released on bond, subject to a temporary restraining order that prohibited him from contacting O'Donnell. Patane subsequently violated the restraining order by attempting to telephone O'Donnell, and officer Tracy Fox began an investigation of the matter. At the same time, a county probation officer informed an agent of the Bureau of Alcohol, Tobacco, and Firearms (ATF) that Patane, a convicted felon, illegally possessed a pistol. The ATF relayed this information to detective Josh Benner. Benner and Fox went to Patane's residence and arrested him for violating the restraining order. Benner attempted to advise respondent of his *Miranda* rights but got no further than the right to remain silent, when Patane interrupted and said he knew his rights. Benner then asked about the pistol and Patane stated "I am not sure I should tell you anything about the [pistol] because I don't want you to take it away from me." Benner persisted and Patane told him that the pistol was in his bedroom and gave Benner permission to retrieve it. A grand jury indicted Patane for possession of a firearm by a convicted felon. A federal district court, however, granted Patane's motion to suppress the firearm on the ground that the officers lacked probable cause to arrest him for violating the restraining order. On appeal, an appellate court reversed the district court's ruling with respect to probable cause, but affirmed the suppression order. The appellate court rejected the government's argument that Supreme Court precedents, in *Oregon v. Elstad*, 470 U.S. 298 (1985), and *Michigan v. Tucker*, 417 U.S. 433 (1974), foreclosed application of the fruit of "the poisonous tree doctrine" of *Wong Sun v. United States*, 371 U.S. 471 (1963), requiring the exclusion of evidence obtained in violation of constitutional rights. Those rulings were, according to the court of appeals, based on the view that *Miranda* announced a prophylactic rule, a position that it found to be incompatible with this Court's decision in *Dickerson v. United States*, 530 U.S. 428 (2000). The court of appeals equated *Dickerson 's* announcement that *Miranda* is a constitutional rule with the proposition that a failure to warn pursuant to *Miranda* is a violation of the Fifth Amendment. The government appealed that decision and the Supreme Court granted review.

The appellate court was reversed by a five-to-four vote. Justice Thomas delivered the opinion of the Court. Justice Kennedy filed a concurring opinion. Justices Souter and Breyer filed dissenting opinions, which Justices Stevens and Ginsburg joined.

□ *Justice THOMAS announced the judgment of the Court and delivered an opinion, in which THE CHIEF JUSTICE and Justice SCALIA join.*

In this case we must decide whether a failure to give a suspect the warnings prescribed by *Miranda v. Arizona*, 384 U.S. 436 (1966), requires suppression of the physical fruits of the suspect's unwarned but voluntary statements. . . . Although we believe that the Court's decisions in *Oregon v. Elstad*, 470 U.S. 298 (1985), and *Michigan v. Tucker*, 417 U.S. 433 (1974), are instructive, the Courts of Appeals have split on the question after our decision in *Dickerson v. United States*, 530 U.S. 428 (2000). Because the *Miranda* rule protects against violations of the Self-Incrimination Clause, which, in turn, is not implicated by the introduction at trial of physical evidence resulting from voluntary statements, we answer the question presented in the negative.

[T]he *Miranda* rule is a prophylactic employed to protect against violations of the Self-Incrimination Clause. The Self-Incrimination Clause, however, is not implicated by the admission into evidence of the physical fruit of a voluntary statement. Accordingly, there is no justification for extending the *Miranda* rule to this context. And just as the Self-Incrimination Clause primarily focuses on the criminal trial, so too does the *Miranda* rule. The *Miranda* rule is not a code of police conduct, and police do not violate the Constitution (or even the *Miranda* rule, for that matter) by mere failures to warn. For this reason, the exclusionary rule articulated in cases such as *Wong Sun* does not apply. Accordingly, we reverse the judgment of the Court of

Appeals and remand the case for further proceedings consistent with this opinion.

[T]he core protection afforded by the Self-Incrimination Clause is a prohibition on compelling a criminal defendant to testify against himself at trial. See, e.g., *Chavez v. Martinez*, 538 U.S. 760 (2003). The Clause cannot be violated by the introduction of nontestimonial evidence obtained as a result of voluntary statements.

[S]tatements taken without *Miranda* warnings (though not actually compelled) can be used to impeach a defendant's testimony at trial, see *Elstad*; *Harris v. New York*, 401 U.S. 222 (1971), though the fruits of actually compelled testimony cannot, see *New Jersey v. Portash*, 440 U.S. 450 (1979). More generally, the *Miranda* rule "does not require that the statements [taken without complying with the rule] and their fruits be discarded as inherently tainted," *Elstad*. Such a blanket suppression rule could not be justified by reference to the "Fifth Amendment goal of assuring trustworthy evidence" or by any deterrence rationale, and would therefore fail our close-fit requirement.

Furthermore, the Self-Incrimination Clause contains its own exclusionary rule. It provides that "[n]o person . . . shall be compelled in any criminal case to be a witness against himself." Unlike the Fourth Amendment's bar on unreasonable searches, the Self-Incrimination Clause is self-executing. We have repeatedly explained "that those subjected to coercive police interrogations have an automatic protection from the use of their involuntary statements (or evidence derived from their statements) in any subsequent criminal trial." *Chavez*. This explicit textual protection supports a strong presumption against expanding the *Miranda* rule any further.

Finally, nothing in *Dickerson*, including its characterization of *Miranda* as announcing a constitutional rule, changes any of these observations. . . .

Our cases also make clear the related point that a mere failure to give *Miranda* warnings does not, by itself, violate a suspect's constitutional rights or even the *Miranda* rule. So much was evident in many of our pre-*Dickerson* cases, and we have adhered to this view since *Dickerson*. See *Chavez*. . . .

It follows that police do not violate a suspect's constitutional rights (or the *Miranda* rule) by negligent or even deliberate failures to provide the suspect with the full panoply of warnings prescribed by *Miranda*. Potential violations occur, if at all, only upon the admission of unwarned statements into evidence at trial. And, at that point, "[t]he exclusion of unwarned statements . . . is a complete and sufficient remedy" for any perceived *Miranda* violation.

Thus, unlike unreasonable searches under the Fourth Amendment or actual violations of the Due Process Clause or the Self-Incrimination Clause, there is, with respect to mere failures to warn, nothing to deter. There is therefore no reason to apply the "fruit of the poisonous tree" doctrine of *Wong Sun*. . . .

Accordingly, we reverse the judgment of the Court of Appeals and remand the case for further proceedings consistent with this opinion.

☐ *Justice SOUTER, with whom Justice STEVENS and Justice GINSBURG join, dissenting.*

The majority repeatedly says that the Fifth Amendment does not address the admissibility of nontestimonial evidence, an overstatement that is beside the point. The issue actually presented today is whether courts should apply the fruit of the poisonous tree doctrine lest we create an incentive for the police to omit *Miranda* warnings before custodial interrogation. In closing their eyes to the consequences of giving an evidentiary advantage to those who ignore *Miranda*, the majority adds an important inducement for interrogators to ignore the rule in that case.

Miranda rested on insight into the inherently coercive character of custodial interrogation and the inherently difficult exercise of assessing the voluntariness of any confession resulting from it. Unless the police give the prescribed warnings meant to counter the coercive atmosphere, a custodial confession is inadmissible, there being no need for the previous time-consuming and difficult enquiry into voluntariness. That inducement to forestall involuntary statements and troublesome issues of fact can only atrophy if we turn around and recognize an evidentiary benefit when an unwarned statement leads investigators to tangible evidence. There is, of course, a price for excluding evidence, but the Fifth Amendment is worth a price, and in the absence of a very good reason, the logic of *Miranda* should be followed: a *Miranda* violation raises a presumption of coercion, *Oregon v. Elstad*, and the Fifth Amendment privilege against compelled self-incrimination extends to the exclusion of derivative evidence, see *United States v. Hubbell*, 530 U.S. 27 (2000) (recognizing "the Fifth Amendment's protection against the prosecutor's use of incriminating information derived directly or indirectly from . . . [actually] compelled testimony"); *Kastigar v. United States*, 406 U.S. 441 (1972). That should be the end of this case. . . .

There is no way to read this case except as an unjustifiable invitation to law enforcement officers to flout *Miranda* when there may be physical evidence to be gained. The incentive is an odd one, coming from the Court on the same day it decides *Missouri v. Seibert*. I respectfully dissent.

■ THE DEVELOPMENT OF LAW

Other Court Rulings on Coerced Confessions and Limiting Miranda

CASE	VOTE	RULING
Yarborough v. Alavardo, 124 S.Ct. 2140 (2004)	5:4	Writing for the Court, Justice Kennedy held that a two-hour-long interview of a juvenile, who

was brought by parents to the police station and who made incriminating statements about a robbery and murder, but who was allowed to leave, and then a month later arrested and charged, was not in police custody for the purposes of *Miranda* and his incriminating statements could be used against him even though he had not been given the *Miranda* warning about his rights. According to Justice Kennedy, the fact that he was a juvenile and other psychological considerations was deemed not relevant to whether he was in police custody. Justices Stevens, Souter, Ginsburg, and Breyer dissented.

B | *Grants of Immunity*

A sharply divided Court upheld Kansas's Sexual Abuse Treatment Program, which requires convicted sexual offenders to sign a form taking responsibility for their sexual offenses as part of their treatment, without also granting them immunity from further prosecution, in *McKune v. Lile*, 536 U.S. 24 (2002). Moreover, Justice Kennedy's opinion commanded the support of only a plurality, with Justice O'Connor concurring in the result but not in his analysis of the Fifth Amendment. Justice Stevens's dissent was joined by Justices Souter, Ginsburg, and Breyer.

9

THE RIGHTS TO COUNSEL
AND OTHER PROCEDURAL
GUARANTEES

A | *The Right to Counsel*

In *Alabama v. Shelton*, 535 U.S. 654 (2002), the Court held that the Sixth
Amendment right to counsel was violated and that suspended sentences, which could result in actual imprisonment, cannot be imposed
when the defendant does not have the assistance of counsel. LeReed
Shelton represented himself in a case of third-degree assault. Upon conviction, he received a suspended sentence and probation. He appealed
but a state court held that the Sixth Amendment is not violated unless
there is a deprivation of liberty. Writing for the Court, Justice Ginsburg
reversed that decision and held that a suspended sentence may not be
imposed unless the defendant has been offered and provided the assistance of counsel at the trial. Justice Scalia, joined by Chief Justice Rehnquist and Justices Kennedy and Thomas, dissented and warned that the
majority had imposed a new requirement and an undue burden on the
states to provide the assistance of counsel.

In *Fellers v. United States*, 124 S.Ct. 1019 (2004), a unanimous Court
reaffirmed that the Sixth Amendment bars the use of incriminating
statements elicited by police from an accused after he has waived his
Miranda rights and after he has been indicted for an offense. Writing for
the Court, Justice O'Connor reaffirmed that the Sixth Amendment
right to counsel bars interrogations or the deliberate elicitation of

information out of the presence of counsel once judicial proceedings have begun, whether by a formal charge, preliminary hearing, indictment, or arraignment.

B | *Plea Bargaining and the Right to Effective Counsel*

■ THE DEVELOPMENT OF LAW

Rulings on Plea Bargaining and Effective Counsel

CASE	VOTE	RULING
Mickens v. Taylor, 535 U.S. 162 (2002)	5:4	The Court rejected a death row inmate's claim that his Sixth Amendment right to effective counsel was violated because his court-appointed attorney had previously represented the murder victim. Justices Stevens, Souter, Ginsburg and Breyer dissented.
Wiggins v. Smith, 539 U.S. 510 (2003)	7:2	The Court overturned a death sentence upon finding that the defendant's attorney failed to investigate and to introduce mitigating factors related to his sexual abuse by his parents and that the failure to do so violated the Sixth Amendment right to effective counsel under *Strickland v. Washington*, 466 U.S. 668 (1984).
Iowa v. Tovar, 124 S.Ct. 1379 (2004)	9:0	Writing for the Court, Justice Ginsburg held that the Sixth Amendment right to counsel is not violated when an accused pleads guilty in a plea bargain without the assistance of an attorney, because he waived the right, was informed of the consequences of pleading guilty, and made a knowing and intelligent act.
United States v. Dominguez Benitez, 124 S.Ct. 2333 (2004)	9:0	Justice Souter rejected a claim that a sentence should be overturned because a federal district court judge failed to warn the defendant that if the court did not accept a plea bargain he could not withdraw his guilty plea, since it was stipulated in the signed agreement and made no difference in the outcome.

D | *The Right to an Impartial Jury Trial*

In another ruling interpreting the Sixth Amendment, the Court cast increasing doubt on the constitutional permissibility of federal and state mandatory sentencing guidelines. In *Apprendi v. New Jersey*, 536 U.S. 466 (2000), the Court struck down New Jersey's law permitting judges to hand down longer sentences for "hate crimes" based on the "preponderance of evidence" standard. A bare majority ruled that enhanced sentences may be imposed only by a jury and on the basis of the stricter "beyond a reasonable doubt" standard. In *Ring v. Arizona*, 536 U.S. 584 (2002), the Court applied the *Apprendi* principle to require juries, not judges, to determine the aggravating circumstances for imposing death sentences. Then, in *Blakely v. Washington*, 124 S.Ct. 2531 (2004), a bare majority struck down Washington's sentencing system for permitting judges to make findings that increase a convicted defendant's sentence beyond the ordinary range for violating the right to trial by a jury. Writing for the Court, Justice Scalia reaffirmed that "any fact that increases the penalty for a crime beyond the prescribed statutory maximum must be submitted to a jury and proved beyond a reasonable doubt." Although Scalia added that "the federal guidelines are not before us, and we express no opinion on them," dissenting Justice O'Connor warned, "Over 20 years of sentencing reform are all but lost, and tens of thousands of criminal judgments are in jeopardy." Chief Justice Rehnquist and Justices Kennedy and Breyer also dissented.

F | *The Rights to Be Informed of Charges to Confront Accusers*

The Court in *Crawford v. Washington*, 124 S.Ct. 1354 (2004), also overturned the ruling in *Ohio v. Roberts*, 448 U.S. 56 (1980), that statements from a witness who was not available for cross-examination could nevertheless be admitted at trial if the judge deemed them reliable. Writing for a unanimous Court, Justice Scalia held that the standard of "reliability" was too subjective and amorphous. In his words, "Dispensing with confrontation because testimony is obviously reliable is akin to dispensing with jury trial because a defendant is obviously guilty. This is not what the Sixth Amendment prescribes." Under the Court's new rule, the prosecution may use statements of absent witnesses only if they were previously cross-examined by the defense at a deposition or in a prior trial.

G | The Guarantee against Double Jeopardy

In *United States v. Lara*, 124 S.Ct. 1628 (2004), the Court held that the federal government may prosecute a Native American in federal court, even after he has been convicted in a tribal court for virtually the same offense: assaulting a federal officer. Writing for the Court, Justice Breyer held that the double jeopardy clause does not bar prosecutions by two sovereign governments and reaffirmed "the inherent power of Indian tribes . . . to exercise criminal jurisdiction over all Indians." Justices Scalia and Souter dissented.

10

CRUEL AND UNUSUAL PUNISHMENT

A | Noncapital Punishment

In its 2002–2003 term the justices considered whether sentences of twenty-five years to life in prison under California's "three-strikes-and-you're-out" law violate the Eighth Amendment when the third strike is for a minor crime. Although about half of the states have three-strikes laws, only California's 1994 law allows misdemeanors to count as strikes. In *Ewing v. California* (excerpted below), Gary Ewing, who had previous convictions for robbery, received a twenty-five-years to life sentence for stealing three golf clubs, each valued at $399. Writing for the Court in a five-to-four ruling, Justice O'Connor held that Ewing's sentence was not grossly disproportionate and therefore did not violate the Eighth Amendment. Justices Scalia and Thomas, concurring, disagreed that disproportional analysis has any place in Eighth Amendment jurisprudence. Justices Stevens, Souter, Ginsburg, and Breyer dissented.

Ewing v. California
538 U.S. 11, 123 S.Ct. 1179 (2003)

In the 1990s, about half the states enacted "three-strikes-and-you're-out" laws, requiring mandatory sentences, including life imprisonment, for individuals convicted of three felonies. California's 1994 law provides that a defendant who has two or more prior felony convictions must receive "an indeterminate term of life imprisonment," with the possibility of parole after twenty-five years of imprisonment. In addition, the law gives prosecutors and judges the discretion to treat certain offenses—known as "wobblers"—as either felonies or misdemeanors, and some crimes that would otherwise be misdemeanors may become wobblers and counted as a felony under the law. For example, a petty theft, a misdemeanor, may become a wobbler and treated as a felony when the defendant previously served prison time for committing a theft-related crime.

In 2000, when on parole from serving a nine-year prison term for committing three burglaries and a robbery, Gary Ewing walked into a pro golf shop and walked out with three golf clubs, priced at $399 each, concealed in his pants leg. An employee observed him limp out of the shop and called the police. The police apprehended him in the parking lot and arrested him. Ewing was charged with and convicted of one count of a felony grand theft of personal property in excess of $400. As required under California's three-strikes law, the prosecutor sought a lifetime prison sentence. At sentencing, Ewing asked the court to reduce the conviction for grand theft, a "wobbler," to a misdemeanor so that he could avoid a three-strikes sentence. The trial judge, however, determined that the theft of the golf clubs should remain a felony and that the four prior strikes for burglary and robbery should stand. Ewing was sentenced to twenty-five years to life in prison. A state appellate court affirmed and the Supreme Court of California denied review, whereupon Ewing appealed to the Supreme Court.

The judgment below was affirmed by a five-to-four vote. Justice O'Connor delivered the opinion for the Court, which Chief Justice Rehnquist and Justice Kennedy joined. Justices Scalia and Thomas filed concurring opinions. Justices Stevens and Breyer filed dissenting opinions, which Justices Souter and Ginsburg joined.

□ *Justice O'CONNOR announced the judgment of the Court and delivered an opinion in which THE CHIEF JUSTICE and Justice KENNEDY join.*

The Eighth Amendment, which forbids cruel and unusual punishments, contains a "narrow proportionality principle" that "applies to noncapital sentences." *Harmelin v. Michigan*, 501 U.S. 957 (1991). We have most recently addressed the proportionality principle as applied to terms of years in a series of cases beginning with *Rummel v. Estelle*, [445 U.S. 263 (1980)].

In *Rummel*, we held that it did not violate the Eighth Amendment for a State to sentence a three-time offender to life in prison with the possibility of parole. Like Ewing, Rummel was sentenced to a lengthy prison term under a recidivism statute. Rummel's two prior offenses were a 1964 felony for "fraudulent use of a credit card to obtain $80 worth of goods or services," and a 1969 felony conviction for "passing a forged check in the amount of $28.36." His triggering offense was a conviction for felony theft—"obtaining $120.75 by false pretenses."

This Court ruled that "having twice imprisoned him for felonies, Texas was entitled to place upon Rummel the onus of one who is simply unable to bring his conduct within the social norms prescribed by the criminal law of the State." The recidivism statute "is nothing more than a societal decision that when such a person commits yet another felony, he should be subjected to the admittedly serious penalty of incarceration for life, subject only to the State's judgment as to whether to grant him parole." . . .

In *Hutto v. Davis*, 454 U.S. 370 (1982), the defendant was sentenced to two consecutive terms of 20 years in prison for possession with intent to distribute nine ounces of marijuana and distribution of marijuana. We held that such a sentence was constitutional: "In short, *Rummel* stands for the proposition that federal courts should be reluctant to review legislatively mandated terms of imprisonment, and that successful challenges to the proportionality of particular sentences should be exceedingly rare."

Three years after *Rummel*, in *Solem v. Helm*, 463 U.S. 277 (1983), we held that the Eighth Amendment prohibited "a life sentence without possibility of parole for a seventh nonviolent felony." The triggering offense in *Solem* was "uttering a 'no account' check for $100." We specifically stated that the Eighth Amendment's ban on cruel and unusual punishments "prohibits . . . sentences that are disproportionate to the crime committed," and that the "constitutional principle of proportionality has been recognized explicitly in this Court for almost a century." The *Solem* Court then explained that three factors may be relevant to a determination of whether a sentence is so disproportionate that it violates the Eighth Amendment: "(i) the gravity of the offense and the harshness of the penalty; (ii) the sentences imposed on other criminals in the same jurisdiction; and (iii) the sentences imposed for commission of the same crime in other jurisdictions."

Applying these factors in *Solem*, we struck down the defendant's sentence of life without parole. We specifically noted the contrast between that sentence and the sentence in *Rummel*, pursuant to which the defendant was eligible for parole. . . .

The proportionality principles in our cases . . . guide our application of the Eighth Amendment in the new context that we are called upon to consider.

For many years, most States have had laws providing for enhanced sentencing of repeat offenders. Yet between 1993 and 1995, "three strikes" laws effected a sea change in criminal sentencing throughout the Nation. These laws responded to widespread public concerns about crime by targeting the class of offenders who pose the greatest threat to public safety: career criminals. . . .

Throughout the States, legislatures enacting three strikes laws made a deliberate policy choice that individuals who have repeatedly engaged in serious or violent criminal behavior, and whose conduct has not been deterred by more conventional approaches to punishment, must be isolated from society in order to protect the public safety. Though three strikes laws may be relatively new, our tradition of deferring to state legislatures in making and implementing such important policy decisions is longstanding.

Our traditional deference to legislative policy choices finds a corollary in the principle that the Constitution "does not mandate adoption of any one penological theory." A sentence can have a variety of justifications, such as incapacitation, deterrence, retribution, or rehabilitation. Some or all of these justifications may play a role in a State's sentencing scheme. Selecting the sentencing rationales is generally a policy choice to be made by state legislatures, not federal courts.

When the California Legislature enacted the three strikes law, it made a judgment that protecting the public safety requires incapacitating criminals who have already been convicted of at least one serious or violent crime. Nothing in the Eighth Amendment prohibits California from making that choice. . . .

Against this backdrop, we consider Ewing's claim that his three strikes sentence of 25 years to life is unconstitutionally disproportionate to his offense of "shoplifting three golf clubs." We first address the gravity of the offense compared to the harshness of the penalty. At the threshold, we note that Ewing incorrectly frames the issue. The gravity of his offense was not merely "shoplifting three golf clubs." Rather, Ewing was convicted of felony grand theft for stealing nearly $1,200 worth of merchandise after previously having been convicted of at least two "violent" or "serious" felonies. Even standing alone, Ewing's theft should not be taken lightly. His crime was certainly not "one of the most passive felonies a person could commit." To the contrary, the Supreme Court of California has noted the "seriousness" of grand theft in the context of proportionality review.

That grand theft is a "wobbler" under California law is of no moment. Though California courts have discretion to reduce a felony grand theft charge to a misdemeanor, it remains a felony for all purposes "unless and until the trial court imposes a misdemeanor sentence." . . .

Ewing's sentence is justified by the State's public-safety interest in incapacitating and deterring recidivist felons, and amply supported by his own long, serious criminal record. Ewing has been convicted of numerous misdemeanor and felony offenses, served nine separate terms of incarceration, and committed most of his crimes while on probation or parole. His prior "strikes" were serious felonies including robbery and three residential burglaries. To be sure, Ewing's sentence is a long one. But it reflects a rational legislative judgment, entitled to deference, that offenders who have committed serious or violent felonies and who continue to commit felonies must be incapacitated. . . .

We hold that Ewing's sentence of 25 years to life in prison, imposed for the offense of felony grand theft under the three strikes law, is not grossly disproportionate and therefore does not violate the Eighth Amendment's prohibition on cruel and unusual punishments. The judgment of the California Court of Appeal is affirmed.

□ *Justice SCALIA, concurring in the judgment.*

In my concurring opinion in *Harmelin v. Michigan*, I concluded that the Eighth Amendment's prohibition of "cruel and unusual punishments" was aimed at excluding only certain modes of punishment, and was not a "guarantee against disproportionate sentences." Out of respect for the principle of *stare decisis*, I might nonetheless accept the contrary holding of *Solem v. Helm*—that the Eighth Amendment contains a narrow proportionality principle—if I felt I could intelligently apply it. This case demonstrates why I cannot.

Proportionality—the notion that the punishment should fit the crime—is inherently a concept tied to the penological goal of retribution. "It becomes difficult even to speak intelligently of 'proportionality,' once deterrence and rehabilitation are given significant weight," *Harmelin*—not to mention giving weight to the purpose of California's "three strikes" law: incapacitation. In the present case, the game is up once the plurality has acknowledged that "the Constitution does not mandate adoption of any one penological theory," and that a "sentence can have a variety of justifications, such as incapacitation, deterrence, retribution, or rehabilitation." That acknowledgment having been made, it no longer suffices merely to assess "the gravity of the offense compared to the harshness of the penalty;" that classic description of the proportionality principle (alone and in itself quite resistant to policy-free, legal analysis) now becomes merely the "first" step of the inquiry. Having completed that step (by a discussion which, in all fairness, does not convincingly establish that 25-years-to-life is a "proportionate" punishment for stealing three golf clubs), the plurality must then add an analysis to show that "Ewing's sentence is justified by the State's public-safety interest in incapacitating and deterring recidivist felons."

Which indeed it is—though why that has anything to do with the principle of proportionality is a mystery. Perhaps the plurality should revise its terminology, so that what it reads into the Eighth Amendment is not the unstated proposition that all punishment should be reasonably proportionate to the gravity of the offense, but rather the unstated proposition that all punishment should reasonably pursue the multiple purposes of the criminal law. That formulation would make it clearer than ever, of course, that the plurality is not applying law but evaluating policy.

Because I agree that petitioner's sentence does not violate the Eighth Amendment's prohibition against cruel and unusual punishments, I concur in the judgment.

☐ *Justice THOMAS, concurring in the judgment.*

I agree with Justice SCALIA's view that the proportionality test announced in *Solem v. Helm* is incapable of judicial application. Even were *Solem's* test perfectly clear, however, I would not feel compelled by *stare decisis* to apply it. In my view, the Cruel and Unusual Punishments Clause of the Eighth Amendment contains no proportionality principle. See *Harmelin v. Michigan* (opinion of SCALIA, J.). . . .

☐ *Justice STEVENS, with whom Justice SOUTER, Justice GINSBURG and Justice BREYER join, dissenting.*

The concurrences prompt this separate writing to emphasize that proportionality review is not only capable of judicial application but also required by the Eighth Amendment.

"The Eighth Amendment succinctly prohibits 'excessive' sanctions." *Atkins v. Virginia*, 536 U.S. 304 (2002). It "would be anomalous indeed" to suggest that the Eighth Amendment makes proportionality review applicable in the context of bail and fines but not in the context of other forms of punishment, such as imprisonment. *Solem v. Helm*. Rather, by broadly prohibiting excessive sanctions, the Eighth Amendment directs judges to exercise their wise judgment in assessing the proportionality of all forms of punishment.

The absence of a black-letter rule does not disable judges from exercising their discretion in construing the outer limits on sentencing authority that the Eighth Amendment imposes. After all, judges are "constantly called upon to draw . . . lines in a variety of contexts," and to exercise their judgment to give meaning to the Constitution's broadly phrased protections. For example, the Due Process Clause directs judges to employ proportionality review in assessing the constitutionality of punitive damages awards on a case-by-case basis. See, e.g., *BMW of North America, Inc. v. Gore*, 517 U.S. 559 (1996). . . . Throughout most of the Nation's history—before guideline sentencing became so prevalent—federal and state trial judges imposed specific sentences pursuant to grants of authority that gave them uncabined discretion within broad ranges. Likewise, I think it clear that the Eighth Amendment's prohibition of "cruel and unusual punishments" expresses a broad and basic proportionality principle that takes into account all of the justifications for penal sanctions. It is this broad proportionality principle that would preclude reliance on any of the justifications for punishment to support, for example, a life sentence for overtime parking. Accordingly, I respectfully dissent.

☐ *Justice BREYER, with whom Justice STEVENS, Justice SOUTER, and Justice GINSBURG join, dissenting.*

The constitutional question is whether the "three strikes" sentence imposed by California upon repeat-offender Gary Ewing is "grossly disproportionate" to his crime. The sentence amounts to a real prison term of at least 25 years. The sentence-triggering criminal conduct consists of the theft of three golf clubs priced at a total of $1,197. The offender has a criminal history that includes four felony convictions arising out of three separate burglaries (one armed). In *Solem v. Helm*, the Court found grossly disproportionate a somewhat longer sentence imposed on a recidivist offender for triggering criminal conduct that was somewhat less severe. In my view, the differences are not determinative, and the Court should reach the same ultimate conclusion here. . . .

Justice SCALIA and Justice THOMAS argue that we should not review for gross disproportionality a sentence to a term of years. Otherwise, we make it too difficult for legislators and sentencing judges to determine just when their sentencing laws and practices pass constitutional muster. I concede that a bright-line rule would give legislators and sentencing judges more guidance. But application of the Eighth Amendment to a sentence of a term of years requires a case-by-case approach. And, in my view, like that of the plurality, meaningful enforcement of the Eighth Amendment demands that application—even if only at sentencing's outer bounds.

A case-by-case approach can nonetheless offer guidance through example. Ewing's sentence is, at a minimum, 2 to 3 times the length of sentences that other jurisdictions would impose in similar circumstances. That sentence itself is sufficiently long to require a typical offender to spend virtually all the remainder of his active life in prison. . . .

In sum, even if I accept for present purposes the plurality's analytical framework, Ewing's sentence (life imprisonment with a minimum term of 25 years) is grossly disproportionate to the triggering offense conduct—stealing three golf clubs—Ewing's recidivism notwithstanding. For these reasons, I dissent.

B | *Capital Punishment*

In *Atkins v. Virginia* (2002) (excerpted below), the Court reconsidered its ruling in *Penry v. Lynaugh* (1989) (excerpted in Vol. 2, Ch. 10), which permitted the execution of murderers who are mentally retarded, and overruled that earlier decision. In its 2004–2005 term the Court will reconsider its earlier decisions, in *Stanford v. Kentucky*, 492 U.S. 361 (1989), and *Wilkins v. Missouri*, 492 U.S. 361 (1989), permitting the execution of death-row inmates who committed murders at the ages of sixteen and seventeen, even though a year earlier, in *Thompson v. Oklahoma*, 487 U.S. 815 (1988), the Court held that Eighth Amendment bars the execution of murderers who were fifteen years old or younger at the time of their crimes. The Court will revisit the permissibility of sentencing minors to death in *Roper v. Simmons* (No. 03-633).

Atkins v. Virginia
536 U.S. 304, 122 S.Ct. 2242 (2002)

In *Ford v. Wainwright*, 477 U.S. 399 (1986), the Court held that the Eighth Amendment bars the execution of death-row inmates who are (or who have gone while on death row) insane. However, in *Penry v. Lynaugh*, 492 U.S. 302 (1989) (excerpted in Vol. 2, Ch. 10), a bare majority upheld the execution of an individual who was mentally retarded. In her opinion for Court, Justice O'Connor emphasized that at the time only one state banned the execution of the mentally retarded and that, even when added to the fourteen states that had rejected capital punishment, this did "not provide sufficient evidence at present of a national consensus" against executing mentally retarded convicts. Subsequently, seventeen other states of the thirty-eight that impose the death penalty enacted laws barring executions of the mentally retarded. And opponents of the death penalty continued to raise the issue in an effort to persuade the Court to reconsider the matter.

In 1998, Daryl Renard Atkins, who has an IQ of fifty-nine—that of a nine- to twelve-year-old—was convicted and sentenced to death for participating in the robbery and murder of a U.S. airman in Virginia. The Virginia Supreme Court affirmed his sentence. This decision was appealed to the Supreme Court. Notably, a number of friend-of-court briefs highlighted the controversy and urged the Court to abandon its earlier ruling; among those filing *amicus* briefs were the European Union, the U.S. Catholic Conference, and the American Psychological Association.

The state supreme court's decision was reversed by a six-to-three vote. Justice Stevens delivered the opinion of the Court. Chief Justice Rehnquist and Justice Scalia filed dissenting opinions, which Justice Thomas joined.

☐ *Justice STEVENS delivered the opinion of the Court.*

Those mentally retarded persons who meet the law's requirements for criminal responsibility should be tried and punished when they commit crimes. Because of their disabilities in areas of reasoning, judgment, and control of their impulses, however, they do not act with the level of moral culpability that characterizes the most serious adult criminal conduct. Moreover, their impairments can jeopardize the reliability and fairness of capital proceedings against mentally retarded defendants. Presumably for these reasons, in the 13 years since we decided *Penry v. Lynaugh*, 492 U.S. 302 (1989), the American public, legislators, scholars, and judges have deliberated over the question whether the death penalty should ever be imposed on a mentally retarded criminal. The consensus reflected in those deliberations informs our answer to the question presented by this case: whether such executions are "cruel and unusual punishments" prohibited by the Eighth Amendment to the Federal Constitution. . . .

The Eighth Amendment succinctly prohibits "excessive" sanctions. . . . A claim that punishment is excessive is judged not by the standards that prevailed in 1685 when Lord Jeffreys presided over the "Bloody Assizes" or when the Bill of Rights was adopted, but rather by those that currently prevail. As CHIEF JUSTICE WARREN explained in his opinion in *Trop v. Dulles*, 356 U.S. 86 (1958): "The basic concept underlying the Eighth Amendment is nothing less than the dignity of man. . . . The Amendment must draw its meaning from the evolving standards of decency that mark the progress of a maturing society."

Proportionality review under those evolving standards should be informed by "objective factors to the maximum possible extent." We have pinpointed that the "clearest and most reliable objective evidence of contemporary values is the legislation enacted by the country's legislatures." *Penry.* Relying in part on such legislative evidence, we have held that death is an impermissibly excessive punishment for the rape of an adult woman, *Coker v. Georgia*, 433 U.S. 584 (1977), or for a defendant who neither took life, attempted to take life, nor intended to take life, *Enmund v. Florida*, 458 U.S. 782 (1982). In *Coker*, we focused primarily on the then-recent legislation that had been enacted in response to our decision 10 years earlier in *Furman v. Georgia*, 408 U.S. 238 (1972) (*per curiam*), to support the conclusion that the "current judgment," though "not wholly unanimous," weighed very heavily on the side of rejecting capital punishment as a "suitable penalty for raping an adult woman." The "current legislative judgment" relevant to our decision in *Enmund* was less clear than in *Coker* but "nevertheless weigh[ed] on the side of rejecting capital punishment for the crime at issue." . . .

Guided by our approach in these cases, we shall first review the judgment of legislatures that have addressed the suitability of imposing the death penalty on the mentally retarded and then consider reasons for agreeing or disagreeing with their judgment.

The parties have not called our attention to any state legislative consideration of the suitability of imposing the death penalty on mentally retarded offenders prior to 1986. In that year, the public reaction to the execution of a mentally retarded murderer in Georgia apparently led to the enactment of the first state statute prohibiting such executions. In 1988, when Congress enacted legislation reinstating the federal death penalty, it expressly provided that a "sentence of death shall not be carried out upon a person who is mentally retarded." In 1989, Maryland enacted a similar prohibition. It was in that year that we decided *Penry*, and concluded that those two state enactments, "even when added to the 14 States that have rejected capital punishment completely, do not provide sufficient evidence at present of a national consensus."

Much has changed since then. [S]tate legislatures across the country began to address the issue. In 1990 Kentucky and Tennessee enacted statutes similar to those in Georgia and Maryland, as did New Mexico in 1991, and Arkansas, Colorado, Washington, Indiana, and Kansas in 1993 and 1994. In 1995, when New York reinstated its death penalty, it emulated the Federal Government by expressly exempting the mentally retarded. Nebraska followed suit in 1998. There appear to have been no similar enactments during the next two years, but in 2000 and 2001 six more States—South Dakota, Arizona, Connecticut, Florida, Missouri, and North Carolina—joined the procession. The Texas Legislature unanimously adopted a similar bill, and bills have passed at least one house in other States, including Virginia and Nevada.

It is not so much the number of these States that is significant, but the consistency of the direction of change. Given the well-known fact that anti-crime legislation is far more popular than legislation providing protections for persons guilty of violent crime, the large number of States prohibiting the execution of mentally retarded persons (and the complete absence of States passing legislation reinstating the power to conduct such executions) provides powerful evidence that today our society views mentally retarded offenders as categorically less culpable than the average criminal. . . .

To the extent there is serious disagreement about the execution of mentally retarded offenders, it is in determining which offenders are in fact retarded. In this case, for instance, the Commonwealth of Virginia disputes that Atkins suffers from mental retardation. Not all people who claim to be mentally retarded will be so impaired as to fall within the range of mentally retarded offenders about whom there is a national consensus. As was our approach in *Ford v. Wainwright*, with regard to insanity, "we leave to the State[s] the task of developing appropriate ways to enforce the constitutional restriction upon its execution of sentences." . . .

[O]ur death penalty jurisprudence provides two reasons consistent with the legislative consensus that the mentally retarded should be categorically excluded from execution. First, there is a serious question as to whether either justification that we have recognized as a basis for the death penalty applies to mentally retarded offenders. *Gregg v. Georgia*, 428 U.S. 153 (1976), identified "retribution and deterrence of capital crimes by prospective offenders" as the social purposes served by the death penalty. Unless the imposition of the death penalty on a mentally retarded person "measurably contributes to one or both of these goals, it 'is nothing more than the purposeless and needless imposition of pain and suffering,' and hence an unconstitutional punishment." *Enmund*.

With respect to retribution—the interest in seeing that the offender gets his "just deserts"—the severity of the appropriate punishment necessarily depends on the culpability of the offender. Since Gregg, our jurisprudence has consistently confined the imposition of the death penalty to a narrow category of the most serious crimes. For example, in *Godfrey v. Georgia*, 446 U.S. 420 (1980), we set aside a death sentence because the petitioner's crimes did not reflect "a consciousness materially more 'depraved' than that of any person guilty of murder." If the culpability of the average murderer is insufficient to justify the most extreme sanction available to the State, the lesser culpability of the mentally retarded offender surely does not merit that form of retribution. Thus, pursuant to our narrowing jurisprudence, which seeks to ensure that only the most deserving of execution are put to death, an exclusion for the mentally retarded is appropriate.

With respect to deterrence—the interest in preventing capital crimes by prospective offenders—"it seems likely that 'capital punishment can serve as a deterrent only when murder is the result of premeditation and deliberation,'" *Enmund*. Exempting the mentally retarded from that punishment will not affect the "cold calculus that precedes the decision" of other potential murderers. Indeed, that sort of calculus is at the opposite end of the spectrum from behavior of mentally retarded offenders. . . . Nor will exempting the mentally retarded from execution lessen the deterrent effect of the death penalty with respect to offenders who are not mentally retarded. Such individuals are unprotected by the exemption and will continue to face the threat of execution. Thus, executing the mentally retarded will not measurably further the goal of deterrence. . . .

The judgment of the Virginia Supreme Court is reversed and the case is remanded for further proceedings not inconsistent with this opinion. It is so ordered.

☐ *Justice SCALIA, with whom the CHIEF JUSTICE and Justice THOMAS join, dissenting.*

Today's decision is the pinnacle of our Eighth Amendment death-is-different jurisprudence. Not only does it, like all of that jurisprudence, find no support in the text or history of the Eighth Amendment; it does not even have support in current social attitudes regarding the conditions that render an otherwise just death penalty inappropriate. Seldom has an opinion of this Court rested so obviously upon nothing but the personal views of its members. . . .

The Court makes no pretense that execution of the mildly mentally retarded would have been considered "cruel and unusual" in 1791. Only the severely or profoundly mentally retarded, commonly known as "idiots," enjoyed any special status under the law at that time. They, like lunatics, suffered a "deficiency in will" rendering them unable to tell right from wrong. W. Blackstone, *Commentaries on the Laws of England* (1769). Due to their incompetence, idiots were "excuse[d] from the guilt, and of course from the punishment, of any criminal action committed under such deprivation of the senses." Instead, they were often committed to civil confinement or made wards of the State, thereby preventing them from "go[ing] loose, to the terror of the king's subjects." Mentally retarded offenders with less severe impairments—those who were not "idiots"—suffered criminal prosecution and punishment, including capital punishment.

The Court is left to argue, therefore, that execution of the mildly retarded is inconsistent with the "evolving standards of decency that mark the progress of a maturing society." *Trop v. Dulles*. Before today, our opinions consistently emphasized that Eighth Amendment judgments regarding the existence of social "standards" "should be informed by objective factors to the maximum possible extent" and "should not be, or appear to be, merely the subjective views of individual Justices." *Coker v. Georgia.*

The Court pays lip service to these precedents as it miraculously extracts a "national consensus" forbidding execution of the mentally retarded from the fact that 18 States—less than half (47%) of the 38 States that permit capital punishment (for whom the issue exists)—have very recently enacted legislation barring execution of the mentally retarded. Even that 47% figure is a distorted one. If one is to say, as the Court does today, that all executions of the mentally retarded are so morally repugnant as to violate our national "standards of decency," surely the "consensus" it points to must be one that has set its righteous face against all such executions. Not 18 States, but only seven—18% of death penalty jurisdictions—have legislation of that scope. Eleven of those that the Court counts enacted statutes prohibiting execution of mentally retarded defendants convicted after, or convicted of crimes committed after, the effective date of the legislation; those already on death row, or consigned there before the statute's effective date, or even (in those States using the date of the crime as the criterion of retroactivity) tried in the future for murders committed many years ago, could be put to death. That is not a statement of absolute moral repugnance, but one of current preference between two tolerable approaches. . . .

But let us accept, for the sake of argument, the Court's faulty count. That bare number of States alone—18—should be enough to convince any reasonable person that no "national consensus" exists. How is it possible that agreement among 47% of the death penalty jurisdictions amounts to "consensus"? Our prior cases have generally required a much higher degree of agreement before finding a punishment cruel and unusual on "evolving standards" grounds. . . .

Moreover, a major factor that the Court entirely disregards is that the legislation of all 18 States it relies on is still in its infancy. The oldest of the statutes is only 14 years old; five were enacted last year; over half were enacted within the past eight years. Few, if any, of the States have had sufficient experience with these laws to know whether they are sensible in the long term. . . .

The Court's thrashing about for evidence of "consensus" includes reliance upon the margins by which state legislatures have enacted bans on execution of the retarded. Presumably, in applying our Eighth Amendment "evolving-standards-of-decency" jurisprudence, we will henceforth weigh not only how many States have agreed, but how many States have agreed by how much. Of course if the percentage of legislators voting for the bill is significant, surely the number of people represented by the legislators voting for the bill is also significant: the fact that 49% of the legislators in a State with a population of 60 million voted against the bill should be more impressive than the fact that 90% of the legislators in a state with a population of 2 million voted for it. (By the way, the population of the death penalty States that exclude the mentally retarded is only 44% of the population of all death penalty States.) This is quite absurd. . . .

But the Prize for the Court's Most Feeble Effort to fabricate "national consensus" must go to its appeal (deservedly relegated to a footnote) to the views of assorted professional and religious organizations, members of the so-called "world community," and respondents to opinion polls. I agree with the CHIEF JUSTICE that the views of professional and religious organizations and the results of opinion polls are irrelevant. Equally irrelevant are the practices of the "world community," whose notions of justice are (thankfully) not always those of our people. . . .

Today's opinion adds one more to the long list of substantive and procedural requirements impeding imposition of the death penalty imposed under this Court's assumed power to invent a death-is-different jurisprudence. None of those requirements existed when the Eighth Amendment was adopted, and some of them were not even supported by current moral consensus. . . .

This newest invention promises to be more effective than any of the others in turning the process of capital trial into a game. One need only read the definitions of mental retardation adopted by the American Association of Mental Retardation and the American Psychiatric Association to realize that the symptoms of this condition can readily be feigned. And whereas the capital defendant who feigns insanity risks commitment to a mental institution until he can be cured (and then tried and executed), *Jones v. United States*, 463 U.S. 354 (1983), the capital defendant who feigns mental retardation risks nothing at all. The mere pendency of the present case has brought us petitions by death row inmates claiming for the first time, after multiple habeas petitions, that they are retarded. . . .

☐ *CHIEF JUSTICE REHNQUIST, with whom Justice SCALIA and Justice THOMAS join, dissenting.*

I agree with Justice SCALIA that the Court's assessment of the current legislative judgment regarding the execution of defendants like petitioner more resembles a post hoc rationalization for the majority's subjectively preferred result rather than any objective effort to ascertain the content of an evolving standard of decency. I write separately, however, to call attention to the defects in the Court's decision to place weight on foreign laws, the views of professional and religious organizations, and opinion polls in reaching its conclusion. The Court's suggestion that these sources are relevant to the constitutional question finds little support in our precedents and, in my view, is antithetical to considerations of federalism, which instruct that any "permanent prohibition upon all units of democratic government must [be apparent] in the operative acts (laws and the application of laws) that the people have approved." *Stanford v. Kentucky*, 492 U.S. 361 (1989).

[T]wo sources—the work product of legislatures and sentencing jury determinations—ought to be the sole indicators by which courts ascertain the contemporary American conceptions of decency for purposes of the Eighth Amendment. They are the only objective indicia of contemporary values firmly supported by our precedents. More importantly, however, they can be reconciled with the undeniable precepts that the democratic branches of government and individual sentencing juries are, by design, better suited than courts to evaluating and giving effect to the complex societal and moral considerations that inform the selection of publicly acceptable criminal punishments.

In reaching its conclusion today, the Court . . . adverts to the fact that other countries have disapproved imposition of the death penalty for crimes committed by mentally retarded offenders (citing the Brief for the European Union as *Amicus Curiae* in *McCarver v. North Carolina*, O. T. 2001, No. 00—8727). I fail to see, however, how the views of other countries regarding the punishment of their citizens provide any support for the Court's ultimate determination. While it is true that some of our prior opinions have looked to "the climate of international opinion," *Coker*, to reinforce a conclusion regarding evolving standards of decency; we have since explicitly rejected the idea that the sentencing practices of other countries could "serve to establish the first Eighth Amendment prerequisite, that [a] practice is accepted among our people." *Stanford* (emphasizing that "American conceptions of decency . . . are dispositive"). . . .

There are strong reasons for limiting our inquiry into what constitutes an evolving standard of decency under the Eighth Amendment to the laws passed by legislatures and the practices of sentencing juries in America. Here, the Court goes beyond these well-established objective indicators of contemporary values. It finds "further support to [its] conclusion" that a national consensus has developed against imposing the death penalty on all mentally retarded defendants in international opinion, the views of professional and religious organizations, and opinion polls not demonstrated to be reliable. Believing this view to be seriously mistaken, I dissent.

■ THE DEVELOPMENT OF LAW

Post–Furman *Rulings on Capital Punishment*

CASE	VOTE	RULING
Kelly v. South Carolina, 534 U.S. 246 (2002)	5:4	Writing for the Court, Justice Souter held that, when prosecutors introduce evidence showing

future violent propensities of a convict, due process requires a jury instruction that, instead of a death sentence, a sentence of lifetime imprisonment would be imposed without the possibility of parole.

Mickens v. Taylor, 535 U.S. 162 (2002)	5:4	The Court rejected a death-row inmate's claim that his Sixth Amendment right to effective

counsel was violated, and his murder conviction tainted, by the fact that his court-appointed attorney had previously represented the murder victim. Writing for the Court, Justice Scalia observed that it made "little policy sense" to presume that the verdict was unreliable because the trial judge had not inquired into the potential for conflict of interest. Justices Stevens, Souter, Ginsburg, and Breyer dissented.

Ring v. Arizona, 536 U.S. 584 (2002)	7:2	Writing for the Court, Justice Ginsburg struck Arizona's law and those in four other states—Colo-

rado, Idaho, Montana, and Nebraska—permitting judges alone, and not juries, to decide whether "aggravating" factors in a murder warrant the imposition of capital punishment. That death-penalty statute was deemed to violate the Sixth Amendment right to a jury trial and to its determination of the facts in a case. In so ruling, the Court extended *Apprendi v. New Jersey*, 530 U.S. 466 (2000), which invalidated a state law permitting judges to hand down longer sentences for "hate crimes," and overturned a prior decision. Chief Justice Rehnquist and Justice O'Connor dissented.

United States v. Bass, 536
U.S. 516 (2002)

9:0

In a two-page unsigned opinion, the Court rejected a racial bias claim against the government's seeking a death sentence on the ground that statistics showing that 80 percent of federal death penalty prosecutions involve minority defendants does not establish differential treatment in cases similar to those of other black defendants. Under *United States v. Armstrong*, 517 U.S. 456 (1996), defendants claiming selective prosecution must show evidence of both discriminatory intent and effect. Here, in response to the government's notice of intent to seek the death penalty, the defendant filed a motion to dismiss or, alternatively, for discovery of information relating to the government's capital charging practices. He did so on the basis of a 2000 Department of Justice study that found that "blacks [are charged] with a death-eligible offense more than twice as often as [the government] charges whites" and that plea bargains are made with white more often than with black defendants. A federal district court granted the motion and was affirmed by an appellate court. The Supreme Court reversed in holding that "raw statistics regarding overall charges say nothing about charges brought against similarly situated defendants" and fail to establish discriminatory intent in charges of capital punishment.

Sattazahn v. Pennsylvania,
537 U.S. 101 (2003)

5:4

Justice Scalia held that a death-row inmate did not suffer double jeopardy as a result of a judge's sentencing him to life imprisonment, after the jury became deadlocked on a death sentence, and a second jury in a subsequent trial unanimously imposed the death penalty. Justices Stevens, Souter, Ginsburg, and Breyer dissented.

Miller-El v. Cockrell,
537 U.S. 322 (2003)

8:1

Justice Kennedy held that a death-row inmate should be allowed to apply for a writ of *habeas corpus* based on a claim that the prosecutor's office was historically "suffused with bias" in excluding blacks from juries. Justice Thomas dissented on the ground that evidence of historical bias was "entirely circumstantial" and not "clear and convincing."

Banks v. Dretke,
124 S.Ct. 1256 (2004)

7:2

Writing for the Court, Justice Ginsburg held that a death-row inmate was entitled to appeal his death sentence because at trial the prosecution withheld evidence that his attorney could have used to discredit a key prosecution witness. Dissenting Justices Scalia and Thomas agreed, but disagreed with the majority's overturning of the death sentence.

Schriro v. Summerlin,   5:4   Writing for the Court, Justice
124 S.Ct. 2519 (2004)   Scalia held that the ruling in *Ring
v. Arizona,* 536 U.S. 584 (2002),
holding that the Sixth Amendment requires juries (not judges) to determine
the aggravating circumstances for imposing death sentences, was a new procedural rule and that such rules do not apply retroactively to death sentences
that are already final, unless they are fundamental and likely to diminish the
chance of an accurate conviction.

II

THE RIGHT OF PRIVACY

B | *Privacy and Personal Autonomy*

Lawrence v. Texas
539 U.S. 558, 123 S.Ct. 2472 (2003)

On the night of September 17, 1998, the Harris County Texas police department received a frantic call from someone who claimed that there was a man with a gun "going crazy" in the Houston apartment of John Geddes Lawrence. Officers responded and arrived and entered the apartment. They found no intruder, but instead found Lawrence and Tyron Garner engaged in sodomy. They arrested them for violating the state's "homosexual conduct" law, which makes it a misdemeanor for any person to engage "in deviant sexual intercourse with another individual of the same sex." A few weeks later, Lawrence and Garner were tried and found guilty of "deviant homosexual conduct," and each was fined $200. They appealed and challenged the statute's constitutionality. A three-judge appeals panel ruled two to one that the convictions "impermissibly discriminate on the basis of sex" and violated the Equal Rights Amendment of the state constitution. But in March 2001, the full Texas Court of Appeals reversed and upheld the state's "homosexual conduct" law. Lawrence appealed that decision to the Texas Court of Criminal Appeals, which denied review, and subsequently filed an appeal to the U.S. Supreme Court, which granted review.

The state court's decision was reversed by a vote of six to three. Justice Kennedy delivered the opinion of the Court. Justice O'Connor filed a concurring opinion. Justices Scalia and Thomas filed dissenting opinions, which Chief Justice Rehnquist joined.

☐ *Justice KENNEDY delivered the opinion of the Court.*

Liberty protects the person from unwarranted government intrusions into a dwelling or other private places. In our tradition the State is not omnipresent in the home. And there are other spheres of our lives and existence, outside the home, where the State should not be a dominant presence. Freedom extends beyond spatial bounds. Liberty presumes an autonomy of self that includes freedom of thought, belief, expression, and certain intimate conduct. The instant case involves liberty of the person both in its spatial and more transcendent dimensions.

The question before the Court is the validity of a Texas statute making it a crime for two persons of the same sex to engage in certain intimate sexual conduct. . . .

We conclude the case should be resolved by determining whether the petitioners were free as adults to engage in the private conduct in the exercise of their liberty under the Due Process Clause of the Fourteenth Amendment to the Constitution. For this inquiry we deem it necessary to reconsider the Court's holding in *Bowers* [*v. Hardwick*, 478 U.S. 186 (1986)].

There are broad statements of the substantive reach of liberty under the Due Process Clause in earlier cases, including *Pierce v. Society of Sisters*, 268 U.S. 510 (1925), and *Meyer v. Nebraska*, 262 U.S. 390 (1923); but the most pertinent beginning point is our decision in *Griswold v. Connecticut*, 381 U.S. 479 (1965).

In *Griswold* the Court invalidated a state law prohibiting the use of drugs or devices of contraception and counseling or aiding and abetting the use of contraceptives. The Court described the protected interest as a right to privacy and placed emphasis on the marriage relation and the protected space of the marital bedroom.

After *Griswold* it was established that the right to make certain decisions regarding sexual conduct extends beyond the marital relationship. In *Eisenstadt v. Baird*, 405 U.S. 438 (1972), the Court invalidated a law prohibiting the distribution of contraceptives to unmarried persons. The case was decided under the Equal Protection Clause, but with respect to unmarried persons, the Court went on to state the fundamental proposition that the law impaired the exercise of their personal rights.

The opinions in *Griswold* and *Eisenstadt* were part of the background for the decision in *Roe v. Wade*, 410 U.S. 113 (1973). As is well known, the case involved a challenge to the Texas law prohibiting abortions, but the laws of other States were affected as well. Although the Court held the woman's rights were not absolute, her right to elect an abortion did have real and substantial protection as an exercise of her liberty under the Due Process Clause. The Court cited cases that protect spatial freedom and cases that go well beyond it. *Roe* recognized the right of a woman to make certain fundamental decisions affecting her destiny and confirmed once more that the protection of liberty under the Due Process Clause has a substantive dimension of fundamental significance in defining the rights of the person. . . .

This was the state of the law with respect to some of the most relevant cases when the Court considered *Bowers v. Hardwick.* The facts in *Bowers* had some similarities to the instant case. A police officer, whose right to enter seems not to have been in question, observed Hardwick, in his own bedroom, engaging in intimate sexual conduct with another adult male. The conduct was in violation of a Georgia statute making it a criminal offense to engage in sodomy. One difference between the two cases is that the Georgia statute prohibited the conduct whether or not the participants were of the same sex, while the Texas statute, as we have seen, applies only to participants of the same sex. Hardwick was not prosecuted, but he brought an action in federal court to declare the state statute invalid. He alleged he was a practicing homosexual and that the criminal prohibition violated rights guaranteed to him by the Constitution. The Court, in an opinion by Justice WHITE, sustained the Georgia law. Chief Justice BURGER and Justice POWELL joined the opinion of the Court and filed separate, concurring opinions. Four Justices dissented.

The Court began its substantive discussion in *Bowers* as follows: "The issue presented is whether the Federal Constitution confers a fundamental right upon homosexuals to engage in sodomy and hence invalidates the laws of the many States that still make such conduct illegal and have done so for a very long time." That statement, we now conclude, discloses the Court's own failure to appreciate the extent of the liberty at stake. To say that the issue in *Bowers* was simply the right to engage in certain sexual conduct demeans the claim the individual put forward, just as it would demean a married couple were it to be said marriage is simply about the right to have sexual intercourse. The laws involved in *Bowers* and here are, to be sure, statutes that purport to do no more than prohibit a particular sexual act. Their penalties and purposes, though, have more far-reaching consequences, touching upon the most private human conduct, sexual behavior, and in the most private of places, the home. The statutes do seek to control a personal relationship that, whether or not entitled to formal recognition in the law, is within the liberty of persons to choose without being punished as criminals.

This, as a general rule, should counsel against attempts by the State, or a court, to define the meaning of the relationship or to set its boundaries absent injury to a person or abuse of an institution the law protects. It suffices for us to acknowledge that adults may choose to enter upon this relationship in the confines of their homes and their own private lives and still retain their dignity as free persons. When sexuality finds overt expression in intimate conduct with another person, the conduct can be but one element in a personal bond that is more enduring. The liberty protected by the Constitution allows homosexual persons the right to make this choice. . . .

At the outset it should be noted that there is no long-standing history in this country of laws directed at homosexual conduct as a distinct matter. Beginning in colonial times there were prohibitions of sodomy derived from the English criminal laws passed in the first instance by the Reformation Parliament of 1533. The English prohibition was understood to include relations between men and women as well as relations between men and men. Thus early American sodomy laws were not directed at homosexuals as such but instead sought to prohibit nonprocreative sexual activity more generally. This does not suggest approval of homosexual conduct. It does tend to show that this particular form of conduct was not thought of as a separate category from like conduct between heterosexual persons.

Laws prohibiting sodomy do not seem to have been enforced against consenting adults acting in private. A substantial number of sodomy prosecutions and convictions for which there are surviving records were for predatory acts against those who could not or did not consent, as in the case of a minor or the victim of an assault. . . .

The policy of punishing consenting adults for private acts was not much discussed in the early legal literature. We can infer that one reason for this was the very private nature of the conduct. Despite the absence of prosecutions, there may have been periods in which there was public criticism of homosexuals as such and an insistence that the criminal laws be enforced to discourage their practices. But far from possessing "ancient roots," *Bowers*, American laws targeting same-sex couples did not develop until the last third of the 20th century. The reported decisions concerning the prosecution of consensual, homosexual sodomy between adults for the years 1880–1995 are not always clear in the details, but a significant number involved conduct in a public place.

It was not until the 1970s that any State singled out same-sex relations for criminal prosecution, and only nine States have done so.

In summary, the historical grounds relied upon in *Bowers* are more complex than the majority opinion and the concurring opinion by Chief Justice BURGER indicate. Their historical premises are not without doubt and, at the very least, are overstated.

It must be acknowledged, of course, that the Court in *Bowers* was making the broader point that for centuries there have been powerful voices to condemn homosexual conduct as immoral. The condemnation has been shaped by religious beliefs, conceptions of right and acceptable behavior, and respect for the traditional family. For many persons these are not trivial concerns but profound and deep convictions accepted as ethical and moral principles to which they aspire and which thus determine the course of their lives. These considerations do not answer the question before us, however. The issue is whether the majority may use the power of the State to enforce these views on the whole society through operation of the criminal law. "Our obligation is to define the liberty of all, not to mandate our own moral code." *Planned Parenthood of Southeastern Pa. v. Casey*, 505 U.S. 833 (1992).

Chief Justice BURGER joined the opinion for the Court in *Bowers* and further explained his views as follows: "Decisions of individuals relating to homosexual conduct have been subject to state intervention throughout the history of Western civilization. Condemnation of those practices is firmly rooted in Judeao-Christian moral and ethical standards." As with Justice WHITE's assumptions about history, scholarship casts some doubt on the sweeping nature of the statement by Chief Justice BURGER as it pertains to private homosexual conduct between consenting adults. In all events we think that our laws and traditions in the past half century are of most relevance here. These references show an emerging awareness that liberty gives substantial protection to adult persons in deciding how to conduct their private lives in matters pertaining to sex. . . .

In *Bowers* the Court referred to the fact that before 1961 all 50 States had outlawed sodomy, and that at the time of the Court's decision 24 States and the District of Columbia had sodomy laws. Justice POWELL pointed out that these prohibitions often were being ignored, however. Georgia, for instance, had not sought to enforce its law for decades.

The sweeping references by Chief Justice BURGER to the history of Western civilization and to Judeo-Christian moral and ethical standards did not take account of other authorities pointing in an opposite direction. A committee advising the British Parliament recommended in 1957 repeal of laws punishing homosexual conduct. *The Wolfenden Report* (1963). Parliament enacted the substance of those recommendations 10 years later.

Of even more importance, almost five years before *Bowers* was decided the European Court of Human Rights considered a case with parallels to *Bowers* and to today's case. An adult male resident in Northern Ireland alleged he was a practicing homosexual who desired to engage in consensual homosexual conduct. The laws of Northern Ireland forbade him that right. He alleged that he had been questioned, his home had been searched, and he feared criminal prosecution. The court held that the laws proscribing the conduct were invalid under the European Convention on Human Rights. *Dudgeon v. United Kingdom*, 45 Eur. Ct. H. R. (1981). Authoritative in all countries that are members of the Council of Europe (21 nations then, 45 nations now), the decision is at odds with the premise in *Bowers* that the claim put forward was insubstantial in our Western civilization.

In our own constitutional system the deficiencies in *Bowers* became even more apparent in the years following its announcement. The 25 States with laws prohibiting the relevant conduct referenced in the *Bowers* decision are reduced now to 13, of which 4 enforce their laws only against homosexual conduct. In those States where sodomy is still proscribed, whether for same-sex or heterosexual conduct, there is a pattern of nonenforcement with respect to consenting adults acting in private. The State of Texas admitted in 1994 that as of that date it had not prosecuted anyone under those circumstances.

Two principal cases decided after *Bowers* cast its holding into even more doubt. In *Planned Parenthood of Southeastern Pa. v. Casey*, 505 U.S. 833 (1992), the Court reaffirmed the substantive force of the liberty protected by the Due Process Clause. The *Casey* decision again confirmed that our laws and tradition afford constitutional protection to personal decisions relating to marriage, procreation, contraception, family relationships, child rearing, and education. . . . Persons in a homosexual relationship may seek autonomy for these purposes, just as heterosexual persons do. The decision in *Bowers* would deny them this right.

The second post-*Bowers* case of principal relevance is *Romer v. Evans*, 517 U.S. 620 (1996). There the Court struck down class-based legislation directed at homosexuals as a violation of the Equal Protection Clause. *Romer* invalidated an amendment to Colorado's constitution which named as a solitary class persons who were homosexuals, lesbians, or bisexual either by "orientation, conduct, practices or relationships," and deprived them of protection under state antidiscrimination laws. We concluded that the provision was "born of animosity toward the class of persons affected" and further that it had no rational relation to a legitimate governmental purpose. . . .

Equality of treatment and the due process right to demand respect for conduct protected by the substantive guarantee of liberty are linked in important respects, and a decision on the latter point advances both interests. If protected conduct is made criminal and the law which does so remains unexamined for its substantive validity, its stigma might remain even if it were not enforceable as drawn for equal protection reasons. When homosexual conduct is made criminal by the law of the State, that declaration in and of itself is an invitation to subject homosexual persons to discrimination both in the public and in the private spheres. The central holding of *Bowers* has been brought in question by this case, and it should be addressed. Its continuance as precedent demeans the lives of homosexual persons. . . .

The foundations of *Bowers* have sustained serious erosion from our recent decisions in *Casey* and *Romer*. When our precedent has been thus weakened, criticism from other sources is of greater significance. In the United States criticism of *Bowers* has been substantial and continuing, disapproving of its reasoning in all respects, not just as to its historical assumptions. The courts of five different States have declined to follow it in interpreting provisions in their own state constitutions parallel to the Due Process Clause of the Fourteenth Amendment.

To the extent *Bowers* relied on values we share with a wider civilization, it should be noted that the reasoning and holding in *Bowers* have been rejected elsewhere. The European Court of Human Rights has followed not *Bowers* but its own decision in *Dudgeon v. United Kingdom*. Other nations, too, have taken action consistent with an affirmation of the protected right of homosexual adults to engage in intimate, consensual conduct. The right the petitioners seek in this case has been accepted as an integral part of human freedom in many other countries. There has been no showing that in this country the governmental interest in circumscribing personal choice is somehow more legitimate or urgent.

The doctrine of *stare decisis* is essential to the respect accorded to the judgments of the Court and to the stability of the law. It is not, however, an inexorable command. *Payne v. Tennessee*, 501 U.S. 808 (1991). In *Casey* we noted that when a Court is asked to overrule a precedent recognizing a constitutional liberty interest, individual or societal reliance on the existence of that liberty cautions with particular strength against reversing course. The holding in *Bowers*, however, has not induced detrimental reliance comparable to some instances where recognized individual rights are involved. Indeed, there has been no individual or societal reliance on *Bowers* of the sort that could counsel against overturning its holding once there are compelling reasons to do so. *Bowers* itself causes uncertainty, for the precedents before and after its issuance contradict its central holding.

The rationale of *Bowers* does not withstand careful analysis. *Bowers* was not correct when it was decided, and it is not correct today. It ought not to remain binding precedent. *Bowers v. Hardwick* should be and now is overruled.

The present case does not involve minors. It does not involve persons who might be injured or coerced or who are situated in relationships where consent might not easily be refused. It does not involve public conduct or prostitution. It does not involve whether the government must give formal recognition to any relationship that homosexual persons seek to enter. The case does involve two adults who, with full and mutual consent from each other, engaged in sexual practices common to a homosexual lifestyle. The petitioners are entitled to respect for their private lives. The State cannot demean their existence or control their destiny by making their private sexual conduct a crime. Their right to liberty under the Due Process Clause gives them the full right to engage in their conduct without intervention of the government. The Texas statute furthers no legitimate state interest which can justify its intrusion into the personal and private life of the individual.

Had those who drew and ratified the Due Process Clauses of the Fifth Amendment or the Fourteenth Amendment known the components of liberty in its manifold possibilities, they might have been more specific. They did not presume to have this insight. They knew times can blind us to certain truths and later generations can see that laws once thought necessary and proper in fact serve only to oppress. As the Constitution endures, persons in every generation can invoke its principles in their own search for greater freedom.

The judgment of the Court of Appeals for the Texas Fourteenth District is reversed, and the case is remanded for further proceedings not inconsistent with this opinion.

It is so ordered.

212 | THE RIGHT OF PRIVACY

☐ *Justice O'CONNOR, concurring in the judgment.*

The Court today overrules *Bowers v. Hardwick.* I joined *Bowers,* and do not join the Court in overruling it. Nevertheless, I agree with the Court that Texas's statute banning same-sex sodomy is unconstitutional. Rather than relying on the substantive component of the Fourteenth Amendment's Due Process Clause, as the Court does, I base my conclusion on the Fourteenth Amendment's Equal Protection Clause. . . .

The statute at issue here makes sodomy a crime only if a person "engages in deviate sexual intercourse with another individual of the same sex." Sodomy between opposite-sex partners, however, is not a crime in Texas. That is, Texas treats the same conduct differently based solely on the participants. Those harmed by this law are people who have a same-sex sexual orientation and thus are more likely to engage in behavior prohibited by Section 21.06. The Texas statute makes homosexuals unequal in the eyes of the law by making particular conduct—and only that conduct—subject to criminal sanction. It appears that prosecutions under Texas's sodomy law are rare.

And the effect of Texas's sodomy law is not just limited to the threat of prosecution or consequence of conviction. Texas's sodomy law brands all homosexuals as criminals. . . .

This case raises a different issue than *Bowers*: whether, under the Equal Protection Clause, moral disapproval is a legitimate state interest to justify by itself a statute that bans homosexual sodomy, but not heterosexual sodomy. It is not. Moral disapproval of this group, like a bare desire to harm the group, is an interest that is insufficient to satisfy rational basis review under the Equal Protection Clause. Indeed, we have never held that moral disapproval, without any other asserted state interest, is a sufficient rationale under the Equal Protection Clause to justify a law that discriminates among groups of persons. . . .

That this law as applied to private, consensual conduct is unconstitutional under the Equal Protection Clause does not mean that other laws distinguishing between heterosexuals and homosexuals would similarly fail under rational basis review. Texas cannot assert any legitimate state interest here, such as national security or preserving the traditional institution of marriage. Unlike the moral disapproval of same-sex relations—the asserted state interest in this case—other reasons exist to promote the institution of marriage beyond mere moral disapproval of an excluded group.

A law branding one class of persons as criminal solely based on the State's moral disapproval of that class and the conduct associated with that class runs contrary to the values of the Constitution and the Equal Protection Clause, under any standard of review. I therefore concur in the Court's judgment that Texas's sodomy law banning "deviate sexual intercourse" between consenting adults of the same sex, but not between consenting adults of different sexes, is unconstitutional.

☐ *Justice SCALIA, with whom The CHIEF JUSTICE and Justice THOMAS join, dissenting.*

"Liberty finds no refuge in a jurisprudence of doubt." *Planned Parenthood of Southeastern Pa. v. Casey,* 505 U.S. 833 (1992). That was the Court's sententious response, barely more than a decade ago, to those seeking to overrule

Roe v. Wade, 410 U.S. 113 (1973). The Court's response today, to those who have engaged in a 17-year crusade to overrule *Bowers v. Hardwick*, 478 U.S. 186 (1986), is very different. The need for stability and certainty presents no barrier. . . .

I begin with the Court's surprising readiness to reconsider a decision rendered a mere 17 years ago in *Bowers v. Hardwick*. I do not myself believe in rigid adherence to *stare decisis* in constitutional cases; but I do believe that we should be consistent rather than manipulative in invoking the doctrine. Today's opinions in support of reversal do not bother to distinguish—or indeed, even bother to mention—the paean to *stare decisis* coauthored by three Members of today's majority in *Planned Parenthood v. Casey*. There, when *stare decisis* meant preservation of judicially invented abortion rights, the widespread criticism of *Roe* was strong reason to reaffirm it. Today, however, the widespread opposition to *Bowers*, a decision resolving an issue as "intensely divisive" as the issue in *Roe*, is offered as a reason in favor of overruling it. Gone, too, is any "enquiry" (of the sort conducted in *Casey*) into whether the decision sought to be overruled has "proven 'unworkable,'" *Casey*.

Today's approach to *stare decisis* invites us to overrule an erroneously decided precedent (including an "intensely divisive" decision) if: (1) its foundations have been "eroded" by subsequent decisions; (2) it has been subject to "substantial and continuing" criticism; and (3) it has not induced "individual or societal reliance" that counsels against overturning. The problem is that *Roe* itself—which today's majority surely has no disposition to overrule—satisfies these conditions to at least the same degree as *Bowers*. . . .

What a massive disruption of the current social order, therefore, the overruling of *Bowers* entails. Not so the overruling of *Roe*, which would simply have restored the regime that existed for centuries before 1973, in which the permissibility of and restrictions upon abortion were determined legislatively State by State. *Casey*, however, chose to base its *stare decisis* determination on a different "sort" of reliance. "[P]eople," it said, "have organized intimate relationships and made choices that define their views of themselves and their places in society, in reliance on the availability of abortion in the event that contraception should fail." This falsely assumes that the consequence of overruling *Roe* would have been to make abortion unlawful. It would not; it would merely have permitted the States to do so. Many States would unquestionably have declined to prohibit abortion, and others would not have prohibited it within six months (after which the most significant reliance interests would have expired). Even for persons in States other than these, the choice would not have been between abortion and childbirth, but between abortion nearby and abortion in a neighboring State.

To tell the truth, it does not surprise me, and should surprise no one, that the Court has chosen today to revise the standards of *stare decisis* set forth in *Casey*. It has thereby exposed *Casey's* extraordinary deference to precedent for the result-oriented expedient that it is.

Having decided that it need not adhere to *stare decisis*, the Court still must establish that *Bowers* was wrongly decided and that the Texas statute, as applied to petitioners, is unconstitutional. . . .

Our opinions applying the doctrine known as "substantive due process" hold that the Due Process Clause prohibits States from infringing fundamental liberty interests, unless the infringement is narrowly tailored to serve a compelling state interest. We have held repeatedly, in cases the Court today does not overrule, that only fundamental rights qualify for this so-called "heightened scrutiny" protection—that is, rights which are "'deeply rooted in this Nation's history and tradition.'"

Bowers held, first, that criminal prohibitions of homosexual sodomy are not subject to heightened scrutiny because they do not implicate a "fundamental right" under the Due Process Clause. Noting that "[p]roscriptions against that conduct have ancient roots," that "[s]odomy was a criminal offense at common law and was forbidden by the laws of the original 13 States when they ratified the Bill of Rights," and that many States had retained their bans on sodomy, *Bowers* concluded that a right to engage in homosexual sodomy was not "'deeply rooted in this Nation's history and tradition.'"

The Court today does not overrule this holding. Not once does it describe homosexual sodomy as a "fundamental right" or a "fundamental liberty interest," nor does it subject the Texas statute to strict scrutiny. Instead, having failed to establish that the right to homosexual sodomy is "'deeply rooted in this Nation's history and tradition,'" the Court concludes that the application of Texas's statute to petitioners' conduct fails the rational-basis test, and overrules *Bowers'* holding to the contrary.

I shall address that rational-basis holding presently. First, however, I address some aspersions that the Court casts upon *Bowers'* conclusion that homosexual sodomy is not a "fundamental right"—even though, as I have said, the Court does not have the boldness to reverse that conclusion.

The Court's description of "the state of the law" at the time of *Bowers* only confirms that *Bowers* was right. The Court points to *Griswold v. Connecticut* (1965). But that case expressly disclaimed any reliance on the doctrine of "substantive due process," and grounded the so-called "right to privacy" in penumbras of constitutional provisions other than the Due Process Clause.

Roe v. Wade recognized that the right to abort an unborn child was a "fundamental right" protected by the Due Process Clause. The *Roe* Court, however, made no attempt to establish that this right was "'deeply rooted in this Nation's history and tradition'"; instead, it based its conclusion that "the Fourteenth Amendment's concept of personal liberty . . . is broad enough to encompass a woman's decision whether or not to terminate her pregnancy" on its own normative judgment that anti-abortion laws were undesirable. . . .

After discussing the history of antisodomy laws, the Court proclaims that, "it should be noted that there is no long-standing history in this country of laws directed at homosexual conduct as a distinct matter." This observation in no way casts into doubt the "definitive [historical] conclusion," on which *Bowers* relied: that our Nation has a longstanding history of laws prohibiting sodomy in general—regardless of whether it was performed by same-sex or opposite-sex couples. It is (as *Bowers* recognized) entirely irrelevant whether the laws in our long national tradition criminalizing homosexual sodomy were "directed at homosexual conduct as a distinct matter." Whether homosexual sodomy was prohibited by a law targeted at same-sex sexual relations or by a more general law prohibiting both homosexual and heterosexual sodomy, the only relevant point is that it was criminalized—which suffices to establish that homosexual sodomy is not a right "deeply rooted in our Nation's history and tradition." The Court today agrees that homosexual sodomy was criminalized and thus does not dispute the facts on which *Bowers* actually relied.

Next the Court makes the claim, again unsupported by any citations, that "[l]aws prohibiting sodomy do not seem to have been enforced against consenting adults acting in private." The key qualifier here is "acting in private"—since the Court admits that sodomy laws were enforced against consenting adults (although the Court contends that prosecutions were "infrequent"). I do not know what "acting in private" means; surely consensual sodomy, like heterosexual intercourse, is rarely performed on stage. If all the Court means by "acting in private" is "on private premises, with the doors closed and windows covered," it is entirely unsurprising that evidence of enforcement would be hard to come by. Surely that lack of evidence would not sustain the proposition that consensual sodomy on private premises with the doors closed and windows covered was regarded as a "fundamental right," even though all other consensual sodomy was criminalized. There are 203 prosecutions for consensual, adult homosexual sodomy reported in the West Reporting system and official state reporters from the years 1880–1995. There are also records of 20 sodomy prosecutions and 4 executions during the colonial period. *Bowers'* conclusion that homosexual sodomy is not a fundamental right "deeply rooted in this Nation's history and tradition" is utterly unassailable.

Realizing that fact, the Court instead says: "[W]e think that our laws and traditions in the past half century are of most relevance here. These references show an emerging awareness that liberty gives substantial protection to adult persons in deciding how to conduct their private lives in matters pertaining to sex." Apart from the fact that such an "emerging awareness" does not establish a "fundamental right," the statement is factually false. States continue to prosecute all sorts of crimes by adults "in matters pertaining to sex": prostitution, adult incest, adultery, obscenity, and child pornography. Sodomy laws, too, have been enforced "in the past half century," in which there have been 134 reported cases involving prosecutions for consensual, adult, homosexual sodomy. In relying, for evidence of an "emerging recognition," upon the American Law Institute's 1955 recommendation not to criminalize "'consensual sexual relations conducted in private,'" the Court ignores the fact that this recommendation was "a point of resistance in most of the states that considered adopting the Model Penal Code."

In any event, an "emerging awareness" is by definition not "deeply rooted in this Nation's history and tradition[s]," as we have said "fundamental right" status requires. Constitutional entitlements do not spring into existence because some States choose to lessen or eliminate criminal sanctions on certain behavior. Much less do they spring into existence, as the Court seems to believe, because foreign nations decriminalize conduct. The *Bowers* majority opinion never relied on "values we share with a wider civilization," but rather rejected the claimed right to sodomy on the ground that such a right was not "'deeply rooted in this Nation's history and tradition.'" *Bowers'* rational-basis holding is likewise devoid of any reliance on the views of a "wider civilization." The Court's discussion of these foreign views (ignoring, of course, the many countries that have retained criminal prohibitions on sodomy) is therefore meaningless *dicta*.

I turn now to the ground on which the Court squarely rests its holding: the contention that there is no rational basis for the law here under attack. This proposition is so out of accord with our jurisprudence—indeed, with the jurisprudence of any society we know—that it requires little discussion.

The Texas statute undeniably seeks to further the belief of its citizens that certain forms of sexual behavior are "immoral and unacceptable," *Bowers*— the same interest furthered by criminal laws against fornication, bigamy, adultery, adult incest, bestiality, and obscenity. *Bowers* held that this was a legitimate state interest. The Court today reaches the opposite conclusion.

The Texas statute, it says, "furthers no legitimate state interest which can justify its intrusion into the personal and private life of the individual." The Court embraces instead Justice STEVENS' declaration in his *Bowers* dissent, that "the fact that the governing majority in a State has traditionally viewed a particular practice as immoral is not a sufficient reason for upholding a law prohibiting the practice." This effectively decrees the end of all morals legislation. If, as the Court asserts, the promotion of majoritarian sexual morality is not even a legitimate state interest, none of the above-mentioned laws can survive rational-basis review.

Finally, I turn to petitioners' equal-protection challenge, which no Member of the Court save Justice O'CONNOR embraces: On its face Section 21.06(a) applies equally to all persons. Men and women, heterosexuals and homosexuals, are all subject to its prohibition of deviate sexual intercourse with someone of the same sex. To be sure, Section 21.06 does distinguish between the sexes insofar as concerns the partner with whom the sexual acts are performed: men can violate the law only with other men, and women only with other women. But this cannot itself be a denial of equal protection, since it is precisely the same distinction regarding partner that is drawn in state laws prohibiting marriage with someone of the same sex while permitting marriage with someone of the opposite sex. . . .

Today's opinion is the product of a Court, which is the product of a law-profession culture, that has largely signed on to the so-called homosexual agenda, by which I mean the agenda promoted by some homosexual activists directed at eliminating the moral opprobrium that has traditionally attached to homosexual conduct. One of the most revealing statements in today's opinion is the Court's grim warning that the criminalization of homosexual conduct is "an invitation to subject homosexual persons to discrimination both in the public and in the private spheres." It is clear from this that the Court has taken sides in the culture war, departing from its role of assuring, as neutral observer, that the democratic rules of engagement are observed. Many Americans do not want persons who openly engage in homosexual conduct as partners in their business, as scoutmasters for their children, as teachers in their children's schools, or as boarders in their home. They view this as protecting themselves and their families from a lifestyle that they believe to be immoral and destructive. The Court views it as "discrimination" which it is the function of our judgments to deter. So imbued is the Court with the law profession's anti-anti-homosexual culture, that it is seemingly unaware that the attitudes of that culture are not obviously "mainstream"; that in most States what the Court calls "discrimination" against those who engage in homosexual acts is perfectly legal; that proposals to ban such "discrimination" under Title VII have repeatedly been rejected by Congress; that in some cases such "discrimination" is mandated by federal statute (mandating discharge from the armed forces of any service member who engages in or intends to engage in homosexual acts); and that in some cases such "discrimination" is a constitutional right, see *Boy Scouts of America v. Dale*, 530 U.S. 640 (2000).

Let me be clear that I have nothing against homosexuals, or any other group, promoting their agenda through normal democratic means. Social perceptions of sexual and other morality change over time, and every group has the right to persuade its fellow citizens that its view of such matters is the best. That homosexuals have achieved some success in that enterprise is attested to by the fact that Texas is one of the few remaining States that criminalize private, consensual homosexual acts. But persuading one's fellow citizens is one thing, and imposing one's views in absence of democratic majority will is something else. I would no more require a State to criminalize homosexual acts—or, for that matter, display any moral disapprobation of them—than I would forbid it to do so. What Texas has chosen to do is well within the range of traditional democratic action, and its hand should not be stayed through the invention of a brand-new "constitutional right" by a Court that is impatient of democratic change. It is indeed true that "later generations can see that laws once thought necessary and proper in fact serve only to oppress," and when that happens, later generations can repeal those laws. But it is the premise of our system that those judgments are to be made by the people, and not imposed by a governing caste that knows best.

☐ *Justice THOMAS, dissenting.*

I join Justice SCALIA's dissenting opinion. I write separately to note that the law before the Court today "is . . . uncommonly silly." *Griswold v. Connecticut* (1965) (STEWART, J., dissenting). If I were a member of the Texas Legislature, I would vote to repeal it. Punishing someone for expressing his sexual preference through noncommercial consensual conduct with another adult does not appear to be a worthy way to expend valuable law enforcement resources.

  Notwithstanding this, I recognize that as a member of this Court I am not empowered to help petitioners and others similarly situated. My duty, rather, is to "decide cases 'agreeably to the Constitution and laws of the United States.'" And, just like Justice STEWART, I "can find [neither in the Bill of Rights nor any other part of the Constitution a] general right of privacy," or as the Court terms it today, the "liberty of the person both in its spatial and more transcendent dimensions."

■ IN COMPARATIVE PERSPECTIVE

Canadian Courts Forbid Discrimination against Homosexuals and Same-Sex Marriages

In *Egan v. Canada*, 2 S.C.R. 513 (1995), the Supreme Court of Canada held, "on the basis historical, social, political and economic disadvantage suffered by homosexuals" and the emerging consensus among legislatures, as well as previous judicial decisions, that sexual orientation was embraced by the equality guarantee of Section 15(1) of Canada's Charter of Rights and Freedom, which provides: "Every individual is equal before and under the law and has the right to the equal protection and equal benefit of the law without discrimination and, in particular, without discrimination based on race, national or ethnic origin, colour, religion, sex, age or mental or physical disability."

Later decisions of the Canadian Supreme Court expanded protection for gays and lesbians. In *Vriend v. Alberta*, 1 S.C.R. 493 (1998), for instance, the Court held that Alberta's human rights code must give protection to homosexuals in employment in order to comply with the guarantee of Section 15(1). See also *M. v. H.*, 2 S.C.R. 3 (1999).

More recently, a lower court judge declared Quebec's prohibition against same-sex marriages invalid, in *Hendricks v. Quebec*, J.Q. No. 3816 (S.C.) (2002). Likewise, the British Columbia Court of Appeal declared the common law definition of marriage unconstitutional and required the substitution of the words "two persons" for "one man and one woman," in *EGALE Canada Inc. v. Attorney General of Canada*, B.C.J. 994 (2003). And in *Halpern v. Attorney General of Canada*, No. C39172 (June 10, 2003), the Court of Appeal for Ontario held that Section 15(1) bars discrimination against same-sex marriages.

Writing for the Court in *Halpern*, Chief Justice Roy McMurtry rejected the government's position against recognizing same-sex marriages, upon reasoning:

> No one is disputing that marriage is a fundamental societal institution. Similarly, it is accepted that, with limited exceptions, marriage has been understood to be a monogamous opposite-sex union. What needs to be determined, however, is whether there is a valid objective to maintaining marriage as an exclusively heterosexual institution. Stating that marriage is heterosexual because it always has been heterosexual is merely an explanation for the opposite-sex requirement of marriage; it is not an objective that is capable of justifying the infringement of a Charter guarantee.
>
> We now turn to the more specific purposes of marriage advanced by [the government]: (i) uniting the opposite sexes; (ii) encouraging the birth and raising of children of the marriage; and (iii) companionship.

The first purpose, which results in favouring one form of relationship over another, suggests that uniting two persons of the same sex is of lesser importance.... [A] purpose that demeans the dignity of same-sex couples is contrary to the values of a free and democratic society and cannot be considered to be pressing and substantial. A law cannot be justified on the very basis upon which it is being attacked.

The second purpose of marriage, as advanced by [the government], is encouraging the birth and raising of children. Clearly, encouraging procreation and childrearing is a laudable goal that is properly regarded as pressing and substantial. However, the AGC must demonstrate that the objective of maintaining marriage as an exclusively heterosexual institution is pressing and substantial: see *Vriend* [*v. Alberta*].

We fail to see how the encouragement of procreation and childrearing is a pressing and substantial objective of maintaining marriage as an exclusively heterosexual institution. Heterosexual married couples will not stop having or raising children because same-sex couples are permitted to marry. Moreover, an increasing percentage of children are being born to and raised by same-sex couples.

The [government] submits that the union of two persons of the opposite sex is the only union that can "naturally" procreate. In terms of that biological reality, same-sex couples are different from opposite-sex couples. In our view, however, "natural" procreation is not a sufficiently pressing and substantial objective to justify infringing the equality rights of same-sex couples. As previously stated, same-sex couples can have children by other means, such as adoption, surrogacy and donor insemination. A law that aims to encourage only "natural" procreation ignores the fact that same-sex couples are capable of having children.

Similarly, a law that restricts marriage to opposite-sex couples, on the basis that a fundamental purpose of marriage is the raising of children, suggests that same-sex couples are not equally capable of childrearing. The [government] has put forward no evidence to support such a proposition. Neither is the [government] advocating such a view; rather, it takes the position that social science research is not capable of establishing the proposition one way or another. In the absence of cogent evidence, it is our view that the objective is based on a stereotypical assumption that is not acceptable in a free and democratic society that prides itself on promoting equality and respect for all persons.

The third purpose of marriage advanced by the [government] is companionship. We consider companionship to be a laudable goal of marriage. However, encouraging companionship cannot be considered a pressing and substantial objective of the omission of the impugned law. Encouraging companionship between only persons of the opposite sex perpetuates the view that persons in same-sex relationships are not equally capable of providing companionship and forming lasting and loving relationships.

Accordingly, it is our view that the [government] has not demonstrated any pressing and substantial objective for excluding same-sex couples from the institution of marriage. For that reason, we conclude that the violation of the Couples' rights under Section 15(1) of the Charter cannot be saved. . . .

Note: the full text of the opinion in *Halpern v. Attorney General of Canada* is available on the website of the Court of Appeal of Ontario at www.ontariocourts.on.ca/decisions.

12

THE EQUAL PROTECTION OF
THE LAWS

A | Racial Discrimination
and State Action

In its 2002–2003 term the Court decided whether a referendum to stay
the implementation of an approved plan for low-income housing violated the Fourteenth Amendment, in *City of Cuyahoga Falls v. Buckeye
Community Hope Foundation* 538 U.S. 188 (2003). Buckeye Community
Hope Foundation purchased property in Cuyahoga Falls and submitted
a plan to develop affordable housing to the city's planning commission,
which granted approval, as did the city council. Subsequently, members
of the public voiced concerns about crime and drugs, safety, and the
"different class" of people associated with low-income housing, and
submitted a referendum petition to present the issue of the housing
development to the voters. The board of elections approved the petition
and stayed implementation of the plan. The foundation sued, claiming
violations of the Fourteenth Amendment and the Fair Housing Act. A
federal district court dismissed the claims, but the Court of Appeals for
the Sixth Circuit found that it had erred in dismissing the equal
protection claim and concluded that the foundation had presented
sufficient evidence to raise the claim that opposition to the low-income
housing project reflected racial bias and that the city gave effect to that
racial bias in allowing the referendum to stay the previously approved
plan. That decision was appealed and the Supreme Court granted
certiorari.

Writing for the Court, Justice O'Connor held that Buckeye Community Hope Foundation failed to establish a racially discriminatory intent, as required for an Equal Protection violation, in claiming an injury from the referendum petitioning process, instead of the referendum itself, which never went into effect. In other words, the foundation failed to show that the referendum process was motivated by racial animus.

C | *Affirmative Action and Reverse Discrimination*

In two widely watched cases challenging the University of Michigan's affirmative action programs, the Court revisited the issue of whether achieving diverse student bodies is permissible and withstands Fourteenth Amendment challenges, as Justice Powell held in *Regents of the University of California v. Bakke*, 438 U.S. 265 (1978) (excerpted in Vol. 2, Ch. 12). By a six-to-three vote in *Gratz v. Bollinger* (excerpted below) the justices struck down the college's program based on a point system. But splitting five to four in *Grutter v. Bollinger* (excerpted below), the justices upheld the law school's program for achieving a "critical mass" of students from groups that have historically been discriminated against.

Gratz v. Bollinger
539 U.S. 244, 123 S.Ct. 2411 (2003)

The University of Michigan receives over 13,000 applications for admission into its College of Literature, Science, and Arts, and admits approximately 3,950 students each year. In order to achieve a diverse student body, the college gave preference to applicants from "underrepresented minority groups," including African Americans, Hispanics, and Native Americans. In the mid-1990s the college used different admissions criteria and set aside a number of seats in each entering class in order to achieve a numerical target. In 1998–1999, however, the college changed its policy in favor of a point system. Under that system the college used a "selection index" or ranking on a 150-point scale in three categories: test scores, academic record, and other factors. As many as 110 of those points were based on test scores and academic achievements. A maximum of 40 points were assigned for other factors, including 20 points for students from underrepresented minority groups or from socioeconomically disadvantaged families; 16 points for state residents from rural areas; four points for children of alumni. In general, applicants in the range of 100 to 150 points were admitted; those between 95 and 99 were admitted or postponed; 90 to 94 postponed or delayed; 75 to 89 delayed or postponed; and 74 and below were delayed or rejected.

In 1995, Jennifer Gratz applied for admission. Her high school grade point average was 3.8 and her ACT standardized test score was 25. The college initially delayed her admission and then placed her on an extended wait list. Under the college's guidelines at the time all underrepresented minority applicants with Ms. Gratz's credentials were admitted, regardless of whether they were in- or out-of-state residents. Ms. Gratz filed a class action lawsuit challenging the constitutionality of the admissions program. In December 2000, a federal district court held that the college's admissions system in 1995–1998 violated the Fourteenth Amendment, but held that its use of a point system was permissible and advanced a compelling governmental interest in promoting diversity in higher education. Ms. Gratz appealed that decision.

The lower court was reversed by a vote of six to three. Chief Justice Rehnquist delivered the opinion of the Court. Justices O'Connor, Breyer, and Thomas filed concurring opinions. Justices Stevens, Souter, and Ginsburg filed dissenting opinions.

□ *CHIEF JUSTICE REHNQUIST delivered the opinion of the Court.*

We granted *certiorari* in this case to decide whether "the University of Michigan's use of racial preferences in undergraduate admissions violate[s] the Equal Protection Clause of the Fourteenth Amendment, Title VI of the Civil Rights Act of 1964." Because we find that the manner in which the University considers the race of applicants in its undergraduate admissions guidelines violates these constitutional and statutory provisions, we reverse that portion of the District Court's decision upholding the guidelines. . . .

Beginning with the 1998 academic year, the OUA [Office of Undergraduate Admissions] dispensed with the Guidelines tables and the SCUGA point system in favor of a "selection index," on which an applicant could score a maximum of 150 points. This index was divided linearly into ranges generally calling for admissions dispositions as follows: 100–150 (admit); 95–99 (admit or postpone); 90–94 (postpone or admit); 75–89 (delay or postpone); 74 and below (delay or reject).

Each application received points based on high school grade point average, standardized test scores, academic quality of an applicant's high school, strength or weakness of high school curriculum, in-state residency, alumni relationship, personal essay, and personal achievement or leadership. Of particular significance here, under a "miscellaneous" category, an applicant was entitled to 20 points based upon his or her membership in an underrepresented racial or ethnic minority group. The University explained that the "'development of the selection index for admissions in 1998 changed only the mechanics, not the substance of how race and ethnicity were considered in admissions.'" . . .

During 1999 and 2000, the OUA used the selection index, under which every applicant from an underrepresented racial or ethnic minority group was awarded 20 points. Starting in 1999, however, the University established an Admissions Review Committee (ARC), to provide an additional level of consideration for some applications. Under the new system, counselors may, in their discretion, "flag" an application for the ARC to review after determining that the applicant (1) is academically prepared to succeed at the University, (2) has achieved a minimum selection index score, and (3) possesses a quality or characteristic important to the University's composition of its freshman class, such as high class rank, unique life experiences, challenges, circumstances, interests or talents, socioeconomic disadvantage, and underrepresented race, ethnicity, or geography. After reviewing "flagged" applications, the ARC determines whether to admit, defer, or deny each applicant. . . .

It is by now well established that "all racial classifications reviewable under the Equal Protection Clause must be strictly scrutinized." *Adarand Constructors, Inc. v. Peña*, 515 U.S. 200 (1995). This "'standard of review . . . is not dependent on the race of those burdened or benefited by a particular classification.'" Thus, "any person, of whatever race, has the right to demand that any governmental actor subject to the Constitution justify any racial classification subjecting that person to unequal treatment under the strictest of judicial scrutiny."

To withstand our strict scrutiny analysis, respondents must demonstrate that the University's use of race in its current admission program employs "narrowly tailored measures that further compelling governmental interests." Because "[r]acial classifications are simply too pernicious to permit any but the most exact connection between justification and classification," *Fullilove v. Klutznick*, 448 U.S. 448 (1980), our review of whether such requirements have been met must entail "'a most searching examination.'" We find that the University's policy, which automatically distributes 20 points, or one-fifth of the points needed to guarantee admission, to every single "underrepresented minority" applicant solely because of race, is not narrowly tailored to achieve the interest in educational diversity that respondents claim justifies their program.

In *Bakke*, Justice POWELL reiterated that "[p]referring members of any one group for no reason other than race or ethnic origin is discrimination for its own sake." He then explained, however, that in his view it would be permissible for a university to employ an admissions program in which "race or ethnic background may be deemed a 'plus' in a particular applicant's file." . . .

Justice POWELL's opinion in *Bakke* emphasized the importance of considering each particular applicant as an individual, assessing all of the qualities that individual possesses, and in turn, evaluating that individual's ability to contribute to the unique setting of higher education. The admissions program Justice POWELL described, however, did not contemplate that any single characteristic automatically ensured a specific and identifiable contribution to a university's diversity. Instead, under the approach Justice POWELL described, each characteristic of a particular applicant was to be considered in assessing the applicant's entire application.

The current LSA policy does not provide such individualized consideration. The LSA's policy automatically distributes 20 points to every single applicant from an "underrepresented minority" group, as defined by the University. The only consideration that accompanies this distribution of points is a factual review of an application to determine whether an individual is a member of one of these minority groups. Moreover, unlike Justice POWELL's example, where the race of a "particular black applicant" could be considered without being decisive, the LSA's automatic distribution of 20 points has the effect of making "the factor of race . . . decisive" for virtually every minimally qualified underrepresented minority applicant. . . .

We conclude, therefore, that because the University's use of race in its current freshman admissions policy is not narrowly tailored to achieve respondents' asserted compelling interest in diversity, the admissions policy violates the Equal Protection Clause of the Fourteenth Amendment. We further find that the admissions policy also violates Title VI. Accordingly, we reverse that portion of the District Court's decision granting respondents summary judgment with respect to liability and remand the case for proceedings consistent with this opinion.

□ *Justice O'CONNOR, concurring.*

Unlike the law school admissions policy the Court upholds today in *Grutter v. Bollinger*, the procedures employed by the University of Michigan's (University) Office of Undergraduate Admissions do not provide for a meaningful individualized review of applicants. . . . The selection index thus precludes admissions counselors from conducting the type of individualized consideration the Court's opinion in *Grutter* requires: consideration of each applicant's individualized qualifications, including the contribution each individual's race or ethnic identity will make to the diversity of the student body, taking into account diversity within and among all racial and ethnic groups. . . .

Although the Office of Undergraduate Admissions does assign 20 points to some "soft" variables other than race, the points available for other diversity contributions, such as leadership and service, personal achievement, and geographic diversity, are capped at much lower levels. Even the most outstanding national high school leader could never receive more than five points for his or her accomplishments—a mere quarter of the points automatically assigned to an underrepresented minority solely based on the fact of his or her race. [T]he selection index, by setting up automatic, predetermined point allocations for the soft variables, ensures that the diversity contributions of applicants cannot be individually assessed. This policy stands in sharp contrast to the law school's admissions plan, which enables admissions officers to make nuanced judgments with respect to the contributions each applicant is likely to make to the diversity of the incoming class. . . .

□ *Justice GINSBURG, with whom Justice SOUTER joins, dissenting.*

In the wake "of a system of racial caste only recently ended" large disparities endure. Unemployment, poverty, and access to health care vary disproportionately by race. Neighborhoods and schools remain racially divided. African-American and Hispanic children are all too often educated in poverty-stricken and underperforming institutions. Adult African-Americans and Hispanics generally earn less than whites with equivalent levels of education. Equally credentialed job applicants receive different receptions depending on their race. Irrational prejudice is still encountered in real estate markets and consumer transactions. "Bias both conscious and unconscious, reflecting traditional and unexamined habits of thought, keeps up barriers that must come down if equal opportunity and nondiscrimination are ever genuinely to become this country's law and practice."

The Constitution instructs all who act for the government that they may not "deny to any person . . . the equal protection of the laws." In implementing this equality instruction, as I see it, government decisionmakers may properly distinguish between policies of exclusion and inclusion.

Our jurisprudence ranks race a "suspect" category, "not because [race] is inevitably an impermissible classification, but because it is one which usually, to our national shame, has been drawn for the purpose of maintaining racial inequality." But where race is considered "for the purpose of achieving equality," no automatic proscription is in order. For, "[t]he Constitution is both color blind and color conscious. To avoid conflict with the equal protection clause, a classification that denies a benefit, causes harm, or imposes a burden must not be based on race. In that sense, the Constitution is color blind. But the Constitution is color conscious to prevent discrimination being perpetuated and to undo the effects of past discrimination."

The mere assertion of a laudable governmental purpose, of course, should not immunize a race-conscious measure from careful judicial inspection. Close review is needed "to ferret out classifications in reality malign, but masquerading as benign," and to "ensure that preferences are not so large as to trammel unduly upon the opportunities of others or interfere too harshly with legitimate expectations of persons in once-preferred groups."

Examining in this light the admissions policy employed by the University of Michigan's College of Literature, Science, and the Arts (College), and for the reasons well stated by Justice SOUTER, I see no constitutional infirmity. . . .

□ *Justice SOUTER, with whom Justice GINSBURG joins as to Part II, dissenting.*

Grutter reaffirms the permissibility of individualized consideration of race to achieve a diversity of students, at least where race is not assigned a preordained value in all cases. On the other hand, Justice POWELL's opinion in *Regents of Univ. of Cal. v. Bakke*, 438 U.S. 265 (1978), rules out a racial quota or set-aside, in which race is the sole fact of eligibility for certain places in a class. Although the freshman admissions system here is subject to argument on the merits, I think it is closer to what *Grutter* approves than to what *Bakke* condemns, and should not be held unconstitutional on the current record.

The record does not describe a system with a quota like the one struck down in *Bakke*, which "insulate[d]" all nonminority candidates from competition from certain seats. The plan here, in contrast, lets all applicants compete for all places and values an applicant's offering for any place not only on grounds of race, but on grades, test scores, strength of high school, quality of course of study, residence, alumni relationships, leadership, personal character, socioeconomic disadvantage, athletic ability, and quality of a personal essay. A nonminority applicant who scores highly in these other categories can readily garner a selection index exceeding that of a minority applicant who gets the 20-point bonus. . . .

The Court nonetheless finds fault with a scheme that "automatically" distributes 20 points to minority applicants because "[t]he only consideration that accompanies this distribution of points is a factual review of an application to determine whether an individual is a member of one of these minority groups." The objection goes to the use of points to quantify and compare characteristics, or to the number of points awarded due to race, but on either reading the objection is mistaken.

The very nature of a college's permissible practice of awarding value to racial diversity means that race must be considered in a way that increases some applicants' chances for admission. Since college admission is not left entirely to inarticulate intuition, it is hard to see what is inappropriate in assigning some stated value to a relevant characteristic, whether it be reasoning ability, writing style, running speed, or minority race. Justice POWELL's plus factors necessarily are assigned some values. The college simply does by a numbered scale what the law school accomplishes in its "holistic review," *Grutter*, the distinction does not imply that applicants to the undergraduate college are denied individualized consideration or a fair chance to compete on the basis of all the various merits their applications may disclose. . . .

Grutter v. Bollinger
539 U.S. 306, 123 S.Ct. 2325 (2003)

In 1992 the University of Michigan Law School adopted an admissions policy based on an index score representing a composite of an applicant's Law School Admissions Test (LSAT) score and undergraduate grade point average. The policy also affirmed the law school's "commitment to racial and ethnic diversity with special reference to the inclusion of students from groups which have been historically discriminated against, like African Americans, Hispanics, and Native Americans," who, without some preference, "might not be represented in [the] student body in meaningful numbers." Accordingly, the law school makes "special efforts" to increase the number and achieve a "critical mass" of such students.

Barbara Grutter, an unsuccessful white applicant and a 43-year-old business woman, challenged the constitutionality of the law school's admission program for relying on race and ethnicity as "predominant" factors and for favoring minority groups and giving them "a significantly greater chance of admission than students with similar credentials." A federal district court held that the law school's admissions program violated the Fourteenth Amendment, but the Court of Appeals for the Sixth Circuit reversed and concluded that the school's interest in achieving a diverse student body was compelling under *Regents of the University of California v. Bakke*, 438 U.S. 265 (1978). Ms. Grutter appealed that decision.

The appellate court's decision was affirmed by a vote of five to four. Justice O'Connor delivered the opinion of the Court. Justice Ginsburg filed a concurring opinion. Justices Scalia and Thomas filed opinions concurring and dissenting in part. Chief Justice Rehnquist and Justice Kennedy filed dissenting opinions.

□ *Justice O'CONNOR delivered the opinion of the Court.*

The Law School ranks among the Nation's top law schools. It receives more than 3,500 applications each year for a class of around 350 students. Seeking to "admit a group of students who individually and collectively are among the most capable," the Law School looks for individuals with "substantial promise for success in law school" and "a strong likelihood of succeeding in the practice of law and contributing in diverse ways to the well-being of others." More broadly, the Law School seeks "a mix of students with varying backgrounds and experiences who will respect and learn from each other." In 1992, the dean of the Law School charged a faculty committee with crafting a written admissions policy to implement these goals. In particular, the Law School sought to ensure that its efforts to achieve student body diversity complied with this Court's most recent ruling on the use of race in university admissions. See *Regents of Univ. of Cal. v. Bakke*, 438 U.S. 265 (1978). Upon the unanimous adoption of the committee's report by the Law School faculty, it became the Law School's official admissions policy.

The hallmark of that policy is its focus on academic ability coupled with a flexible assessment of applicants' talents, experiences, and potential "to contribute to the learning of those around them." The policy requires admissions officials to evaluate each applicant based on all the information available in the file, including a personal statement, letters of recommendation, and an essay describing the ways in which the applicant will contribute to the life and diversity of the Law School. In reviewing an applicant's file, admissions officials must consider the applicant's undergraduate grade point average (GPA) and Law School Admissions Test (LSAT) score because they are important (if imperfect) predictors of academic success in law school. The policy stresses that "no applicant should be admitted unless we expect that applicant to do well enough to graduate with no serious academic problems."

The policy makes clear, however, that even the highest possible score does not guarantee admission to the Law School. Nor does a low score automatically disqualify an applicant. Rather, the policy requires admissions officials to look beyond grades and test scores to other criteria that are important to the Law School's educational objectives. So-called "'soft' variables" such as "the enthusiasm of recommenders, the quality of the undergraduate institution, the quality of the applicant's essay, and the areas and difficulty of undergraduate course selection" are all brought to bear in assessing an "applicant's likely contributions to the intellectual and social life of the institution." . . .

We granted *certiorari* to resolve the disagreement among the Courts of Appeals on a question of national importance: Whether diversity is a compelling interest that can justify the narrowly tailored use of race in selecting applicants for admission to public universities.

We last addressed the use of race in public higher education over 25 years ago. In the landmark *Bakke* case, we reviewed a racial set-aside program that reserved 16 out of 100 seats in a medical school class for members of certain minority groups. The decision produced six separate opinions, none of which commanded a majority of the Court. . . .

Since this Court's splintered decision in *Bakke*, Justice POWELL's opinion announcing the judgment of the Court has served as the touchstone for constitutional analysis of race-conscious admissions policies. Public and private universities across the Nation have modeled their own admissions programs on Justice POWELL's views on permissible race-conscious policies. . . .

We have held that all racial classifications imposed by government "must be analyzed by a reviewing court under strict scrutiny." This means that such classifications are constitutional only if they are narrowly tailored to further compelling governmental interests.

Strict scrutiny is not "strict in theory, but fatal in fact." Although all governmental uses of race are subject to strict scrutiny, not all are invalidated by it. As we have explained, "whenever the government treats any person unequally because of his or her race, that person has suffered an injury that falls squarely within the language and spirit of the Constitution's guarantee of equal protection." But that observation "says nothing about the ultimate validity of any particular law; that determination is the job of the court applying strict scrutiny." When race-based action is necessary to further a compelling governmental interest, such action does not violate the constitutional guarantee of equal protection so long as the narrow-tailoring requirement is also satisfied.

Context matters when reviewing race-based governmental action under the Equal Protection Clause. Not every decision influenced by race is equally objectionable and strict scrutiny is designed to provide a framework for carefully examining the importance and the sincerity of the reasons advanced by the governmental decisionmaker for the use of race in that particular context.

With these principles in mind, we turn to the question whether the Law School's use of race is justified by a compelling state interest. . . . The Law School's educational judgment that such diversity is essential to its educational mission is one to which we defer. The Law School's assessment that diversity will, in fact, yield educational benefits is substantiated by respondents and their *amici*. . . .

As part of its goal of "assembling a class that is both exceptionally academically qualified and broadly diverse," the Law School seeks to "enroll a 'critical mass' of minority students." The Law School's interest is not simply "to assure within its student body some specified percentage of a particular group merely because of its race or ethnic origin." That would amount to outright racial balancing, which is patently unconstitutional. . . .

The Law School's claim of a compelling interest is further bolstered by its *amici*, who point to the educational benefits that flow from student body diversity. In addition to the expert studies and reports entered into evidence at trial, numerous studies show that student body diversity promotes learning outcomes, and "better prepares students for an increasingly diverse workforce and society, and better prepares them as professionals."

These benefits are not theoretical but real, as major American businesses have made clear that the skills needed in today's increasingly global marketplace can only be developed through exposure to widely diverse people, cultures, ideas, and viewpoints. . . .

We have repeatedly acknowledged the overriding importance of preparing students for work and citizenship, describing education as pivotal to "sustaining our political and cultural heritage" with a fundamental role in maintaining the fabric of society. *Plyler v. Doe*, 457 U.S. 202 (1982). This Court has long recognized that "education . . . is the very foundation of good citizenship." *Brown v. Board of Education*, 347 U.S. 483 (1954). For this reason, the diffusion of knowledge and opportunity through public institutions of higher education must be accessible to all individuals regardless of race or ethnicity. The United States, as *amicus curiae*, affirms that "[e]nsuring that public institutions are open and available to all segments of American society, including people of all races and ethnicities, represents a paramount government objective."

Moreover, universities, and in particular, law schools, represent the training ground for a large number of our Nation's leaders. Individuals with law degrees occupy roughly half the state governorships, more than half the seats in the United States Senate, and more than a third of the seats in the United States House of Representatives. The pattern is even more striking when it comes to highly selective law schools. A handful of these schools accounts for 25 of the 100 United States Senators, 74 United States Courts of Appeals judges, and nearly 200 of the more than 600 United States District Court judges. . . .

Even in the limited circumstance when drawing racial distinctions is permissible to further a compelling state interest, government is still "constrained in how it may pursue that end: [T]he means chosen to accomplish the [government's] asserted purpose must be specifically and narrowly framed to accomplish that purpose." *Shaw v. Hunt*, 517 U.S. 899 (1996). The purpose of the narrow tailoring requirement is to ensure that "the means chosen 'fit' . . . th[e] compelling goal so closely that there is little or no possibility that the motive for the classification was illegitimate racial prejudice or stereotype."

Since *Bakke*, we have had no occasion to define the contours of the narrow-tailoring inquiry with respect to race-conscious university admissions programs. That inquiry must be calibrated to fit the distinct issues raised by the use of race to achieve student body diversity in public higher education. . . .

To be narrowly tailored, a race-conscious admissions program cannot use a quota system—it cannot "insulat[e] each category of applicants with certain desired qualifications from competition with all other applicants." Instead, a university may consider race or ethnicity only as a " 'plus' in a particular applicant's file," without "insulat[ing] the individual from comparison with all other candidates for the available seats." In other words, an admissions program must be "flexible enough to consider all pertinent elements of diversity in light of the particular qualifications of each applicant, and to place them on the same footing for consideration, although not necessarily according them the same weight."

We find that the Law School's admissions program bears the hallmarks of a narrowly tailored plan. . . . We are satisfied that the Law School's admissions program, like the Harvard plan described by Justice POWELL, does not operate as a quota. . . . Justice POWELL's distinction between the medical school's rigid 16-seat quota and Harvard's flexible use of race as a "plus" factor is instructive. Harvard certainly had minimum goals for minority enrollment, even if it had no specific number firmly in mind. . . .

Here, the Law School engages in a highly individualized, holistic review of each applicant's file, giving serious consideration to all the ways an applicant might contribute to a diverse educational environment. The Law School affords this individualized consideration to applicants of all races. . . .

What is more, the Law School actually gives substantial weight to diversity factors besides race. The Law School frequently accepts nonminority applicants with grades and test scores lower than underrepresented minority applicants (and other nonminority applicants) who are rejected. This shows that the Law School seriously weighs many other diversity factors besides race that can make a real and dispositive difference for nonminority applicants as well. By this flexible approach, the Law School sufficiently takes into account, in practice as well as in theory, a wide variety of characteristics besides race and ethnicity that contribute to a diverse student body. . . .

We are mindful, however, that "[a] core purpose of the Fourteenth Amendment was to do away with all governmentally imposed discrimination based on race." *Palmore v. Sidoti*, 466 U.S. 429 (1984). Accordingly, race-conscious admissions policies must be limited in time. This requirement reflects that racial classifications, however compelling their goals, are potentially so dangerous that they may be employed no more broadly than the interest demands. . . .

In the context of higher education, the durational requirement can be met by sunset provisions in race-conscious admissions policies and periodic reviews to determine whether racial preferences are still necessary to achieve student body diversity. Universities in California, Florida, and Washington State, where racial preferences in admissions are prohibited by state law, are currently engaged in experimenting with a wide variety of alternative approaches. Universities in other States can and should draw on the most promising aspects of these race-neutral alternatives as they develop. The requirement that all race-conscious admissions programs have a termination point "assure[s] all citizens that the deviation from the norm of equal treatment of all racial and ethnic groups is a temporary matter, a measure taken in the service of the goal of equality itself." *Richmond v. J. A. Croson Co.* . . .

It has been 25 years since Justice POWELL first approved the use of race to further an interest in student body diversity in the context of public higher education. Since that time, the number of minority applicants with high grades and test scores has indeed increased. We expect that 25 years from now, the use of racial preferences will no longer be necessary to further the interest approved today.

In summary, the Equal Protection Clause does not prohibit the Law School's narrowly tailored use of race in admissions decisions to further a compelling interest in obtaining the educational benefits that flow from a diverse student body. Consequently, petitioner's statutory claims based on Title VI also fail. The judgment of the Court of Appeals for the Sixth Circuit, accordingly, is affirmed.

□ *Justice GINSBURG, with whom Justice BREYER joins, concurring.*

However strong the public's desire for improved education systems may be, it remains the current reality that many minority students encounter markedly inadequate and unequal educational opportunities. Despite these inequalities, some minority students are able to meet the high threshold requirements set for admission to the country's finest undergraduate and graduate educational institutions. As lower school education in minority communities improves, an increase in the number of such students may be anticipated. From today's

vantage point, one may hope, but not firmly forecast, that over the next generation's span, progress toward nondiscrimination and genuinely equal opportunity
will make it safe to sunset affirmative action.

☐ *CHIEF JUSTICE REHNQUIST, with whom Justice SCALIA, Justice
KENNEDY, and Justice THOMAS join, dissenting.*

As we have explained many times, "'[a]ny preference based on racial or ethnic
criteria must necessarily receive a most searching examination.'" *Adarand.* Our
cases establish that, in order to withstand this demanding inquiry, respondents
must demonstrate that their methods of using race "'fit'" a compelling state
interest "with greater precision than any alternative means." *Bakke.*

In practice, the Law School's program bears little or no relation to its
asserted goal of achieving "critical mass." . . . From 1995 through 2000, the
Law School admitted between 1,130 and 1,310 students. Of those, between 13
and 19 were Native American, between 91 and 108 were African-Americans,
and between 47 and 56 were Hispanic. If the Law School is admitting between
91 and 108 African-Americans in order to achieve "critical mass," thereby preventing African-American students from feeling "isolated or like spokespersons
for their race," one would think that a number of the same order of magnitude
would be necessary to accomplish the same purpose for Hispanics and Native
Americans. Similarly, even if all of the Native American applicants admitted in
a given year matriculate, which the record demonstrates is not at all the case,
how can this possibly constitute a "critical mass" of Native Americans in a class
of over 350 students? In order for this pattern of admission to be consistent
with the Law School's explanation of "critical mass," one would have to believe
that the objectives of "critical mass" offered by respondents are achieved with
only half the number of Hispanics and one-sixth the number of Native Americans as compared to African-Americans. But respondents offer no race-specific
reasons for such disparities. Instead, they simply emphasize the importance of
achieving "critical mass," without any explanation of why that concept is
applied differently among the three underrepresented minority groups.

These different numbers, moreover, come only as a result of substantially
different treatment among the three underrepresented minority groups, as is
apparent in an example offered by the Law School and highlighted by the
Court: The school asserts that it "frequently accepts nonminority applicants
with grades and test scores lower than underrepresented minority applicants
(and other nonminority applicants) who are rejected." Specifically, the Law
School states that "[s]ixty-nine minority applicants were rejected between
1995 and 2000 with at least a 3.5 [Grade Point Average (GPA)] and a [score
of] 159 or higher on the [Law School Admissions Test (LSAT)]" while a
number of Caucasian and Asian-American applicants with similar or lower
scores were admitted.

Review of the record reveals only 67 such individuals. Of these 67
individuals, 56 were Hispanic, while only 6 were African-American, and only
5 were Native American. This discrepancy reflects a consistent practice. For
example, in 2000, 12 Hispanics who scored between a 159–160 on the LSAT
and earned a GPA of 3.00 or higher applied for admission and only 2 were
admitted. Meanwhile, 12 African-Americans in the same range of qualifications applied for admission and all 12 were admitted. Likewise, that same
year, 16 Hispanics who scored between a 151–153 on the LSAT and earned a
3.00 or higher applied for admission and only 1 of those applicants was admitted.

Twenty-three similarly qualified African-Americans applied for admission and 14 were admitted. . . .

[T]he correlation between the percentage of the Law School's pool of applicants who are members of the three minority groups and the percentage of the admitted applicants who are members of these same groups is far too precise to be dismissed as merely the result of the school paying "some attention to [the] numbers." [F]rom 1995 through 2000 the percentage of admitted applicants who were members of these minority groups closely tracked the percentage of individuals in the school's applicant pool who were from the same groups. . . . For example, in 1995, when 9.7% of the applicant pool was African-American, 9.4% of the admitted class was African-American. By 2000, only 7.5% of the applicant pool was African-American, and 7.3% of the admitted class was African-American. This correlation is striking. Respondents themselves emphasize that the number of underrepresented minority students admitted to the Law School would be significantly smaller if the race of each applicant were not considered. But, as the examples above illustrate, the measure of the decrease would differ dramatically among the groups. The tight correlation between the percentage of applicants and admittees of a given race, therefore, must result from careful race based planning by the Law School. . . .

I do not believe that the Constitution gives the Law School such free rein in the use of race. The Law School has offered no explanation for its actual admissions practices and, unexplained, we are bound to conclude that the Law School has managed its admissions program, not to achieve a "critical mass," but to extend offers of admission to members of selected minority groups in proportion to their statistical representation in the applicant pool. But this is precisely the type of racial balancing that the Court itself calls "patently unconstitutional." . . .

□ *Justice KENNEDY, dissenting.*

The Court, in a review that is nothing short of perfunctory, accepts the University of Michigan Law School's assurances that its admissions process meets with constitutional requirements. The majority fails to confront the reality of how the Law School's admissions policy is implemented. The dissenting opinion by The CHIEF JUSTICE, which I join in full, demonstrates beyond question why the concept of critical mass is a delusion used by the Law School to mask its attempt to make race an automatic factor in most instances and to achieve numerical goals indistinguishable from quotas. . . . It remains to point out how critical mass becomes inconsistent with individual consideration in some more specific aspects of the admissions process.

About 80 to 85 percent of the places in the entering class are given to applicants in the upper range of Law School Admissions Test scores and grades. An applicant with these credentials likely will be admitted without consideration of race or ethnicity. With respect to the remaining 15 to 20 percent of the seats, race is likely outcome determinative for many members of minority groups. That is where the competition becomes tight and where any given applicant's chance of admission is far smaller if he or she lacks minority status. At this point the numerical concept of critical mass has the real potential to compromise individual review.

The Law School has not demonstrated how individual consideration is, or can be, preserved at this stage of the application process given the instruction to attain what it calls critical mass. In fact the evidence shows otherwise. There was little deviation among admitted minority students during the years from 1995 to 1998. The percentage of enrolled minorities fluctuated only by 0.3%, from 13.5% to 13.8%. The number of minority students to whom offers were extended varied by just a slightly greater magnitude of 2.2%, from the high of 15.6% in 1995 to the low of 13.4% in 1998. . . .

The narrow fluctuation band raises an inference that the Law School subverted individual determination, and strict scrutiny requires the Law School to overcome the inference. Whether the objective of critical mass "is described as a quota or a goal, it is a line drawn on the basis of race and ethnic status," and so risks compromising individual assessment. . . .

To be constitutional, a university's compelling interest in a diverse student body must be achieved by a system where individual assessment is safeguarded through the entire process. There is no constitutional objection to the goal of considering race as one modest factor among many others to achieve diversity, but an educational institution must ensure, through sufficient procedures, that each applicant receives individual consideration and that race does not become a predominant factor in the admissions decisionmaking. . . .

☐ *Justice SCALIA, with whom Justice THOMAS joins, concurring in part and dissenting in part.*

Unlike a clear constitutional holding that racial preferences in state educational institutions are impermissible, or even a clear anticonstitutional holding that racial preferences in state educational institutions are OK, today's *Grutter-Gratz* split double header seems perversely designed to prolong the controversy and the litigation. Some future lawsuits will presumably focus on whether the discriminatory scheme in question contains enough evaluation of the applicant "as an individual," and sufficiently avoids "separate admissions tracks" to fall under *Grutter* rather than *Gratz*. Some will focus on whether a university has gone beyond the bounds of a "'good faith effort'" and has so zealously pursued its "critical mass" as to make it an unconstitutional de facto quota system, rather than merely "'a permissible goal.'" Other lawsuits may focus on whether, in the particular setting at issue, any educational benefits flow from racial diversity. Still other suits may challenge the bona fides of the institution's expressed commitment to the educational benefits of diversity that immunize the discriminatory scheme in *Grutter*. And still other suits may claim that the institution's racial preferences have gone below or above the mystical *Grutter*-approved "critical mass." Finally, litigation can be expected on behalf of minority groups intentionally shortchanged in the institution's composition of its generic minority "critical mass." I do not look forward to any of these cases. The Constitution proscribes government discrimination on the basis of race, and state-provided education is no exception.

☐ *Justice THOMAS, with whom Justice SCALIA joins as to Parts I–VII, concurring in part and dissenting in part.*

No one would argue that a university could set up a lower general admission standard and then impose heightened requirements only on black applicants. Similarly, a university may not maintain a high admission standard and grant exemptions to favored races. The Law School, of its own choosing, and for its own purposes, maintains an exclusionary admissions system that it knows produces racially disproportionate results. Racial discrimination is not a permissible solution to the self-inflicted wounds of this elitist admissions policy.

The majority upholds the Law School's racial discrimination not by interpreting the people's Constitution, but by responding to a faddish slogan of the cognoscenti. Nevertheless, I concur in part in the Court's opinion. First, I agree with the Court insofar as its decision, which approves of only one racial classification, confirms that further use of race in admissions remains unlawful. Second, I agree with the Court's holding that racial discrimination in higher education admissions will be illegal in 25 years. I respectfully dissent from the remainder of the Court's opinion and the judgment, however, because I believe that the Law School's current use of race violates the Equal Protection Clause and that the Constitution means the same thing today as it will in 300 months. . . .

D | *Nonracial Classifications and the Equal Protection of the Law*

(1) *Gender-Based Discrimination*

■ THE DEVELOPMENT OF LAW

Rulings Dealing with Gender Discrimination and Statutory Interpretation

CASE	VOTE	RULING
*United States v. Dominguez Benitez,*124 S.Ct. 2333 (2004)	9:0	Justice Souter rejected a claim that a sentence should be overturned because a federal district

court judge failed to warn the defendant that if the court did not accept a plea bargain he could not withdraw his guilty plea, since it was stipulated in the signed agreement and made no difference in the outcome.

(2) *Discrimination against Gays and Lesbians*

Lawrence v. Texas, 539 U.S. 558, 123 S. Ct. 2472 (2003), striking down Texas's law making homosexual sodomy a crime, is excerpted in Chapter 11.

INDEX OF CASES

Cases printed in boldface are excerpted on the page(s) printed in boldface.

Other Books by David M. O'Brien

Storm Center:
The Supreme Court in American Politics
6th ed.

Constitutional Law and Politics:
Vol. 1. *Struggles for Power and Governmental Accountability*
Vol. 2. *Civil Rights and Civil Liberties*
5th ed.

Animal Sacrifice and Religious Freedom:
Church of Lukumi Babalu Aye v. City of Hialeah

Abortion and American Politics
(with Barbara H. Craig)

Judicial Roulette

What Process Is Due?
Courts and Science-Policy Disputes

Views from the Bench:
The Judiciary and Constitutional Politics
(with Mark Cannon)

The Politics of Technology Assessment:
Institutions, Processes and Policy Disputes
(with Donald Marchand)

The Public's Right to Know:
The Supreme Court and the First Amendment

Privacy, Law, and Public Policy

The Politics of American Government
3rd ed.
(with Stephen J. Wayne, G. Calvin Mackenzie, and Richard Cole)

To Dream of Dreams:
Religious Freedom and Constitutional Politics in Postwar Japan
(with Yasuo Ohkoshi)

Judges on Judging
2nd ed.
(editor)

The Lanahan Readings on Civil Rights and Civil Liberties
2nd ed.
(editor)

Judicial Independence in the Age of Democracy:
Critical Perspectives from Around the World
(with Peter Russell)

Government by the People
20th ed.
(with James MacGregor Burns, J. W. Peltason, Thomas E. Cronin, David B. Magleby, and Paul Light)